The Spiritual Awakening Guide

Kundalini, Psychic Abilities, and the Conditioned Layers of Reality

The Spiritual
Awakening Guide

Kundalini, Psychic Abilities, and the
Conditioned Layers of Reality

Mary Mueller Shutan

 FINDHORN PRESS

Published in 2015 by Findhorn Press, Scotland

ISBN 978-1-84409-671-8

Edited by Patricia Kot
Cover illustration by Mary Shutan
Cover design by Richard Crookes
Interior design by Damian Keenan
Printed and bound in the USA

DISCLAIMER
The information in this book is given in good faith and is neither
intended to diagnose any physical or mental condition nor to serve
as a substitute for informed medical advice or care.
Please contact your health professional for medical advice and
treatment. Neither author nor publisher can be held liable by any
person for any loss or damage whatsoever which may arise from the
use of this book or any of the information therein.

Published by
Findhorn Press
117-121 High Street,
Forres IV36 1AB,
Scotland, UK

t +44 (0)1309 690582
f +44 (0)131 777 2711
e info@findhornpress.com
www.findhornpress.com

Contents

DEDICATION

To my family, my pets, my readers and editors,
my teachers and mentors…
and to anyone who is ready and willing
to look beyond illusion.

Introduction

It is a strange world we live in. Most of us live life in an unconscious manner and in a relatively disassociated state. We look to the future and to the past and feel discomfort and a sense of disconnect to the present. In this state of slumber and disconnect, we allow for things that are not of vital importance to overwhelm and cloud our lives. Shopping, television, drugs, alcohol, gossip, technology, and other pursuits allow us to remain anesthetized, disassociated, and asleep. We have cluttered our existences with things and experiences that lack importance. We let the external cloud us until we no longer understand what we are thinking or what we are doing with our lives. Many of us no longer have a place for ourselves in our very own lives. At some level, even for the most unconscious and disembodied of us, we recognize that our lives are not working—that we have somehow gotten away from the things that we are here to do and what is of vital importance to our very souls. We have the rare glimpse or memory of who we are and who we are meant to be, and it is devastating because it is so far from what we have become.

In this unconscious state it is all about getting by—working at jobs that are draining, hated, or do not suit our unique talents; relationships that we have grown out of; and to-do lists that have us focus on what we have yet to get done. We focus on the past and the future without consideration of the present. It is considered normal to lose the passion and imagination of our youth. It is considered normal to sleepwalk through life, struggling to get by, and to be deeply unhappy with what has happened to our lives.

But what would happen if we were to wake up from our collective slumber, to understand not only the patterns that drive us but also the patterns that create our realities? Remembering and becoming who we truly are is life changing. Breaking free from the unconscious personal, family, and collective patterns of society is revolutionary. And for many of us, this process of awakening, remembering, and breaking free has begun.

When I began undergoing a spiritual awakening it was a difficult experience. I did not understand what I was seeing and feeling, and there was little source material out there to understand the process. I began to realize the difficulties and struggle of being on a spiritual path. At the same time I began experiencing ever-widening glimpses of peace, harmony, joy, flow, and guidance to remember and become who I truly am meant to be in this world. Most literature on spiritual awakening is aspirational, focused ultimately on feel-good, ego-based, self-help sort of material. This literature has a place in society but it ultimately strays from the difficulties of this path and clear, pragmatic, and concise directions for modern-day living while undergoing an awakening. Simply put, there are countless books out there for people who aspire to become awakened, but few resources are out there for those of us who are already experiencing awakenings. Ultimately, I have created what I was lacking in my own awakening process—details of the process, types of awakenings, difficulties and joys, and how to work through an awakening while still remaining a part of modern society.

Part 1 goes through each of the twelve layers of conditioned reality that cover an awakened state. These layers of conditioned reality—everything from our own trauma and abuse to past lives, ancestral issues, and more global or cosmic forces—can be navigated with the tools and understandings provided in this book. Everything from the first steps of being on a spiritual path to awakening and post-awakening states are discussed with clarity and pragmatic, real-world advice. Part 2 goes over gradual and milder forms of spiritual awakening. Part 3 gets into the more difficult and sudden types of awakenings. These sudden awakenings are where we find ourselves in a spiritual process that completely revolutionizes our existence, creating significant issues in functioning and drastic changes in our mind, body, and spirit within a short period of time. Part 4 goes through some of the more common experiences during the awakening process.

The intent of this book is not about one singular journey. It is about the path—the hardships, joys, fears, and depths of emotion and feeling that come with being awake, free, and truly alive in a world that is not. Going through the awakening process for all its difficulties is something to be cherished, but it is also something that needs to be properly understood in order to work with and be present during. I have written this book in an effort to detail the process of awakening in modern society—a world that no longer understands and cannot relate to texts and experiences from hundreds, if not thousands, of years ago. I do not have a religion to sell you. I am not a guru. But I hope that you find yourself within these pages and know that you are not alone, that your experiences are similar to those who have gone through spiritual awakenings for thousands of years.

Although there is something of a divide in the definition of what being "awake" truly means from a variety of spiritual traditions, there are commonalities in the journey of awakening. Once awakened, the meaning of our awakened state is ours and ours alone. Once truly in contact with the divine, and with the divinity within us, the questions cease, and our path expands into having no path at all. But until then we need teachers, literature, and others who have walked this path to show us how to navigate it. I am in full realization in creating this book that every experience described will not be exactly the same and that even similar paths vary wildly. This book is not a step-by-step manual or a checklist for you to go through. Rather, it is a resource to help you understand your experiences, to help you work with your spiritual path, and to get you to develop your own resources and understandings of your own, unique path to awakening.

I wish to thank my guides, teachers, and the healing institutions that have taught me so much. I also wish to thank my husband, David, and the many students, patients, and clients who have crossed my path. Like anyone on this path, I am constantly a student who realizes that in all I know, I know very little.

PART 1

Awakening and the Twelve Layers of Conditioned Reality

The Awakening Process

For many of us, awakening is something that is actively searched for. Years of meditation practice, yoga, workshops, and healing methods all have led us to awakening. This is the ideal path—one of gradual changes, deep understandings of a spiritual nature, and a context and container, such as a meditation group or teacher who can guide us through the process, provide us with understandings, and allay any fears that come up along the path.

For others, awakening occurs as a result of the searching process but lacks the appropriate teacher or guide to the experience. We find ourselves awakening through spiritual pursuits but find that our teacher, the other students, and our friends are not, and then have nowhere to turn for real assistance during the process.

Some of us who are awake were simply born into an awakened state. When we are born this way, we may gradually lose this state or put ourselves to sleep when we come to an age where we understand that it is not culturally appropriate to be awake in a world that is not. In an effort to be "normal"—relating and similar in understandings to our family members, friends, and community—we shut down our awareness. It is common for many of us awakening as adults to remember the specific moment we shut ourselves down or started to wear a mask to appear normal. A few of us who are born awake stay that way, simply deepening our experiences and understandings as we mature.

For many of us awakening occurs gradually and is a step-by-step process. Others of us awaken suddenly, resulting in dramatic physical, psychological, and spiritual changes within a short period of time that may require hospitalization, medication, and create a significant inability to function. Along with differing types of awakenings there are also variances to the degrees of awakened state. These can range from feeling energy for the first time to states of understanding the rhythms and flows of the universe and beyond.

In the process of awakening we may find ourselves in a seemingly endless loop of existential crises—wondering what our purpose is now that we are more awake. We are seekers, not understanding our purpose and the why or how of how we have become the way we are. We do not understand why those around us do not understand to the same level that we understand. We are stuck in various stages of awakening and are unable to find our way out.

However an awakening begins, it is the start of an inner calling, a chance to do something great to contribute to humanity. It is a signal to become a teacher, a leader of others, a healer, a force of compassion and wisdom in the world. It is the start of something important, it is a call to service, it is a realization and awakening to who we truly are, to our power, and to who we could be if we were not restricted by ourselves, society, and other sources. We become in line with our soul, and our physical reality, mental and emotional outlook, and our day-to-day existences change to match who we are meant to be in this world. We have the ability in an awakened state to bring our own unique power and truth to the world in a way that no other individual, even another awakened individual, can.

The Sleeper

In ordinary, conditioned reality (the reality that most people agree upon), most people are sleeping. There is a comfort to this state. The objective is to just get through—to get by. We go to jobs we dislike, stay in relationships because it is easier than not staying, and re-live the same patterns of trauma over and over again. At some point there is a loss of that spark, that sense of knowing of what we want to do or should be doing with our lives. If there are moments of crisis, of questioning, they are met with behaviors to put us back to sleep.

For those of us who are asleep there is a lack of the present moment. There are fears of what is to come, what might happen, and a collection of traumas and issues from the past that we have not processed (worked through) or let go of. In this state we are living in the past, the future, but not the present.

This lack of presence shows up in our physical body—we are disassociated and disembodied from our physical bodies. Most of us do not have the faintest idea of what we actually look like in a mirror but instead will focus on the areas we have disassociated from—our abdomens, feet, legs, chest.

When we are asleep we have moments that make us question spiritual matters, such as death, birth, or traumas, that keep showing up in an attempt to be resolved. There is a tendency toward behavior that puts us back to sleep when we experience these. Television, shopping, technology, drugs, alcohol, food, and sex are all tools used to put ourselves back to sleep when the present moment is creating discomfort or to fill up the parts of ourselves we have disassociated from. This tendency to want to anesthetize ourselves from anything unpleasant is not just in the sleeper category but is apparent in most states of the spiritual journey.

There is a comfort to being asleep. We know what to expect because it is largely the same week after week, year after year. We all know those who have the same routine, job, the same lunch every day, know their place in the community, church, and have the same friends for 30 years. There are of course ups and downs at this level for everyone—job loss, death, and financial issues—but overall it is the same linear line from birth to death. Variation from this line causes discomfort, anxiety, and fear, but the safety of the routine and patterns that have been created are frequently enough for us in the sleeper state and will provide an expected existence for most of us when at this level.

Although there can be a sense of spirituality in the sleeper state, it is often not a personal sense. There is no personal revelation or investment into religion or spirituality. These pursuits, if done at all, are completed out of a sense of duty and are simply societal conventions. When we are asleep we do not recognize that we are following the constraints of society, of our family, and of collective conditioning. While there are moments of joy, of happiness, for the most part we don't understand there is another way to live and freedom from the constraints and patterns of our lives. We do not believe that we have any other options, because that is what we have been brought up to believe, and that is what life proves to us over and over.

There is comfort in the known and a cognitive dissonance, an inability to process and rejection of anything that does not fit in our worldview. There is a set of black and white rules, and we are content with the understanding of what we perceive the rules to be. We feel that we understand what is expected out of us in life, and what to expect out of life in return. Life is always a struggle—to be happy, money, relationships—but there is an understanding and clarity in this struggle. We know Truth because it has been handed down to us—through family, community, and society—and there is little questioning of this Truth. Anything that we do not know, any experience we have not had, is simply a lie.

There is a focus on the physical and material world for the sleeper. Along with acquiring material goods and what is expected of us by collective conditioning (house, children, gadgets, cars) there is also a focus on the physical realm—what can be seen, touched/felt, tasted, and heard. There is little focus on spiritual or emotional realms, and little room for the magical, unexplainable, or causes that have not directly impacted us.

For some of us in the sleeper category, there is a glimmer of awareness and an understanding that there could be more out there, but we are unable or unaware of how to achieve it. Life events like death, divorce, job loss, disease/diagnosis, or self-inquiry through therapy or other means has made us want more out of life than what we have been given. We either use that opportunity to put ourselves back to sleep, or we bring ourselves to the next category, that of being somewhat awake.

The Somewhat Awakened

Those of us who are somewhat awake will often have the same wants and needs as those who are asleep. We have an understanding of our place in society and what is expected of us but are looking for more out of life. There is a realization that there is more beyond our individual struggles. There is a love and heart-centered space for others that can come through by being part of a family, a community, being religious, or seeing evidence of safe love between others—such as the ever popular kitten- and puppy-type videos online.

We enjoy many of the same things that the asleep group does—material and physical things—and have many of the same struggles. But although we struggle being somewhat awakened, it is not the same "me first" variety as those in the asleep group. We are able to look at others with some compassion and understanding. We have an understanding that there is something larger than us—a faith or spiritual understanding that can guide us in times of need. We participate in religious and spiritual activities not out of a sense of societal obligation, but because we feel the need for something greater than ourselves and find this force to be a fulfilling and necessary part of our existence.

We also have an understanding of our emotions and have an understanding that our past and childhood have contributed and made us who we are. We are able to understand basic patterns of our lives. For example, women in this category who have bad relationship after bad relationship have an understanding that it comes from lack of parental affection, or even childhood abuse, and that they are playing out that pattern in their adult relationships. Sometimes we have the ability to get out of these basic patterns, but there is typically an understanding of the pattern without the ability to know how to change the pattern. The woman gets out of the relationship only to find one that is slightly less abusive, or find someone and repeat the same pattern again and again.

When we are somewhat awake we are able to dedicate ourselves to others and have an understanding of spirituality and religion. We are aware of the existence of some of our patterns but we are unable to change many of them. Although there is physical, mental, spiritual, and emotional awareness, at some level we are still caught in the parameters of societal conditioning and understanding of what we can or cannot do with our lives. We have begun the questioning process but are not awake enough to do anything beyond what has been taught to us through our conditioning. So we feel resigned to our fate, our wounds, our jobs and relationships. The fact that we are awake enough to know that our lives may have turned out differently if we grew up in another community, or had different parents, only fuels the fire of "what ifs" and constant mental chatter that plague us in this state. We are not living in the present—we are living in the wounds of our past, and in the future of what-ifs and daydreams.

Those who are somewhat awakened more than others seem to be of the daydream type, with a focus on putting the awake and aware part of ourselves back to sleep through gossip, Internet, television, and a constant stream of thoughts, mental conditioning, and what-ifs—dreaming of if we only had a different life, different body, were a different person, or had a different family or different experiences growing up. We are in a constant, often brutal, state of negativity about ourselves and about the world.

Ego Awakening

It is important to understand that many who are teaching or claiming to be "awake" or "enlightened" are doing so on a somewhat awake or between awake and asleep level. This false, or ego awakening is an illusion that can cause a great deal of harm. Careful differentiation of gurus, teachers, and ourselves is needed so that we do not fall into this category, which is increasingly and unfortunately common.

The end goal of spirituality when we are undergoing an ego awakening is often monetary gain or physical, material pursuits. When we wake up there is a shedding or letting go of material things, a realization that physical, material goods are not needed beyond simple necessities. There is also a general sense of happiness with how things are and what one has. This is not to say that an awakened person does not have possessions but that falsely awakened people often cling to the material world. Their main focus is spiritual enlightenment in order to get a new car or to become wealthy. There is a tendency for teachers in this category to charge huge fees for things like workshops, and while all teachers should get paid (and very much need to eat and live in the material, physical world) the main focus for these teachers is on money.

The ego awakened will often have just the amount of material to appear spiritual or to have spiritual understandings, but the end result of this brief search is that they now know all of the answers in the universe. Anyone who has tasted an awakened state knows that there is no way to understand everything in the universe. The easiest way to spot someone in this category is if they go around talking about how enlightened or awake they are, paired with a lack of humility, little to no compassion, and an inability to see themselves as still learning.

If we claim superiority, feel the need to be special, and talk down to others, we are in this category. Each one of us is special—we are a soul with a beautiful reason for being here and are filled with love, light, darkness, beauty, and power—just like everybody else. We simply remember while others do not. While we may know more about a specific topic, or have more spiritual understandings, there is no reason to feel like we should be placed on a pedestal due to our awakened state because there is always so much yet to learn and there is always someone out there that knows more or is further along than we are or who can see things in a different way.

Real spiritual understanding is a constantly evolving process. What I am writing about today might be completely different if I were to write it tomorrow. What you know right now should be much different than what you know six months from now. The ego- awakened stop themselves from progressing. If you know everything there is no need to know more. For those who are awakened, the process of being "awake" is actually the beginning of the journey—it is an ever-deepening process of learning. For those with humility, this process will constantly be amazing and constantly unfold. The ego-awakened stop their journey because their egos have told them that they are superior and they are unwilling to understand how small they are or how little they know.

The ego-awakened create a world in which they are a guru or teacher so they can feed the patterns of wounding that they do not yet want to face. When someone becomes a teacher, they are likely doing it because they wish to assist others. It, in fact, is an understandable progression of the path of an awakened soul as well as a falsely awakened one. But the difference here is in humility. A truly awakened teacher will teach the student to find his or her own path rather than telling him or her which path to follow. An awakened teacher will come from a place of humility and wish for the student to rise to the level of the teacher or beyond in his or her understandings.

The falsely awakened will no longer ask for help because they feel that would destroy their facade of enlightenment. They maintain that their lives are perfect and are unwilling to be real about their difficulties and actual experiences. This often has disastrous results, as the ego-awakened are likely in a great deal of pain that they cannot express to anyone because that would expose them. Those who follow them believe their falsehoods and believe that if they only follow their gurus, their lives will be wonderful. This creates a situation in which the ego-awakened finds students who can never achieve the same heights as their guru because the ego-awakened guru hasn't actually reached that state.

If someone is undergoing an ego awakening there is a repeating of rhetoric, words, and phrases that are not their own and a reliance on others. We all need community, peers who understand and love us. We all need teachers to be catalysts and support us. But awakening allows for us to understand the divinity within ourselves. People undergoing false awakenings frequently align themselves with gurus, teachers, and cultures and begin adopting them as their own. Instead of becoming fully themselves they adopt another culture or teaching without infusing their own understandings into the work. They quote others because they lack the direct experience. They need teachers to give them experiences and to provide them with answers.

There is a certain amount of ego that comes through with having moments of initial awakenings. The type of knowledge and understandings, both personal and about the cosmos, can cause us to feel very different about ourselves than we once did.

We have a different vantage point than we once did of the world. This is expected on the spiritual path at all levels of awakening. With a false awakening we remain with that feeling of separation, often feeling that we are better than those around us, that we have or hold some type of secret knowledge, and that we know the secrets of the cosmos. People in this category can align themselves with groups saying that theirs is the only way to achieve enlightenment, or they might remain in this singular state of ego-heightened awareness or separation, not realizing that they can move beyond it.

Ego awakenings maintain a false illusion of oneness. The experience of oneness is much different than many people talk about, either because it is indescribable or they lack direct experience of it. While we all are one, we are not the same. The ideas that all of our opinions are valid, that we should be ego-less, that we should not judge anyone, that we all have the same understanding levels, and many other illusions come from this state. In awakened states we understand—can see, sense, feel—the current layer of conditioning people are operating at. We feel compassion for others and their struggles (as well as our own). But there is this false ideal that in oneness we all are equal, that we can all access the same information, and that all of our opinions are equally valid that is perpetuated in false awakenings. We all filter oneness through all of the layers of conditioned reality and Self. To put this simply, we should be more willing to listen to a biochemist with a doctorate discuss tRNA than someone with only basic high school biology who has never heard of it before. The ability to discern with compassion who has a doctorate and who is still in spiritual kindergarten comes with awakening.

The last way that ego awakening presents itself is through false emotion. In the awakening process we come across a bliss that is basically indescribable. It is like falling in love, a constant opening and unfolding and learning. What this bliss has translated to in new-age literature is a sort of permanent happiness. An awakened state is not a constant state of love and light; it is not a constant state of oneness—there are ebbs and flows that come with awakening. Those undergoing ego awakening have created the illusion that everything needs to be happiness. Many of us who begin awakening do it in a manner that we are no longer grounded in our bodies. We begin creating illusions and delusions from this state. Any sort of struggle, emotion, or negativity in the world is seen as "bad" and there is an unwillingness to look at or see any sort of darkness, struggle, or difficulty in our lives or the world. Being in an awakened state means constant bliss—but it does not mean we no longer struggle or have issues. It does not mean we no longer need to participate in the world. We are intended to be within the confines of a physical body for a reason, and we are in our external reality and day-to-day lives for a reason.

By far, the ego-awakened category is the most prevalent awakening in modern society. This category can happen from any stage or through any experience of awakening.

Many teachers out there are ego-awakened and are simply miming and mimicking what they have read and heard from others. Do not be fooled by them. Take all teachings (including this book) as simply a way of lighting the way of your own path. Find your own way; let it ever deepen and widen.

Many of us go through similar stages and experiences as we work our way through the different layers of consensual reality and get in touch with the divine. We may go straight through—releasing our issues, then family issues, past lives, ancestral issues, society, communal, and cultural issues before working through archetypal issues, world issues, shadow self and Destroyer, grid systems, and entering divine flow and beyond. Some of these categories may come all at once, some may not come at all, and it is most likely we will go back and forth between categories. Obviously, some of these categories overlap. Although this next section is set up as if it were neat and clean categories, the truth is that our experiences are not this tidy. As we discuss the following states, it is important to know that none of our spiritual journeys are a checklist, and these are not boxes to fill in. By being honest and assessing where we truthfully are in our own unfolding, we can continue to learn and grow.

Between Awake and Asleep

For most of us the first awakening comes as a peak experience, such as attending a rock concert or being in a powerful spot in nature where we momentarily experience a sense of oneness. We are able to, for the first time, see ourselves as if from a different vantage point or suddenly have the understanding that there is a force much larger than ourselves.

There is, at first, an understanding that there are patterns larger than us that control our lives. In this category we begin exploring some of these patterns. The patterns of the Self—emotions, traumas, and wounds of the past—are all common themes for therapy and are typically the first patterns to arise. When we first begin waking up, our "stuff" begins rising to the surface.

Processing is the reliving, re-experiencing, and release of stagnation in the body. This stagnation may be physical issues, traumas, and other emotional issues; the conditioned layers of reality; and anything else that is covering an awakened state. Processing can be confusing for us, as we may not have the knowledge that we are undergoing a spiritual process and do not know why past traumas and other issues are arising. Processing is a release of these energies out of the physical body so we can become a clearer channel.

Processing often begins gradually, as emotions and traumas from the Self come up. Then experiences of other layers of conditioned reality—our family systems, ancestry, past lives, and global patterns—begin to emerge to be processed through us. Every pattern or layer of conditioned reality we clear brings us closer to understanding who we really are. When we become conscious of these obscuring layers, working through and clearing them, we acquire the freedom to be who we truly are.

In more complex or sudden awakenings, many experiences and the blockages of many layers rise to the surface at the same time. The experience of having many things come up to clear at the same time is extraordinarily difficult, especially when we have little idea of what is going on. The sudden awakening has the advantage of going through emotions, trauma, physical, mental, emotional, and spiritual wounding at an astonishing rate, but it is difficult to maintain balance, functioning, and assistance from others who have enough knowledge to help navigate us through spiritual transitions that are more sudden and dramatic in scope.

The First Stage of Awakening

When we have an experience that shows us how small we are in the universe it creates a recognition and understanding that we are a part of the collective whole, or something bigger than just ourselves. The sensation and sudden understanding that the universe is a very large place and we are just a speck in comparison is a catalyst that propels us into awakening. This experience is often understandably memorable, and after experiencing it we will begin to seek it out again and again because it is so awe-inspiring. This experience can happen at any time or any place—for many it is an experience of looking at the night sky, or being somewhere like the Grand Canyon. For others it might be the collective energy of being at a rock concert, skydiving, having the perfect cup of coffee, or even taking the dog for the walk.

This sensation is also the first moment of understanding that there is a force out there that is guiding us or has some sort of collective intelligence. It is our first glimpse of the vastness of the universe, and of being a small part of this vastness. With this experience there are feelings of being at the right place at the right time, happiness, joy, and feeling in sync with the flow of the universe. All of our fear, anger, and pain are momentarily taken away. We are happy and childlike. Then this moment passes and we return to ordinary reality and our ordinary fears and pains. But even having this experience for a moment awakens us to the fact that there is something more out there. This experience and its accompanying emotions are a catalyst to spiritual awakening.

Understanding that we are a small part of the universe allows for the understanding to come through that we are a part of a whole. This may be actually feeling a sensation of oneness for the first time. Although this is a flickering oneness, meaning that it does not last but for a moment, the impression of oneness is such a heightened recall of who we truly are that it creates a lasting impression and propels us to further spiritual experiences. We begin to have synchronicities, experiences, and events that are in alignment with our understandings and are messages from the divine. These experiences are meaningful, poetic, and deeply individual. During the awakening process, people, events, jobs, places, and everything that is meant for us to see or be a part of begins to be magnetized to us.

When we start awakening our individual life issues begin rising to the surface. This means that everything from our birth (or even in-utero experiences) to where we currently are in the present moment begins to come to the surface to be processed and released. We carry all unhealed material in our physical bodies. Trauma that we were unable to work through at the time because it was too overwhelming, emotions that could not be processed because they were too big or scary, and experiences that were shoved down by alcohol, drugs, or other behaviors that numbed rather than worked through overwhelming events are all in this category.

This may first appear as simply recalling past events that we have not thought of for a while. This means that we may have a birthday party in which we were embarrassed or an argument between our mother and father from when we were a young child come up with all of the memories and emotions that these experiences created. This experience may be surprisingly physical, and we may feel pain or discomfort in the area of the body that housed the event that we are releasing. For more sensitive people this may appear as a multi-sensory experience, with dreams, images, thoughts, emotions, and even tastes coming up from the memories that are releasing.

For others, several events or everything from our personal life that still has an energetic charge will begin releasing at once, leading to a physical, emotional/mental, and spiritual crisis that is difficult to navigate. This can understandably be confusing as a range of emotions and experiences come up and the physical body will have difficulty clearing so much material at once. When many things come up at once we go into a state of overwhelm and have further trauma that will need to be cleared. For those of us who are going through difficult awakenings it is understandable how many of us resort to numbing substances when too much material comes up at once to process. This is especially true if we do not know what is occurring is a spiritual process or the memories coming up are of very difficult experiences that we may not have the resources to navigate.

For those of us who are going through this type of sudden awakening, personal memories as well as other layers of conditioned reality—family, ancestral, karmic, former lives, societal, and so on—can begin to release at the same time, often resulting in the need for hospitalization, medical attention, or at the very least a break from work, school, or ordinary life. It is often difficult for those of us going through sudden or severe types of awakenings to understand what is happening to us or to find a resource that is able to understand and take care of the physical and spiritual symptoms that emerge.

When we begin processing the understanding emerges that we are more than physical beings—we are emotional, mental, and spiritual beings in a physical container. We also begin understanding that when we have a trauma or event that we feel a charge from (meaning that we feel a strong emotion from it) it stays in our physical bodies until we are able to neutralize or release it. In gradual awakenings this is a conscious process and often a decision on our part to work through past trauma and uncomfortable material. In a sudden or more dramatic awakening process these experiences, traumas, and charged material will come up to be released and begin to process without our understanding or consent.

The Twelve Layers

We are constructed of many layers. For simplicity, the discussion here is of twelve—going from the outermost layer to the innermost. If we picture our reality and idea of who we are as a series of nesting dolls, the twelfth layer would be the largest and the most external. Each layer we become aware of and work through is one nesting doll removed, one step closer to uncovering who we truly are. By consciously knowing about and working through these layers we can release them and take steps further to fully awakening. As mentioned prior, for some, this process is going through each layer gradually—removing one nesting doll at a time. For others there is a sudden removal of five, or ten, nesting dolls at once. Each layer has its own traumas, emotions, wounding, and patterns that cover the awakened state. Each layer has its own beliefs and understandings that create our reality and obscure who we truly are and what the world actually is. Let us awaken to who we are and the true nature of the world without all of the illusions, patterns, and traumas that confine and separate us.

Twelfth Layer:
Releasing the Self

The twelfth layer of conditioned reality is that of the Self. The Self (with a capitalized *S*) is our experience of the world from an in-utero state to our current age. Since we can recall many of our experiences, can express them in a logical way, and it is within our social constructs and accepted notions of reality that our experiences and traumas create who we are today, we do not need to expand ourselves too much to begin the processing of this outer layer.

In this stage we are able to let go of past negative or charged life experiences. This is a more gradual way of releasing, but it can be overwhelming if we do not know why past experiences are coming to our conscious minds or if what is coming up was an intense experience. In our current world we find it to be relatively acceptable to go to a therapist to work through emotions and traumas, and may not define this as a spiritual process. Although working through emotions and stories is helpful, if we do not understand the awakening process we may remain purely in logical and emotional realms, retelling and reliving stories again and again instead of clearing and working with them on a spiritual level.

A man who came to see me related releasing experiences in his bed at night, viewing them as if he were viewing short films about his life. He would relive them and the emotions, physical sensations, and thoughts and conversations he had during them. Others may feel an individual body part, like the neck or lower abdomen, begin to release with the emotions and experiences that were held in that area of their body coming up.

In the gradual awakening, experience by experience will be released until we have come to near the end of our own issues. It is misinformed to say that once awake or once the level of the Self is worked through that we will never have issues of a personal nature again or we don't have more to work through on this level. This is a difficult illusion to destroy, but the idea that once we are awake that we never experience conflict, emotions, or pain is simply untrue. In actuality, the experience of being awake allows us to fully experience these emotions, embody them, understand them, and then process and release them. It is a much different experience than allowing anger to pile up, to let fear weigh us down, and to let our experiences be skewed by our emotions and traumas. But to pretend that if we were being mugged that we would not experience fear or that if we broke a leg we would not feel pain just because we are "awake" is untrue. Quite simply, stuff still happens. The perspective shift that occurs when awakening allows us to view what is happening in our lives from a place of understanding and compassion, without the stored wounds of the Self creating further difficulties, magnifying, or obscuring our view of the situation. Even in an awakened person there are still issues that arise at the Self layer. The difference is that once this layer is mostly moved past, this process is conscious … we understand what is arising and can consciously work with it. When we have worked through much of the Self, or are going through a sudden awakening in which another layer begins to arise, we begin to encounter the eleventh layer, that of past lives.

Eleventh Layer:
Past Lives

At some point we will have released enough of our own issues that we begin working on other patterns that are impacting us. For some of us this will be in the form of past lives. Past-life issues may come up gradually or if we are going through a sudden awakening we may have past lives, ancestral issues, and other layers all come up to process and clear all at the same time.

It is not unusual for some of us to resist the clearing of past lives due to religious upbringing. If we are conditioned to not have the belief structure to support that we have had past lives, it is extremely difficult to understand and acknowledge that this type of energy can have an impact on us. Those of us who have more open cosmologies may still not have the knowledge base to realize that the experiences and energies we are processing are past lives. Many of us begin processing past-life energies long before we can accept or understand what is occurring.

What is more difficult about releasing the experiences of our past lives is that we do not have a physical reference point for them. Although we now have an understanding that we are clearing out patterns of the past we do not remember past lives the same way as the patterns from the direct experience of our own lives. When we clear our own lives, we have distinct memories that allow us to understand and directly associate them with the feelings and traumas coming up. When the memory of getting made fun of by a boy we liked at school or having whiplash from getting in a car accident comes up, these distinct memories from our own history allow for us to make logical sense out of what is coming up. Psychotherapy is filled with people with emerging memories at the level of the Self from early childhood and beyond. Unfortunately, when patterns that are not immediately accessible through personal history begin emerging, it is quite easy to block these experiences from clearing or to tell ourselves that we are not experiencing them at all.

How do past-life patterns emerge? Past-life issues are typically body-part specific, such as feeling our throat release and suddenly having an understanding that our throat was cut in a past life, or understanding that our pelvic pain is rooted in a miscarriage or death during giving birth in a past life. These traumas and patterns can release in any manner, such as having visions, dreams, or sudden senses of knowing.

For example, say that in a past life you got stabbed in the back. In our present day reality you may hurt your back in that area at the gym lifting weights, you may have a friend "backstab" you unexpectedly, or you may have a sudden bout of rapid heartbeat or sensation of something heavy in the chest. You are being shown that this area of your body has something happening to it that needs to clear and find relief. In past-life emergence, one area of our body will get injured, be in pain, or suffer trauma again and again. People who have been in ten car accidents may simply be horrible drivers or they may have experienced a death in a past life in a car that needs to be released.

Often past lives begin to appear as dreams or vague recollections that are not of our lives. They can be brief flashes or entire elaborate scenes. Many times we will feel how our past self died in our own body. Dying in wars, hangings, tar and feathering, childbirth, plagues, and all sorts of details about things many had no idea about until we research the subject are common in past-life recall. A man told me of specifics of how a train works after never having been on one when he began getting past-life recall. These are all not terribly unusual, and they come through when we are ready to release them.

Our body will know when it can begin to access a deeper layer of clearing beyond the Self layer. The more that we work in our daily lives to heal and look beyond our current layer of conditioned reality, the more our body can wake up from the illusions of these layers and out of sleep. When we consciously work through our issues through self-enquiry, meditation, and keeping an open mind, past-life energies will naturally appear at the right time in our lives to process and clear.

What is interesting about the releasing of past lives is how physical they seem to be. Past lives localize in a specific area of the body often associated with the issues or reasons for dying and often release in the same manner. A specific localized pain will show up and we will either begin to get flashes of another person or life or will begin to have very strange dreams that have nothing to do with our present life or current psychology. The dreams that come up for past-life experiencers can best be described as feeling oddly personal but yet removed, as if watching a movie that we are somehow deeply invested in.

Many women and men are carrying their past lives with them which have transferred aspects of the disease or issues with a localized body part to their current lives and body. I have now worked with countless women who have had diagnosed gynecological conditions clear up or get better with realizing past-life, dying-in-childbirth-type scenarios. One woman who came to me had severe endometriosis to the extent that she had to take a week off work each month due to depression and pain issues. Nothing she had tried worked, but when she realized that she had died in childbirth in a previous life and her child had passed a few moments later, she began hysterically crying. Later she contacted me and said that her period had started the next day with a lot of clotting and pain. After that session, during her next cycles she was down to only being in pain on the day of her period and the day before, and the pharmaceuticals and methods of treating her condition now worked for her when they had not before.

This patient had a glimpse at how powerfully the effects of a past life can impact the body. Just to be clear, once something is entrenched physically, simply clearing a past life is not likely to fully resolve a physical issue. But once the past life has released and the spiritual issues are resolved, the physical and emotional interventions can work when they had not previously been able to, or work better than they had before.

For past lives it is often easiest to find out the object associated with the past life. Simply ask for it. If you are at this stage of awakening the object will often appear. This object can be the manner of death (such as a knife or rope), or a localized area of issues in your current physical body. There is a reason that this past life is hanging out in the body. For many past lives, the reason is that it hasn't cleared its death state yet.

Many of us keep our past lives without releasing them because they are interesting. We research, dig into our own psyches, go to hypnotherapy, meditate, and construct whole new illusions or experiences about what may or may not have happened to us in a previous life. This can be quite funny, as most of us construct illusions of being Cleopatra instead of allowing for the real past-life energy to emerge. When we simply notice it as if we are reading an interesting story and do not try to embellish or make it more interesting, we can let it go. We do not need to retell it again and again. We do not need to know if it is true or research it or convince others of it. We can just let it go.

On some level it doesn't matter if our past lives are true or not. The lifting and clearing of any chaotic or blocked energy in the body will allow for us to be clearer and healthier. Each time that we clear something from our physical body it allows for us to become a bit more awakened. Each time we clear something we become more who we truly are without the impact of other energies informing our lives. Although past lives are wonderful to think about or to try to understand, the focus should not be on the past lives. The focus should be on creating a clear channel in our bodies and becoming more awake.

All we need to know from past lives is that we should clear the chaos and blockage from our past lives. This chaos and blockage is represented by an object or memory somewhere in our physical body. By removing and clearing the section of our body where it is housed, we then can integrate that past self, claim the power of that self, and become more powerful and whole in our day-to-day lives.

EXERCISE: How to Clear Past Lives

- Allow the experience to come up. Simply notice it.
- Do not create elaborate fantasies about what is coming up. Simply notice it as interesting.
- Note the area of your present-day body that is holding this experience. You will feel pain or discomfort in this area. For some this will be a small area; for others this may take up the whole body.
- Allow yourself to see, feel, or imagine the object (something that has been inserted or remains in your body from the experience).
- Focus on the object or area of the body.
- Tell this object/area that you see and feel it, and you are now truly ready to surrender it.

- Allow it to go. When you can physically imagine yourself removing an object, it can leave, lift off ... however it wants to leave, it is welcome to. If only part of it wants to go, let part of it go.
- Go back to this area later and repeat the process until you are feeling more clear, no longer feel a charge from the incident (emotions or energy), no longer feel pain in this area of your body, or no longer see or feel the object.

Our mind will want to know why—why it is there, what it is doing there, what lessons to learn from it. Our mind will want to keep creating stories. Actual stories might come up. We might learn why we always feared the ocean, why we don't want to have children, why we are so tired, or why we were obsessed with military planes as a child. We can allow these understandings to occur, but recreating our whole existence around them or holding onto them because they are interesting or spiritual holds some of the energy in our body. Let this energy go. As it leaves, we will be shown more understandings and lessons about these energies. Acknowledge these lessons and understandings and simply let them go.

Beyond the manner of death, the other reason that past lives stay energetically locked in our bodies is because there is a lesson or experience that was difficult that we (in our past life) did not get to process appropriately. This could be that our past life had a difficult relationship with a family member or that there was a war, trauma, or some other pattern that did not resolve. Any experience that would cause us as our current-day selves deep regret, trauma, emotions, pain, or struggle would cause our past selves the same. At the end of each lifetime we begin to clear many things—some of them are such strong energies and patterns that they are not able to resolve before our physical death. These patterns and energies then carry over to the next life in order to be resolved appropriately.

It is common for us to find that a relationship with someone or an experience from a past life is being repeated in this lifetime. This is especially common for patterns that did not process in the first stage of awakening—the clearing of personal issues, emotions, and the Self. Similar to energies from the Self, we keep on repeating and bringing experiences to us from past lives in order to heal. Past-life issues are relatively common, especially in patterning, such as when we cannot figure out why we dislike our sister so much, or why we hate a teacher or authority figure, or why we seem to meet the same type of woman or man again and again who is wrong for us, for these types of experiences are rooted in a deeper layer than our current lifetime—that of a past life. It is only by resolving the pattern or experience at the level of the past life that it can fully resolve in our current lives.

When we are clearing past-life issues and find that they do not clear through simple surrender we can work with the past-life pattern meditation below. We may also need to do more clearing work at the previous level (the level of the Self) before a release of past-life issues occurs. It is typical for us to be rather messy, spiritual beings with patterns at varying levels of conditioned reality—some of the past-life issues we experience may not resolve because they are rooted in deeper layers still. We continue progressing through layers with remnants of energy and patterns at the previous layers, flickering back and forth between layers until we get to the root reason for our issues. When we get to the root layer of our issues it will clear through all of the more superficial layers. This means that if we have an issue that is showing up as blocked energy in our past life as well as our current Self we may need to progress all the way to the Seventh Layer of conditioned reality (karmic layer) to fully resolve the issue.

It would be wonderful if we had a clear, linear progression through the layers of conditioned reality but that is never the case. We always must go back and examine all of the layers, even in the awakened state, to work through patterning and blockages. The more awake we become, the more we can see and understand patterns and blocks at a deeper level and have heightened capabilities in clearing them. By being open to looking backward at our spiritual journey we can continue to unfold into awakening and beyond.

EXERCISE: Clearing Past-Life Patterns and Lessons

If you are unable to clear a past life through the previous work, it is likely that there is a pattern or lesson associated with it that you should know about it.

- Get a solid understanding of the past life and the body part involved from the previous exercises.
- Simply ask if there is anything you should know about the pattern. You can ask either the body part directly, a guide, God, you in the past life, or whatever seems appropriate. If there is anything to know, it will be revealed to you.
- Keep attention and listen. It might reveal right then to you. More commonly it will reveal within the next few days.
- Notice synchronicities and issues over the next few days. What do they have in common? The way that this pattern and lesson shows up will emerge if you are paying attention. The right people, places, and emotions will show you clearly what the pattern is.
- When you have noticed issues emerging, write them down. This will provide clarity about what the pattern is.

- Simply ask what the lesson is after you have written down the issues and people who have presented to you over the last few days.
- If you are shown the pattern, people involved, and lesson, let the pattern know that it can release from your physical body. Let it do so.
- Often we make things more complicated than we need to, so just acknowledging the energy of the past life, knowing the pattern, and allowing it to release are enough, but often our egos like ceremony. If you require a ceremony, you can either picture the cord linked to the past life being severed, or the energy of the past life being sent somewhere or picked up by an angel or deity of your choosing.
- Do a recheck of your body, and then you can thank your body and the past life if it feels appropriate.

If we do this exercise and are still feeling energy from this past life or the area of our physical body where it was lodged, we can simply repeat the steps. Again, sometimes deeper layers or other issues need to resolve first. If we feel like this is the case, know that this past-life energy will reemerge and let us know when it is the right time to release.

Once we can express the energy of the blocked or repressed past-life experience we can claim the power and strength as our own. When we have any aspect of ourselves blocked or locked down, our bodies are taxed from dealing with this energy. It takes energy to organize this chaos and traumatic energy into a specific part of our body. Our body walls off this energy in an effort to keep it as small and blocked as possible, because it is not yet ready to deal with the energy. Unfortunately, what happens is that once this energy is walled off it is unable to release properly without guidance.

Dr. John Upledger, one of the innovators of CranioSacral Therapy, referred to this phenomenon as an energy cyst. An energy cyst is simply localized, chaotic energy. When emotional, physical, and/or spiritual trauma occurs, the energy of it enters the physical body. So it does the least amount of damage, we consolidate this energy the best we can to one area in our body. It requires energy to keep this chaotic energy that is filled with emotions and past experiences in its spot. When we free this energy, our bodies are no longer taxed with keeping this energy contained and new energy has the opportunity to flow through areas that were once blocked.

This new energy flow will already be a source of power, and it will integrate appropriately by itself most times. Instead of being a victim, or looking at past-life experiences as negative or something that needs to be cleared, we can instead actively reclaim the power of the experience.

EXERCISE: How to Claim the Power of Past Lives

Once we find that we have completely or even partially cleared a specific part of our body of a past-life object or experience, we can actively integrate and claim the power of the past life.

- Sit with your feet on the floor, imagine the top of your head (your crown chakra) opening like a small gate, and allow for white light to come in. You can ask the divine to do this, a specific angel, deity, or guide if you are familiar with those. Imagine white light and energy flowing through the top of your head to fill in the hole that has been created. The body will likely naturally begin to flow better in the area you have cleared, but bringing in white light will help clear out any residual energy.
- Allow any residual energy to flow out of the bottom of your feet or lift off of your body like smoke.
- When you have done this, ask for the power of the experience to come through to you. Imagine this power as a specific-colored light. Let it flow into your whole body.
- Ask internally what the gift of this past life was. This can be anything. Simply listen, feel, or be open to seeing what the gift is.
- Ask for your past life and present life to be integrated. Allow for the energy freed up to be returned to you in the present moment. Visualize or feel this happening. If you are more sensitive, this can be a profound shift. Even if you do not feel or see this happening know that this experience and integration is important.

Anytime we are going through a significant clearing, working with a spiritual healer who can do integration work may be necessary if we feel really out of balance. We also may need more work to completely clear an area, either doing these activities again or working with deeper layers and patterns that have not yet been explored.

Tenth Layer:
Immediate Family Systems

In a typical progression of awakening, the release of immediate family systems clearing occurs either before, during, or immediately after past lives. Our immediate family system is anyone from our family who has made a direct impact on our existence. This can be mother, father, sister, brother, or grandmother. This patterning occurs even if we have a family member who is not present, or if we are adopted. In the case of adoption there are now two family systems that can be worked with. In the case of death or lack of presence in the life, this absence creates a patterning that must also be resolved.

This awakening begins with the understanding of the Self as not just "I" but also a complete family unit, with mother, father, siblings, pets … and the endless variations that occur within modern family units. At first, there is an understanding that is quite common and broad that the function of the family unit is as important as the function of the Self. This shows up in planning of activities, finances, consideration of each member of the household, and their emotions and experiences of life. One functional whole is the ideal, and each family member is recognized as a part of that whole.

This type of awakening is often the first awakening of bliss and love. Although many of us have difficult family existences, the possibility and love that appears in a new mother or new father at their creation of a child is enough to show that such love is possible in the universe. Although this is, in some ways, a selfish awakening and one of biological imperative since our children are in many ways a representation and continuation of the Self, it does open the possibility and understanding of such love, which is vital in understanding later stages of oneness. The amount of bliss and love that a new parent feels toward his or her child is the amount of bliss and love that can come through in the awakened state.

The immediate family awakening contains a deep connection to partner or spouse. It is not unusual for those going through awakening to begin to process the events, experiences, and energies of the spouse/partner, children, and other members of the household including pets. It is important at this stage to begin a bit of differentiation and understanding of the Self, to know what we would define as "our" processing and which is that of our household or environment. A simple question of "Is this mine?" when we find ourselves feeling angry, irritable, or having issues or experiences come up when we are going through this layer of awakening is typically enough to clarify what we are experiencing. Knowing that when we are awakening we are clearing not only our experiences but that of those around us, starting with immediate family, should ease confusion during this process, and will assist us during later stages of awakening.

An important note and distinction should be made here about when we begin to process energies outside of ourselves. It is easy to begin to take responsibility, to see patterns (for example, the patterns that brought us together with our partners) and to feel emotional over creating these patterns. At some level this is true, and we must take responsibility in order to fully awaken. On another, more pragmatic level, this responsibility and understanding need not extend to fixing or controlling others. When we begin to awaken we are able to see how we have contributed to the patterns of our relationships. What our responsibility is as someone who is increasingly conscious is to clear up our part in it, to look inward to see what wounding or part of these patterns comes from ourselves.

When we get to this level of awakening it is common to divorce, to distance ourselves from family members that we see as "toxic," change our names, and even move to another state or country. It is easy at this level to want to avoid people with significant patterns and to only surround ourselves with "love and light." On some level this may be necessary—we are waking up to patterns of abuse and toxicity that we are no longer able to ignore. If we are in danger or suffering severely as a result of our circumstances, our outer circumstances need to change. However. in most cases this urge to change names, locations, and partners is simply not necessary. The tendency to "fix" our outer circumstances—our names, location, friends, and families—is a real call to look internally at the patterns and wounds that we still carry. This stage of awakening is uncomfortable because we are beginning to see some of the layers of conditioned reality and they make us uncomfortable. In healing ourselves we do not need to change our external circumstances even if we have the urge to do so.

This level can be uncomfortable because we begin to see the patterning and wounds of others. It is easy for us to look outside and see the faults of others. At this level the faults we find in others are often our own wounds. At this level of conditioned reality it is easy to want to tell everyone our "truth," to tell everyone what their wounds are and how to fix them. It is difficult to live in the world because people suddenly seem toxic, and we are awake enough to see the wounds and patterns of our family members and friends. It is important to tell ourselves that each person has a path and their own unique prison. By developing compassion for our family, our community, our world and by understanding the wounds of others, we can continue our own path without driving ourselves crazy about others not taking responsibility for their own issues.

All this level of awakening requires is awareness and a focus on love. By this I mean that it is natural for us to pick up the fear of our children, the anger of our spouse, or the chaos of an elderly parent. The negative patterns of conditioning at this level emerge quite regularly, and it is easy to place the focus on the chaotic or negative energies. Instead, focusing on the love and the oneness of the family unit (even if there are difficulties) and sending love or seeing each family member with love is enough to flow through this level. A clear differentiation of Self is necessary, and beginning to question what is yours and what is not yours is an excellent habit to start. There is nothing to do at this level but realize that we are at this level and remain open enough to move through it.

THE SPIRITUAL AWAKENING GUIDE

EXERCISE: How to Clear Energy That is Not Yours

- Feel the emotion or pain that you are feeling.
- Ask if it is yours. If it is, do other work for yourself.
- If it is not yours, acknowledge the emotion or physical pain.
- Ask for it to leave.
- Put your feet firmly on the floor.
- Imagine the emotion or pain draining out of your legs and into the earth.

One of the simplest ways (beyond the above meditation) to clear energy that is not ours is to simply take a shower or a bath with Epsom salts. Lemon, either as a spray or in a glass of water, can assist with clearing as well. If we are in a household with a lot of immediate family patterns and emotions, clearing our whole house with lemon is wonderful. Sage, copal, and palo santo are herbs known for clearing properties. Taking a broom and sweeping chaotic energy and emotions from the top to bottom of your house, back to front, always sweeping toward and out the door, is a method of clearing that is effective. Keeping a bowl of water out with salt will absorb energies. Simply keeping our homes clean and neat will allow for energies to clear. Recognition of this layer—realizing what energies are ours and what are not, and the understanding and acceptance of the patterns that we are, for the first time, recognizing that are present in our family unit—will allow for us to move through the family line to work with ancestral patterns.

Ninth Layer:
Ancestral Patterns

At a certain point, either out of necessity or simply because we are ready, we will begin to release the ancestral layer of conditioned reality. These patterns may begin to present themselves and we simply become aware of them. By realizing that there is a pattern in place that is affecting us, we then become aware enough at a certain point to decide to break the threads of the pattern, allowing ourselves to break free from them.

We may simply have a growing awareness that when working with the tenth layer (immediate family) that many of our issues stem from a deeper layer, that of our ancestry.

For ancestral patterns, old family stories may come into our lives as if by synchronicity, such as the telling of stories at family gatherings. When this occurs we may begin to become aware about how those stories are still playing out in our lives. At this level of awakening we begin to see how the plight of our ancestors has been passed down to us. Wars, immigration, starvation, plagues, genocides, and family tragedies are common in all of our histories. These unresolved issues and patterns of our ancestors are housed in our bodies and are repeated again and again in our family line until they are cleared. ·

When we begin to understand our ancestral history—the decisions that had to be made, the fears, anger, and traumas of our ancestral line—we can begin to understand how these patterns still exist within us. The decisions of our ancestors are not our own, although we are experiencing the impact of these decisions and are still playing them out in our current lives. Even if we do not consciously know the stories and history of our ancestors, this layer can be cleared.

When I lived in Chicago, I worked with many people who were descendants of the Holocaust. Many were a few generations removed from the Holocaust, although I did have the experience of working with direct descendants a few times. Many of the people I worked with were successful upper-middle-class people living in white suburbia. They had the typical fears and issues one would expect—divorce, material possession and spending issues, self-worth, and depression. But as I worked with these people an interesting pattern emerged. After we were able to process their own emotions and circumstances surrounding their current family, job, and so on a huge pattern of fear and feelings of imprisonment occurred. Some of these women and men admitted to activities that would be thought extremely strange of someone in that class and age group, such as hoarding food, insomnia with dreams of being chased, never feeling settled or grounded, and always feeling the need to be on alert. Although this group had the usual amount of trauma that one would expect of this group, these feelings and images that emerged were not from the Self.

Working through these images, it became crystal clear that many of these patients were descendants of the Holocaust and that the patterns they were experiencing were not their own. They had no reason to hoard food, to feel constantly afraid, or have dreams of being attacked. By clearing not only their emotions but their ancestral line back to the Holocaust and further, the dreams and behaviors subsided and they were able to move forward from these patterns.

At this point of our awakening, symbols, dreams, and images of ancestors may be coming through. Simply pay attention to them. Pay attention to the patterns and traumas of the family line. We may not know all of them because families hide traumas such as incest, murders, suicides, and other issues for good reason. After we understand the patterns of our ancestry we can begin to clear them and then bring forward the power and gifts of our ancestors. It is a much different experience to be empowered by our ancestors rather than have their traumas hold us back.

Ancestral issues are housed within our physical body but do not often appear as physically as past lives or our own issues do. They can wildly vary from person to person, but I have had people report threads, lines, grids, clouds outside the body, blobs, and simply feelings of blockage. The ancestral layer of awakening is typically more emotional than physical. Fear, anger, rage, or grief that is overwhelming without a present-day reason is the most common experience that people report when working with ancestral patterns.

Although we are always in a physical body, the patterns and layers at the ancestral level are much deeper than the layers of Self, past lives, and immediate family. As we go deeper we begin to go beyond the physical to the emotional. This is the proverbial rabbit hole where the beginning of the spiritual path shows up more readily, externally, and physically, and as we progress further it becomes more emotionally and then spiritually based. Even at the deepest level the physical body and emotions are still affected. Each layer goes deeper but we are expanding at the same time outward. This is why the deepest layers are the most inner but have to do with the cosmos.

Another way we become aware of ancestral patterns is by having a long path of healing with a talented healer who is aware of these patterns and this level of existence. Meditation also brings up ancestral patterns if done on a regular basis. To awaken through this level it is necessary to begin a meditation practice if one has not already been established. Regular meditation, stillness, and self-inquiry will allow for us to transcend the layers of conditioned reality and see who we truly are.

For many, ancestral patterns remain unconscious and get enacted day after day with no real understanding. Ancestral patterns are extremely common and resistant to healing. Modern therapy approaches frequently go to the Self, the early childhood experience, and to the immediate family. There is little understanding of how patterns and traumas of our ancestral line affect us and so these wounds often go unhealed for generations.

So what is needed to release ancestral energies? The first thing is to realize the patterns that we carry that are not ours, and are not of our immediate family. While the Holocaust example of tragedy is readily understandable, we all have incidents of war, rape, villages burned, or famine in our ancestral history. Some of these histories we may know—they have been passed down orally through the family lineage through generations or are readily available in history texts. But some of us have no real idea of what was lurking in our family lineage other than the faint idea that it probably wasn't an ideal situation.

Our histories and ancestry form a sort of tapestry. The threads of the tapestry are members of our family line and their stories. Some of the threads that make up this tapestry are of strength and of perseverance. Some of the threads are frayed, stuck together, or too tight because of issues in our ancestry. By coming into awareness of ancestral patterns you will break the threads that make up the tapestry that binds you to these energies.

EXERCISE: Working with the Tapestry of Our Ancestral Line

- Come into awareness of the tapestry that makes up your ancestral line. This line includes your ancestors, your immediate family, and yourself. This tapestry will also include your children.
- Look at the tapestry or feel for it.
- Take a piece of paper and draw your tapestry. If you are visually dominant, you can simply see this. If you feel more, you can ask for the tapestry and allow your hand to draw it spontaneously without you knowing what it looks like beforehand.
- When you look at your tapestry, are there places that look beautiful and strong? Look at these strong places and see or feel what words come to mind about the strength of your ancestors.
- When you look at the tapestry are there places that look frayed, stuck, dark, or weak? Focus on these areas, allow for words or visuals to come through about these places.
- When you find the words or visuals, ask for the patterns to appear if they haven't already. Ask what the patterns are that you are repeating in your daily life.
- Allow for yourself to acknowledge these patterns of your ancestors that are present in your life still. For example, if your ancestor was someone who lost her family in a fire and was never able to cope with the loss, the pattern would be one of loss and grief. This may have been passed down to you as being cautious about fire, about being possessive about your children and partner, or even deciding not to have a family or a partner.
- Once you have realized the pattern, ask for the strength of the pattern. The woman who dealt with losing her family was a survivor. This ancestral pattern was also passed down to you.
- Imagine the ancestor (do not second guess your visual or felt sense of this ancestor being with you—do this even if you feel like you are making this up) and thank them for the beauty of the pattern. Let them know you are clearing the rest of the pattern. Ask them if it is okay that you do so.
- Allow for yourself to either see your higher power, a guide, or yourself gently reworking this tapestry until the part that once held the energy of this problem looks complete to you.

This is an extensive meditation and is not likely something that can be done steps 1–10. If you need to, stop at each step or go back and repeat steps until you are able to get through all ten. It really does require some effort to consciously clear your ancestry, but it is well worth it.

Know that when the time comes for our ancestral patterns to rise we can choose to understand, come to awareness, and accept these energies with gratitude. Then we can understand the whole pattern, the whole tapestry, and take the strength of the situation rather than the fear or negative charge. By forgiving, understanding, and accepting the ancestral energies that run through us we can transform them to strength. This is a layer of conditioning that results in a huge leap forward in consciousness when we work through it. When we work on this deep of a level we can see from a different vantage point—one of the strength and history of our ancestors. We can have our ancestors guide us. We can see the different, more superficial layers from this place of strength and wisdom. We begin to see the world not through our wounds, or our family and ancestral wounds, but from a place of clarity beyond that.

Many of us have taken clearing these sorts of energies too literally. We think that we need to erase the stories, even forget where we have come from and our personal and collective past to awaken. That simply is not true. What we are doing is releasing the negative charge and trauma from the situation. We should be able to look back at our ancestors, our life, our parents, and feel a sense of neutrality as well as love and compassion. If we are feeling anger, revenge, fear, and other emotions the situation still has a charge and has not fully released yet. Our ancestral tapestry is a grid of energy that can be full of chaos and trauma or can be charged with power, informing and empowering us throughout our lives.

EXERCISE: How to Release the Ancestral Line

Ancestral energies may come up and clear quite naturally, or they may require some conscious work. Once the knowledge of the pattern and wound from our ancestry comes up it should clear quite naturally as long as we are not resistant to it leaving or want to keep the pattern for some reason. Simply becoming aware, surrendering the pattern, and clearing it is often enough. When we are conscious enough to know our patterns we can consciously choose to act differently to break the habits and energies of our patterning. However, sometimes a process is necessary to get us out of a stuck place.

- First, you must identify the wound. You do not need to know the exact situation, but you should know the wound. A wound is an emotion or reaction to a situation—it is the loop that still is circulating in your brain. For example, my patients who were a few generations from the Holocaust had a fear around hunger, around not getting enough food, and around starvation. This "looped" through their brains again and again, creating behaviors that did not stem from their own experiences.

- Next, identify the understanding that came from your ancestors. In this case, the ancestors of these patients decided to hoard food, to eat very little, or to eat as much as they could whenever they could. They never knew when they were going to get food next, so they reacted appropriately for the situation.
- Now, see this pattern in your own life. What is your relationship to food? How did this pattern impact you? This pattern may have changed or may have not to play out in your life. Identify the pattern and see how it plays out in your life.
- (Optional step) For those of you who are sensitive, where do you see this pattern in or around you currently?

When you have all of this information you can bring this pattern into full awareness. By doing so, it gives the pattern an opportunity to release and for you to be free of it. Simply with these three (or four) steps in mind, know that you do not have to repeat this loop of behavior, and begin to change your reaction appropriately. This change might occur quite easily, or it might need some negotiation to release. For example, with the Holocaust descendants, once they were able to recognize where the pattern came from, many immediately stopped hoarding. However, for others this habit became so ingrained that they required nutritionists, therapists, spiritual healers, and other professionals to help them negotiate letting go of some of the destructive behaviors they had created as a result of their patterning and to build new, healthy patterns now that they were free to make their own decisions.

Looping

A loop is a way that we react to trauma that is too much for us to process. It is also what we do with subconscious patterns, either patterns that are passed down to us (like from ancestors or past lives) or are more communal patterns, such as largely unspoken patterns around race, religion, and sexuality that are pervasive in our culture.

A loop is simply that—it is a relay in our brains that creates the same situation, emotions, and lessons again and again. It does this for several reasons, the biggest being simply that our minds work in patterns and some looping, or ingrained ways of being, are natural and easier for the brain in order to make sense of the world. Looping can involve thought patterns, emotions, spiritual patterns, or the physical body. Many times it is multi-faceted.

An example of this was a woman who had been in a rather severe car accident where she was in a three-car pileup on the highway. With all of her health-care providers she would begin to move her body to curl inward as if she were in the car again at the moment of impact during the accident when talking about it. In her mind she was still in the car and in the process of being hit. When she came to me she was able to realize that she was reenacting the accident again and again, and we worked a different way out of the loop. This broke the loop and allowed for her brain and body to realize that she no longer required this loop.

The same fears, situations, and types of people will present at all levels of awakening (or even in people who are totally asleep) to show the wounds and loops that are present in us. For those going through awakening this process may either intensify or speed up. Intensification of this means having this loop triggered many times within a short period of time—such as meeting the same type of person over and over again until we finally realize that the people we are meeting are similar to our mother with whom we had significant issues. Speeding up means that we will go through intense periods of processing and that loops may show themselves one after the other, resulting in us meeting all sorts of people and being thrust into many situations that are fairly unpleasant for us.

Although looping is a protective mechanism, it is also how we make sense out of the conditioned layers of reality. We go through the same routines, the same actions again and again because it is easier for us to process mentally. When we experience a trauma or blockage this also creates a loop that we will repeat until we are able to consciously break free from it. In an awakened state, we are either free from these "loops" or conditioned thoughts and behaviors and are totally in the present moment or are very conscious that we are looping.

If this process is occurring, awareness and surrender is key. By consciously knowing what we "loop" and choosing to act, think, and behave differently than the loop has conditioned us to, we can break free from these loops, or ingrained conditioned ways of being, in our lives. Now that we have the knowledge of what is happening, we can clear all of our conditioned looping with the knowledge that we will have much more freedom after each one that we break free from. Free from loops, we can discover who we truly are.

Eighth Layer:
Societal and Collective Conditioning

The layer of societal and collective conditioning may come at any time, and may even come before much of our personal history clearing has occurred. This layer often presents as a grid. What happens at this level is that we perceive ourselves to be awake and that seemingly the whole world is asleep or in one of the less awakened categories.

So what happens when we begin to understand that society is asleep? We begin to notice that television, news, and the people surrounding us are following the same patterns and conversations like a script. At first this realization causes many of us to fall in a depressive state. There is good reason for this. All that we knew and understood to be true is falling away. For some of us this happens gradually, as we wake up and realize that our family, our community, and society at large are asleep. For others it happens instantaneously that the illusions that hold society together fall away.

The realizations at this layer of conditioned reality can be quite alienating, leading to a desire to separate oneself from society. Many of us during this phase drop long-standing relationships and friendships, let go of our possessions, and begin deeply questioning our faith and our lives as a whole. We begin to wake up to the understanding that a great deal of patterns have been placed upon us by the collective dream of society.

During this phase the illusion around society and societal constructs drops. The awakening and letting go of societal and collective patterns is a huge step in the awakening process. We awaken to the collective patterns of religion, sex, gender, race, and others that confine us, and this can be a disturbing realization because we realize the illusions behind societal conditioning but have not yet reached a point where we understand what to do about this new knowledge.

This is also the stage of realizing than more than the Self creates the world. It is a common spiritual misconception that we singularly create the world around us—and that each of us fully creates our own reality. When we awaken to the societal level we can see through this former illusory thinking and realize that collectively we create the world and its conditions.

This level of awakening is the last hugely emotional layer to work through. Anger, rage, grief, depression, and other emotions will surface with a forceful quality to them. When we are experiencing these huge emotions and emotional fluctuations that come at this level, simply knowing that our emotions are releasing so that we can move through this layer of conditioning can carry us through. It is easy to judge ourselves or be ashamed for being "awake" and still carrying a lot of rage and fear. When we know that we are releasing much of our emotional baggage in a short period of time we can better make sense of our experiences. When we understand that we are angry at the collective sleeper state of society we can work to adjust and integrate this new knowledge in a healthy and balanced way. Being patient with ourselves, realizing that we are at this level of awakening, and realizing that the strong emotions and experiences that come at this level are paving the way for further awakening will allow for us to not remain stuck, continually becoming angry or grief-ridden over the illusory separation of us being "awake" and the rest of society being "asleep." When we are willing to go beyond the illusory nature of feeling superior, different, or unique because we are awake in a society that is not, we can move beyond feelings of separation. When we allow ourselves to deeply feel emotions arising without castigating them or deeming them something that an awakened person shouldn't feel we allow for them to come up to release. When we open ourselves up to the possibility that there is something beyond simply knowing that society is a dream or a grid of conditioned reality we have the chance to reconcile and awaken further.

Dark Nights

For many of us this type of awakening leads to a *Dark Night of the Soul*, where we feel a sense of despair, a loss of the comfort and understandings that being asleep provided us. There is a sense of missing the simplicity of being under the patterns and scripts of conditioned reality but also an understanding that there is something beyond the stage that we are at now. Once in the awakening process it is rare that we are content in any of the stages unless we are experiencing an ego awakening or have fully awakened.

Many of us stay in the societal awakening stage for lengthy periods of time. We become angry and disillusioned, realizing that the government, societal norms and rules, and the whole construct of society is patently false. We are blocked by our rage, fear, and anger. If we are able to work through these emotions we can progress. Some of us choose to consciously work through our emotions, seek help for our spiritual depression, and seek further spiritually. Others of us get stuck and are unable to ask for or find help or are afraid of moving forward.

When we experience a Dark Night during this stage of awakening, the sense of depression and feelings of being in a fog or black hole can be overwhelming. There are feelings of helplessness, of apathy, of an overwhelming depression and rage as well as a sense of grief at the realizations that come up. There is an understanding that is false but pervasive in this category that there is nothing we can do. When we have woken up to societal and collective conditioning, everyone but ourselves appears to be asleep. There is both a sense of ego stroking that comes with this as we feel that we alone understand things that nobody else possibly could, but also a sense of paralyzing separation, isolation, loss, and depression. There is the new flickering of understanding coming in that we are but a small part of creating society and the world that makes us feel unable to make a difference.

It is easy to stay at this stage for long periods of time, to isolate, convincing ourselves that the world is a horrible place. There is a conviction that the rest of the world is going to hell and nobody else understands what is going on but us that is pervasive in this stage. This is yet another stage where we are tempted to focus externally on the problems of the sleeping society and the world instead of looking internally. When we

44

are able to again look internally and work through our part of creating societal and collective conditioning we can heal and move through it.

This is the stage where the ego first understands that it is losing ground, and although an experience of isolation occurs, it is typically one of the first stirrings of truly understanding and feeling oneness.

Dark Nights are understandably difficult. They are a period of nothingness, a time where whatever spiritual support or connections to our spiritual or divine nature do not feel present. They are a time of rewiring and preparation for a new stage of understanding and a leap of consciousness. But until we recognize that we are in a Dark Night, we will not understand what is going on. We will just feel miserable, as if God or our higher power has forsaken us. We will go to counselors and receive medications or talk therapy that might help with symptoms, but if the depression and other symptoms of the Dark Night are spiritual in nature, the root of the issue will not be worked through and we will further stagnate.

When we are experiencing a Dark Night it is crucial to reach out to friends and family. Our friends and family might not understand spiritual awakening, but anyone who can provide comfort to us will understand what a bad day is like or what depression is like. When we realize that we are in fact experiencing a Dark Night, we must force ourselves to go out into nature, connect with friends and family, and go into counseling if needed so we can move through this experience. Once we recognize that we are in this place we can understand that we are being prepared to move forward. Even if we cannot consciously connect to our spiritual nature we can understand that it is there and ask for it to move us forward sooner rather than later. Dark Nights can occur when we need down time before moving forward. By giving ourselves this time—resting, watching movies, stopping meditating and other spiritual pursuits, immersing ourselves in daily routines, and letting family and friends know what we are experiencing—it will pass.

For some of us, the Dark Night becomes such a place of stagnation and emptiness that we consider suicide. Our symptoms are severe and we are truly suffering. When we experience this, know that it is important that we are safe until it passes. Asking for help from physical resources such as friends and family, allopathic sources, medication, and even hospitalization is not a sign of failure. Sometimes we need to learn how to ask for help and to be kept safe. Just because we are experiencing something spiritual does not mean that physical sources cannot help us. When we regain functioning and clarity we can work through the issues that caused us to experience our Dark Night in a more balanced state.

For those of us who have awakened to societal and collective conditioning we will now understand that society is a collective dream. As a culture, society, community, neighborhood, and so on we are all collectively dreaming our existences.

As we begin to wake up to this level of existence we begin to understand that we are a tapestry of sorts. Although we each have a personal tapestry and ancestral tapestry, in the community, societal, and world tapestries, we may be just a thread or part of a thread. These threads that compose the tapestry are made up of our thoughts, our fears, our collective conditioning and expectations, and larger influences. Many of us who begin the process of waking up begin to realize that these threads, our lives, are programmed in such a way that we never really do much with our lives. We are collectively woven to be asleep. This tapestry appears as a grid that some of us in this stage are able to see as lines, lights, or streams of energy. Sometimes we are able to see entire grids, although this typically comes later. This may appear out of the corner of our eye, in bed at night, or even during the day in plain view. The grid of societal conditioning is one of the lower ones that makes up the universe, and will appear surrounding us but also penetrating through us.

When we get to a different stage of understanding we can learn how to work with the grids, but in this stage, it is hard not to despair or get wrapped up in emotion. It is easy to stay in judgment, calling ourselves awakened and coming up with long lists and requirements for what others must do to be awakened or calling ourselves a teacher and never progressing after this stage. It is easy to step into destructive behaviors or put ourselves back to sleep in this stage. It is easy to step into ego awakening and create further illusions and delusions that we know all that there is, and how special and important we are. It is easy at this stage to pretend that we know everything because we know a little bit about something. But if we begin to develop compassion for those around us who are asleep, if we have compassion for ourselves and open ourselves to what we do not know with humility, we can move through this difficult stage. When we start to be of service, when we start to feel as if we are making a difference, some of the existential despair will dissipate. When we are willing to look at the judgment and the darkness within ourselves that remains, turning inward, and realizing that we do not know everything, we can further awaken.

As we begin to become aware of societal constructs we will also begin processing them. It is easy to get angry or not know what is going on when we begin to process these energies. Many of us got headaches during the Boston bombings, threw up before 9/11, or get dreams of less newsworthy societal and communal events when we awaken to this stage. Sometimes it is easy to connect to these energies if we watch the news or realize where the energy is coming from. Most of us have dreams, feel ill, or experience pain with little realization of how much societal energies can impact us.

These are more intense energies to clear at this level, and these energies may result in a wide variety of physical and emotional symptoms. It is not unusual for psychic abilities to drastically increase at this time. Headaches, dreams, fatigue, and emotional lability are very common. We are processing not only our own material (yes, there is still that), but also the leftovers from our immediate family, past lives, ancestry, and now society. These energies when clearing can result in great openings physically as we begin to feel flows of energy through our body.

Because we are beginning to feel greater flow there will also be a rising awareness of that which is not flowing—what is still stuck. We will feel this in our physical body and the sensation of physical issues will dramatically increase. For example, if we are feeling flow through everywhere in our body but our hip, our hip will begin to increase in pain. The deeper we go in terms of layers the more access to energy and the greater the flow of energy will be through our bodies. This flow of energy when coming to the hip will hit it like a massive wave hitting a rock. Gradually this rock will be worn down if the waves continue. But in the meantime our physical issues increase as it becomes very clear where in our body energy cannot flow through. When we begin processing and having access and awareness to larger energies, such as societal energies, it is a huge force slamming against whatever stagnation remains in our body. When we are mostly cleared of our patterning these energies can flow through us and we will simply notice them, but at first and for quite a while they might actually be quite painful.

Awareness that these energies are not ours and simply allowing these energies to flow through us without hooking into them is extremely important. We can do this by simply noticing things that are coming up without wanting to know too much of the "why" or creating stories around what is happening to us. We should ask if this is ours and if the answer is "no," allow the energies to pass through into the feet and out the body. The basic tree meditation (found in Part 4 of this book) is a good method to begin processing these energies. Larger flows of energy will clear out the rest of the gunk from the other patterns and issues in your body if we allow them to.

Bodywork can be extremely helpful at this point to release the physical congestion. Zero Balancing, a form of bodywork that works with the physical body, specifically the skeletal structure, as well as the energetic structure and flows of the body, is a wonderful way to work with the energetic, emotional, and physical nature of this stage at the same time.

Spirit Guides and Non-Physical Energies

The amount of energy around and in us when we reach the societal conditioning level of awakening is becoming brighter and larger. We will notice the amount of energy flow through our bodies has increased as well. It is not uncommon for us to temporarily have issues with electronics, static-electricity-type sensations when touching objects, or find that television or computers are making us ill. The ability to heal others with simply touching them, such as in modalities like Reiki or Healing Touch, intensifies at this level, as well as an interest in healing, spirituality, and being of service.

With this comes the attraction of spirits and energies to us. Imagine each of us as a nightlight. The more awakened we are, the brighter of a nightlight we are. Other energies will be attracted to us, and we will be able to see or sense them on some level. For most of us this can be a bit disconcerting. Feeling as if we are never alone, feelings of being watched, or even being touched or spoken to for perhaps the first time are common symptoms.

An increase in psychic abilities or the development of new sensitivities is common. Inability to digest specific foods; intolerance to alcohol and drugs; and hearing, seeing, smelling, tasting, and feeling things that were not in our normal range of perception before happen at this level. This layer allows us to see things a different way than we once did. It is common to be in touch with the outer constructs of reality, such as the archetype level, for the first time. Although the archetype level will be covered in detail later on, know that the archetype level allows for us to get in touch with aspects of ourselves that are more spiritual in nature—power animals, spirit guides, angels, deities, and non-physical teachers.

These archetypes and deeper layers of spiritual conditioning allow for us to begin to access our own inner truth. The guides, animals, deities, and experiences that come through the archetype and lower levels of spiritual existence are Self-created. They are an aspect of us. This is wonderful, because they are intended to teach us about ourselves, guide us to become who we are at our core, become whole, and allow us to stand in our true power.

It is important at this stage to have a consistent meditation practice as well as a physical practice. A consistent meditation practice will allow for us to develop the relationship with our guides and will allow for us to process the amount of energies that are coming through us. A physical practice can obviously keep us healthy, but the main objective in having a physical practice—like hiking, yoga, tai chi, running, and other forms of exercise—is to keep us in our physical body and grounded. It is easy when we begin to have spiritual experiences to allow for them to take us away from the world rather than have them allow us to become more present in the world. By having a physical practice we can begin to integrate our spirituality into our physical body.

There are a lot of us at this stage who stop our awakenings by thinking that spirituality is something separate or different from physical reality. They are not intended to be separate—the spiritual, mental, physical, and emotional levels of ourselves all create, balance, integrate, and work with one another. When we separate the spiritual and the physical we are not able to fully awaken and end up disliking the physical world and have distaste for the physical senses and human experience on Earth. We then constantly chase the next "high" of spirituality at workshops, or through meditation, and are not changing our physical reality. Often we get stuck at the ego level of awakening and start to belittle others who are not as far as we are. If this happens we can get quite miserable in our daily existence because we have some sort of sense of who we truly are and it is not coming through in our lives. Know that the spiritual is intended to flow through physical reality. Taking care of and enjoying the physical body, its emotions and senses, is a good way to be spiritual and embodied at the same time.

When we experience this level of awakening know that although our perspective has changed, and our ideas of the world have changed with it, that this is not a fully awakened state. It is very common to get stuck at the societal level of awakening—to get hooked into developing psychic abilities, developing some compassion for others, but maintaining our judgment of others and ourselves and not changing our daily lives much. It is easy to think that this is the end of things and to let our egos tell us that we are greater or better than others, that we are intended to be a guru or great thinker, and to remain stuck here.

To go beyond this point requires the disintegration of the "I." Releasing the societal level of conditioning is actually a pivot point—it is an understanding of wider constructs and different layers of existence but it does not yet require us to let go to the extent of feeling oneness, or open to the understanding that we are quite small. To go beyond this point requires a disintegration of ego, a letting go of self-importance, and developing compassion for the Self and the world.

Seventh Layer:
Karmic Patterns

Karma (to be very general about the subject) means action, meaning that we at some point had an action that created a reaction and a need to make up for past debts, problems, and trespasses of our former selves. Karma clears similarly to past lives in that we become aware of a pattern and can become aware of the threads linking us to our former selves. Some karma arguably needs to be played out through cosmic order, and we need to do specific things in this lifetime in order to resolve it.

The best manner of clearing karma is to be a good person in this lifetime and clearing the other layers of conditioning and patterning that have come before this. Working with karma is a lifetime process, and if we are in the process of awakening we will be clearing considerable amounts of karma. Unlike some of the other categories in which we can go through the process of realization, understanding the impact it has on us in the present, and then releasing, karma has to do with lessons that have more to do with divine timing than some of the other patterns. Much of this is out of our control and will come up through gradual and intense inner work naturally. There is nothing we need to "do" with karma; it will release in divine timing. Nobody can release it for us. We simply need to surrender, let go of the idea that we have control over every facet of our lives, and not allow for fear to create blockage so it can properly release.

Working on karmic patterns may take a lifetime to clear due to the lessons and understandings we need to gain on a cosmic level. If we are still in our physical bodies, we still have karma to work through. Spiritual lessons and timing are often illogical to us due to the many steps back that we would need to take to understand them. Even at the most awakened levels of being, the knowledge of karma or understanding of it does not clear it. The realization that we are only in control of so much of our existences comes through at this level. There is an eventual understanding that divine timing is in control of this level of existence, and a flow toward the activities, experiences, and relationships that we are intended to without hesitation that will clear karma in the awakened soul.

If we come across a karmic relationship we can work through the loop that will bring us the lesson of the karma, but it may not clear until we fully understand the origins, meaning the past life it was created in, the circumstances, as well as encounter the other energies, people, and situations that came with the karma. This will take place in unique timing—the entirety of the situation may come right away or may take twenty years. It is important to not get stuck in an ego awakening, or claim that all karma has cleared, because then we will no longer recognize when new patterns on a karmic level come up. By keeping ourselves open and humble and realizing that we only have so much control over this layer we can move through it.

For a basic Self lesson (say the experience of breaking your leg) you might have to process the residual pain and some of the emotion coming up surrounding it.

JEFFREY, a man who broke his leg during a skiing accident, came to me because his leg had "not felt right" since he had broken it several years prior. Although testing, physical therapy, and chiropractic adjustments had released the physical attributes of the pain, he was still experiencing an uneasiness, unsteadiness, and lack of overall balance. He was also in the process of becoming more aware about how emotions impacted his body, and was aware of the fact that the religious path of his parents was no longer the correct faith for him.

Through his session with me he was able to understand that his leg was holding residual emotional energy of grief and fear from the incident. This cleared within two sessions but he was still unable to feel totally steady and balanced. We explored other reasoning for this—past life, family systems, and ancestry. All of this showed some material to work with, and as he came to realize that he felt ungrounded from his parents divorcing, his ancestry revealed quite a bit of pain and fear from going through World War II, and a past life showed itself to be an experience as a preacher who no longer felt strong in his faith. It was through working with all of these levels that he began realizing that he was dealing with a karmic pattern of a lack of faith, a weakness that showed itself in his legs and first chakra and affected his balance.

As Jeffrey came to understand many of the reasons for his lack of faith he understood that this was not a quick fix—something he could simply bring awareness to and release. He would likely have to spend this entire lifetime striving to understand how he could bring faith back into his life and resolve the lifetimes and multiple layers of patterning concerning lack of faith. Many karmic lessons have to do with realizing a lesson gradually and over a long period of time and releasing the relationships and experiences that show up to help us work through the pattern in our current lifetime. These lessons are intended to make us a whole, healed person who can truly become full of power and grace.

Karma presents as a deep knowledge of why and how the patterns that came up have done so. We can clear the instances and experiences that karma has created for us through working with the Self and other systems, including past lives, family systems, and so on. When these instances have resolved, we are open to learning the greater lessons behind these patterns and the karma that perhaps originated the patterns and imbalances.

Sixth Layer:
World, Global, and Cosmic Patterns

After societal constructs, world and global energies will present. This again appears as a grid. With this level of awakening we may again feel as if we are seeing things from a different perspective. We have worked the personal, past life, family and ancestral, and some of the societal layers, and we begin to, maybe for the first time, understand that we are the world, and the world is us.

During this stage the ego begins to drop away and feelings of compassion begin to appear without conditions. Since the new understandings allow us to know that we are the world and are a mirror of the world, the judgmental nature of the societal conditioning stage starts to disappear and we begin to feel love or at least compassion toward the world and its inhabitants. This is one of the biggest differentiations between the societal level and the world level of awakening. In the societal level it is still about us—our experiences cause us anger, cause us to feel isolated, or cause a feeling of superiority because we are more awake than most other people. In the global level we have moved past the pivot point of "I" into the beginning stages of divine flow and oneness.

A feeling of compassion for people comes through in this phase and an understanding that people are exactly where they need to be emerges. We also realize that although we are awakening we will always have more to learn and grow. Rather than judgment, a sense of discernment develops. An understanding that many people are in sleeper states and many are in further states of awakening than us develops. Compassion for people for where they are while still having a pragmatic understanding that not all truths are valid, not all opinions are equal, develops.

Deep love and compassion flows through this stage of awakening. Rather than it being about us, or the sense of competitive spirituality that is present in many of the more superficial layers, we may begin to discover that we are not that important. We wake up to the fact that each person, no matter what spiritual state or stage of awakening they are in, is a teacher and a student. Some people teach us who not to be or show us our former selves. Others show us that we can still unfold further. There are many beautiful, individual understandings that come through at this stage about the state of the world and how the world at its core is about compassion and love.

Rather than the existential type of despair that may have come over us waking up to collective and societal conditioning, the sensations of waking up in the global category are again more physical. Our physical bodies are representations of the world. Since we have come to the understanding that we are the world and are beginning to experience true oneness, we may be overwhelmed by the amount of stimuli coming our way from the world.

Societal conditioning is emotional in nature since it is composed of the thoughts, emotions, and understandings of society. It is a largely mental and emotional construct. Therefore, we process these energies through our mental and emotional bodies. Global energies are dense, physical, and land-based. They are composed of the vast history of each country, city, and town. The re-emergence of physical symptoms—aches, pains, and diseases that seemingly come out of nowhere—is quite common with global awakening.

Global awakening is a bit more difficult than some of the personal stages because like the next category, cosmic awakening, it requires taking a few steps back to understand what is going on. Since we have likely been on a spiritual path for a while by the point we get to this, or perhaps came into this world in this stage and remained sensitive to these energies, we understand that what is going on is spiritual or energetic in nature. This stage is difficult because we do not often have the direct links or ability to process logically why we may not be feeling well emotionally or physically.

The reasons for not feeling well are often associated with direct happenings in the world. Bombings, wars, genocides, and so on will present physically in our bodies. Often we do not hear of uprisings, genocides, and other forms of mass destruction that occur in foreign countries so it can be understandably difficult to go from stages of oneness and feelings of joy and bliss that begin to emerge in this stage to having a day or a few hours of feeling completely horrible or unable to get out of bed.

Emerging Into Oneness

Many of us who feel global patterning and the beginnings of oneness remain here because we have woken up to the extent that we have arrived at a flickering oneness state of our journey and do not realize we can go further. Subconsciously there may be an understanding that to move beyond the flickering of oneness requires work, faith, and a deeper level of surrender. To move past this stage requires moving past the ego, the "I" that remains a victim in this world, and fully letting go of that Self into oneness. That is understandably a lot to ask. When we remain in this category for long enough we constantly talk about how sensitive we are and what type of pain we are in today and the spiritual reasons for our pain. Some of us stuck in this category eventually become hermits and are simply unable to function in the world, or we begin to become aware of why we are feeling the headache we are feeling and begin to get perspective and deep insight as to how to work with these energies.

For those of us who are willing to move away from the "I" that wants us to stay in a state of victimhood and pain, we can get perspective on ourselves as a global being. We understand that we are oneness and we are now, and always have been, a physical representation of the world. This means that the entire world is represented in us, in our physical container. So when a major shift, weather pattern, war, and so on happens, we will feel it somewhere in our body. Often we get obsessed with logic and the need to know here. We wish to know why we have a headache or feel off. When we hear of a bombing in Egypt, or that it is Mercury Retrograde, we attribute it to that and complain about how those events are affecting us.

We then logically create a story about how the spiritual happening is causing us misery, thereby holding onto that pain and not allowing the energy to flow through us. We can let go of these energies by letting go of the need to know and the creation of a story surrounding these energies. If we are aware of why we are feeling this way, simply noticing it as an interesting fact rather than holding onto the experience and story of it will allow for it to release. Know that we are processing these energies because we are awake to them.

When we awaken to global energies we become a release valve for them. We have cleared enough of the other layers of conditioned reality that we are able to access, feel, and clear global energies for the world. Violence, chaos, and the joys of the world are able to move through us and are able to be released through us. Although every single person on this planet is a part of the world and contains global energies within them, when we awaken we begin to be a tool of the divine. This means that we are now of service to the divine and can be a tool of release for the pressure cooker of global energies. When we surrender we can allow for the force of these energies to move through us, and we can be of service to the Earth's energetic releases.

As we get further into the layers there is less for us to do. At the layer of Self, immediate family, past lives, and ancestry there is much to do. Conscious clearing of events and traumas that are housed in our bodies make up much of the "gunk" that is blocking us. Once these levels are worked through, the levels of noticing and understanding and states of being come through (rather than doing). Societal conditioning and global energies are grids that come into consciousness. There is nothing to do but become aware and conscious of these energies. What the larger energies, such as global energies, do is bring up pains and uncleared issues within ourselves that remain. These are larger energies and will bring up darker and deeper patterns within the previous layers. When these big flows of energy bring up our own emotions and pain we can work through them consciously with the wisdom taken from having access to the perspective of societal or global energies.

Before we contribute everything in our lives to global energies simply because we have awakened to this state, we can still remain logical beings. If we ate poorly, are having difficulty at work, or had a fight with a family member it is highly likely that we need to work on that level before we ascribe everything to global energies. Although we have reached a state of spiritual awakening, when we drop a hammer on our foot we still need to go to the hospital. At this stage it is easy to lose our physical bodies and our logic. By looking at all of the stages we have gone through when an imbalance or problem arises from outer to inner (Self, past lives, ancestry, society, global) we can take care of the problem with the proper care.

We can begin a questioning process here:

- Is this Self (Is this mine?)
- Is this from my family or friends?
- Is this from a past life?
- Is this from ancestral sources?
- Is this a societal energy?

- Is this a karmic energy?
- Is this a global energy?
- Is this a cosmic energy?

By beginning to question and differentiate these energies, our bodies can begin to discern what is going on and clear them more readily. We can also take personal responsibility for what is ours rather than focusing on spiritual, or external, sources of pain and take care of energies at the appropriate level.

Global energies are quite strong. At first these energies feel like a massive waterfall through us. We may be flooded with images, feel emotions that are not ours, be in pain, or be sick. Non-physical beings and other energies heighten; psychic abilities and sensitivities will increase. Our bodies may develop stronger food aversions, sensitivities, and allergies. These sensitivities to food, people, places, and other energies are because our bodies are feeling huge flows of energies for the first time and anything that we put in our bodies that causes a state of imbalance will be felt in a strong manner by our bodies. We are awakening to what our body really wants and are becoming fully embodied. I am reminded of the story of the *Princess and the Pea* when we get to this layer of conditioned reality. These strong flows point out anything that is in us that is out of balance, and our digestive, immune, nervous, and endocrine systems will need to rebalance to accept and understand these stronger flows of energy.

Depending on how much we have been called in dreamtime we may feel activated. Activation means that a part of ourselves, our awakened self, has been called to be of service in some way. This can understandably be tiring and disorienting while it is happening, even when we fully understand what is going on. Feelings of dizziness, disassociation, as well as feelings of peace and satisfaction come from being activated. In this stage we may find our spiritual selves called during the daytime and will split from our physical bodies or we may find that we physically are called to be of greater service such as working in a soup kitchen, assisting in an animal shelter, or other forms of service for the world.

EXERCISE: Releasing Global Energies

When you are feeling a headache or some other related physical activity due to global issues, notice and speak out loud to it. Maybe you have the understanding that this energy is coming from conflict going on in Syria.

- Say out loud, "My head hurts. I feel a connection to Syria." You do not need to inquire more about it, although it may be tempting. If more is revealed to you for a specific purpose, it will show itself without any effort on your part.

- When you say this, visualize the energy as a color of your choosing and imagine it releasing out of your crown if it is a higher chakra or affecting the upper body or the bottom of your feet if it is an energy affecting your lower body.
- Feel the vibratory quality present in your whole body of this event. Allow for it to gradually come off of your entire body like waves or static, slowly disappearing from your physical body outward until it leaves your field.
- Allow for white light to stream through your crown like a waterfall, allowing any emotions or pains that are not yours to pass through you through the bottoms of your feet.

By recognizing that these energies are not yours, naming them, and allowing for them to pass through you, you will gradually develop a sense of awareness without physical symptoms and they will more readily pass through you. At some point you can activate your light body—the energy that surrounds you going through the top of your head and the bottom of your feet and the energy that surrounds you and forms your field. If you are experiencing your light body and you are having difficulties with global energies, you can simply allow for your light body to come into consciousness and for the light to dissolve or release any of the global energy. In time you will notice this happening automatically and will not need to do anything.

Global energies create a larger grid than societal conditioning. They are both a conditioned layer of reality and also a heightened energy of the world. Further out are archetypal, mythic, and collective consciousness grids. When we are immersed in the two grids closest to the Self (societal and global) deep understandings and leaps forward in consciousness occur. A letting go of the ego and emerging into a non-flickering state of oneness can now happen.

Fifth Layer:
Ego Death

At the level of global awareness and beginnings of oneness we understand that there is divine flow and that we are truly part of the whole. This is a deep and new understanding for us. Most of us intellectually know about this stage beforehand, but the true feeling of oneness is felt and known here. There is an understanding that the people surrounding us are of us and that they are showing us our deepest wounds. There is a deepening of compassion for others and the beginnings of true self-love in this stage. We begin to feel divine flow and oneness, the constant wave of energy flowing through us. At this stage it is still flickering and we will go between feeling divine flow and separating from it. We are dipping our toes into the ocean of divine flow but have not dived in.

We also begin to experience Ego Death. There is a lot of misinformation about Ego Death in modern spiritual culture. There is an understanding of the first stage of Ego Death, where the ego dies and there is no longer a Self that can identify as "I" but not of the fact that the dissolution of "I" and Ego Death is temporary, and of the second phase, where we re-identify with our individual natures and physical bodies.

Ego Death is an extraordinarily difficult experience. There is a struggle to let go of the mind, a struggle to let go of the Self, and the deepest level of surrender to give ourselves up to the undifferentiated flow of divinity. We must choose to dive into divine flow rather than continue to dip our toes in. By letting divine flow fully in we let go of the constraints and identification of the importance of the Self present in the previous levels of conditioned reality.

The amount of joy, bliss, and connection at coming into a state of oneness is indescribable. When we reach this stage it is easy to get lost in this undifferentiated Self. It is also common for us to pull ourselves out of divine flow and back into the constructs of conditioned reality because the understanding and feeling of so much freedom and joy is frightening to the dissolving ego. When we do this we go back to the global stage of awakening; however, we are forever changed by even momentarily entering divine flow.

Many of us lose ourselves at this stage simply because we are conditioned by popular spiritual literature to believe that this is the last stage of awakening. Due to a misunderstanding of this phase we have categorized the ego as being "bad," as if the ego were in one corner and oneness was in the other. This statement is only true in lower stages of understanding where opposites cannot live comfortably with one another. Once oneness has been found there is a temporary dissolution of ego, "I," a death. The further stages of awakening allow for us to reclaim our egos in a balanced way. We are reborn and re-emerge in relation to divine flow. We are intended to be separate selves. We are both oneness and separate. There is no contradiction to this. There is a reason we have a physical body with senses, emotions, and a fully human experience. By allowing for the ego to have this stage of "dying" we can awaken to this relational change where we again have egos and separation from oneness.

It is through this death that we encounter and release our fears over physical death. While we learn that the physical form has a purpose, and begin to appreciate it for perhaps the first time, we also understand that it is a temporary vehicle. The anxieties and fears about physical death, the importance of the "I" and all of our stories and illusions contained in the lower levels cease. We identify as both an individual and as a part of divine flow with no contradictions.

Fourth Layer:
Understanding and Releasing Thoughtforms

We are logical creatures. Many of us live in a world entirely composed of thoughtforms and are embodied only in our heads. In this stage of awakening we let go of our strong mental faculties, the illusions and conditioned layers of reality we create from our thoughts, as well as our need for logic. This stage often occurs in conjunction with the Ego Death stage as a condition of entering into full oneness.

We are taught that everything must have a reason, a cause–effect. In some ways this is true. Often we can see this cause–effect in action. We have a bad childhood with a bad male role model as a father so we choose bad relationships with men in later life. We lack self-love, so we choose situations that will prove to us that we do not deserve love. We are angry so we call to us reasons to be angry. Or even simpler: We forget to buy coffee so we have a caffeine headache. These are all logical, mental reasons for how we are. This is an understanding that is woven through modern psychotherapy—everything that is a factor in your life can be explained and rationalized.

At some point in the awakening process we begin to understand that thoughts, or thoughtforms, weave a web of illusions that is separate from even the conditioned layers of reality. We add on further to these layers of reality with layers upon layers of thoughtforms. These thoughtforms cloud our vision and create a grid that confines us. If we can only imagine our lives being one way, or have a rigid definition of who we are and what we can do, our lives will be this way. Rigid, puritanical, and black/white understandings of the world being only as we see it create our world. These thoughts combined with the thoughts of the millions of other people in the world create our expectations and conformities in religion, sex, class, politics, race, gender, occupation, and in fact the grid systems of the societal and world layers of conditioned reality.

It is during this stage that we begin to let go of these rigid thoughtforms and the thoughtforms of others that create our reality. Opposites begin to make sense; contradictions and duality make sense. Something can be nothing and something, true and false, at the same time. Instead of our old reactions of anger, or frustration, or attempts to cram the thoughts into our old rigid paradigms, we are able to sit comfortably with dualities.

No longer is it our thoughts that create our reality but divine flow. We are a vessel for this flow and it will guide us into becoming a pillar of strength. This switch from an "I"-centered universe allows for us to see, feel, and have compassion for people still struggling with their own rigid thoughtforms. We begin to understand how thoughtforms create the world around us and transcend them. No longer are we imprisoned by the standards and thoughts of others or ourselves—we are free to take what wisdom, teachings, classes, and understandings work for us and leave the rest. There is a freedom from needing this material—books, teachers, and gurus—at this stage. This is the ultimate switch from external—where we quote books and others as pillars of wisdom—to internal, where we recognize ourselves as the ultimate wisdom.

Like many of the other stages, the awareness of thoughtforms is key to transcending this stage. Seeing how our thoughts create our reality and how others around us create theirs will allow for us to transcend living in a world created out of thoughtforms. We can begin to see how the collective thoughts create our world and how we contribute. We can take personal responsibility for our own thoughts and our emotions.

We can understand how our base emotion creates our reality. A base emotion is that emotion we always notice ourselves gravitating toward—for some it is fear, for others it is anger or grief. Fear tends to be the base instinct of all emotions and is the creator of the limitations we impose upon ourselves. In this stage we will intimately know our base emotion. It may seem like this emotion is taunting us, or that we are suddenly in situations that test every single fear that we have. This is even more confusing because we are at a state of awakening where we have released many of our personal issues. Suddenly we experience a wellspring of strong, primal rage or grief and it seems to come out of nowhere and is not connected to an event or experience. It simply is.

This base emotion will go through all of our fears in a desperate attempt to hold on. It will show itself more and more, creating illusions of fear so we will not surrender and bypass this stage. Our base emotion will attempt to sabotage us, to tell us that our spiritual understandings, our path, our experiences are not real and if they are real we do not deserve them.

JOSEPH was a forty-eight-year-old man who contacted me via e-mail and we set up a consultation. He had an experience with the divine where he felt completely loved and cared for. But when he came out of it his whole world began to fall apart. He lost his job, his wife began divorce proceedings, and his child who was a teenager at the time began doing drugs and drinking— something Joseph had a family history of. Through this he could continually hear the divine saying, "Let go and let God," but he was too fearful to fully surrender. He began drinking again. Over the next year he lost his house, his daughter wouldn't talk to him and eventually had to be sent to rehab, and his new job was half of his pay and was not personally fulfilling. He became angry with God, questioning his journey and why everything had to be such a struggle.

One morning he woke up and realized that he was in the arms of the divine; he was in divine unfolding again. He again heard, "Let go and let God" and agreed to surrender out of desperation. He surrendered everything—selling most of his possessions to get treatment for himself and his daughter, leaving his job, and moving in with his elderly mother. He acknowledged his fears and through that he decided to surrender anyway, having faith that there was something beyond fear. After that surrender he began to get pieces of his life back. His daughter began getting treatment and therapy, eventually going to college and having a good relationship with her father. Joseph remarried a woman who also had a strong spiritual path, and he got a job that paid less but was more fulfilling to his sense of purpose on Earth.

Our base, primal emotion keeps us in line and within the confines of constructed reality. It keeps us right where we are, in the known. To realize full awakening we must let go of fear, the base emotion that arises, and have faith. We must surrender and fully immerse ourselves in divine flow. By transcending the fear of the logical brain—which tells us that we constantly need things, that we are going to fail, that anything new is scary so we might as well stay with our routine, our life, as the way it is—we will realize freedom. We do not need to stay in lives we dislike out of fear; we do not need to stay who we are because thoughtforms and conditioned layers of reality created these confines. Once we transcend our fear we begin to taste the freedom that awakening provides.

We are a web, a tapestry of thoughts. These are our own thoughts, our family, ancestry, society, cultural thoughts that make us who we are. They weave together to tell us what to think, what to buy, what we need to be happy, what we need to be a fulfilled human. Advertising and our celebrity culture are our clearest and most obvious examples. They show women and men doing what we are supposed to want to do, impossibly beautiful, often directly giving us messages of how we are supposed to live our lives. It is rare that any of us has the means to follow the path of this super-materialism, so there is a subconscious (or sometimes very conscious) understanding that we always fall short. We are left in a state of perpetual want.

We perpetuate a constant state of negativity in our thoughtforms. We do not like pain or discomfort on any level so we stop ourselves from feeling it. This pain not only still remains in our physical bodies but enters the world at large. This pain, these negative thoughts that we have create a personal and collective shadow. We externalize our pain to the extent that it creates a huge cloud of negativity and negative happenings in the world. If we truly process our emotions and work through our thoughts instead of becoming numb or creating a mask of "love and light" type of spirituality, we are able to integrate these thoughts. When we integrate our thoughts and do not shy away from them we are able to transcend even the darkest or most painful thoughts and emotions.

Personal and Collective Shadow

The shadow is the part of ourselves that is unconscious—the desires, emotions, and traumas that have defined us. It is our darkness, the secret violence, anger, grief, and energy cysts that we are unable or unwilling to process. Collectively, our shadows as well as our conscious selves create the world, its violence, wars, racism, sexism, classism, and rules for appropriate, unspoken conduct.

By individually working with all of the parts of ourselves, including the shadow, we become conscious of all aspects of ourselves and are able to go beyond simplistic thought structures of good and bad, dark and light. In the lightworker community there is a pervasive trend of growing the amount of light one has while ignoring the dark. Anything defined as "dark" or "shadow" is ignored and grows relative to the amount of light one has. It is a regular part of such communities to not want to discuss anything dark, or to have rigid constructs and rules for conduct about what being awake and conscious means. When we ignore our shadow we remain immobilized in spiritual immaturity. We become spiritual bypassers—always looking elsewhere for spirituality, never embodied because we do not want to deal with the real, messy, emotional, traumatic, and "dark" aspects of truly becoming awakened.

The shadow must be realized and worked with to realize an awakened state. There is no part of ourselves that is "bad" or needs to be destroyed. This illusory belief that awakening and enlightenment are constant joy, light, and smiling and that focusing on anything but this is bad creates an even greater personal and collective shadow in the world. Real awakening involves understanding and having compassion for the shadow. It involves embodiment and exploration of all of our emotions, all of our sides. It involves reconciliation and nonjudgment of even what we would define our darkest impulses and emotions. By consciously understanding and working with our shadow we can become whole. Not light and shadow, good and bad, spiritual and physical, but one whole embodied, messy being. Our shadow is not something to work through; it is a part of us. We should love it—we should love the murderous aspects of ourselves, the angry part of ourselves as much as the blissful aspects of ourselves. This is true awakening, and it is beautiful. Each one of us who is able to bring our shadow to this point, each of us who makes our darkness side more conscious and integrated takes a bit away from that collective shadow and our collective society becomes a bit more awakened.

By working with our shadows we become more embodied in our physical forms. We are physical beings intended to fully experience anger, joy, bliss, love, grief … to take great beauty in art, music, and our senses. By not processing and clearing the pathways of the physical body our spirituality is always outside of ourselves. We must look to other teachers, quote books, and become spiritually split, not understanding that the spiritual, mental, and physical bodies are all one. Our spiritual natures are our physical natures—we do not need to journey to awaken. We awaken through embodying our physical selves wholly, through expressing all of our emotions and reconciling each part of the world, our emotions, thoughts, as part of our Self.

The first thing that happens in the thoughtform stage is a noticing of the tapestry of thoughtforms. Perhaps we start noticing that the news is full of fear and negativity. Maybe we start to see how television overall is keeping us wanting things that we can never have. Then we start to notice that we are ever so gradually changing. We notice how friends are judgmental and realize that we used to be exactly like that. We talk with neighbors and realize that they are constantly in competition with one another over achievements, family, and material goods. We see that the world is in a state of disassociated negativity and how we may be part of that. We see how everyone is focused on tearing things and people down. We begin to take responsibility for our own thoughts, even the most troubling ones and identify them as ours. By taking responsibility for all of our thoughts, even the negative ones, and not pushing them aside, we do not have to put on a mask. We can be who we fully are with no excuses.

There are small understandings of thoughtforms that occur throughout awakening, but in the final stages this becomes more dramatic. We begin to separate from sources of thoughtforms that we notice do not make us feel good. Friends and family that we once enjoyed we have grown apart from. We begin to crave solitude. We begin to process our own shadow, our own thoughts, and take responsibility for them. We then may still not choose to be around friends and family or take part in negative environments, but once we reconcile our own thoughts and what they project we are able to once again come out of solitude and rejoin even the most negative of people if we so choose.

This stage of awakening is often a gradual understanding and slow letting go of the threads of this tapestry. These are the very threads that hold us in fear, that keep societies and cultures together, and that make up our collective consciousness. These threads keep us in place, keep us from being totally alive because of expectations and understandings. To break free from them takes time, and it takes courage. To break free from them too quickly means a complete separation from society. This happens to some of us—we move to another country, change our names, or go live with a religious order or simply off the grid.

But for most of us this takes time. Slowly the threads will begin to separate from the tapestry—at first an understanding of the collective sort of thrall we are under emerges. We begin to notice that we are in a collective matrix that is comprised of expectations and understandings. Then we begin to separate ourselves from this, either physically or energetically. We begin to realize by taking a step back that our family, our culture, our society, and our world repeats the same thoughts and events like they are reading from a script that loops over and over again. This is typically a rather unsettling realization. How can we live in a world where we know that everything is repeating, that not only are we looping but the world as a whole is as well? Many separate even more with this knowledge.

> CONNIE, a woman with a beautiful, peaceful smile, explained how this stage affected her. She told me that when she got to this stage, she came into a deep depression. She was at a restaurant when she realized that everything was as if puppets were being pulled by strings. The people surrounding her were following a script, and she no longer desired to follow through with it. She suddenly knew what people were going to say before they did, what the food would taste like, what would happen in the evening because it had all happened before—like it was part of a script she had read fully when everyone else was acting it out without knowing the end. She went home that evening and wept. The whole world to her seemed dark, and she was beginning to see collective thoughtforms like clouds around people and the world. She saw how much they affected us and she wept for the world. She ended up taking a week off of work before she found me online, and I got her to understand that participating in the world with this knowledge would not be easy at first, but it is part of being alive.

If we are able to make it through this drastic realization, there is a re-entry into society. Many of us stay in the stage of separation for quite a long period of time. We are unable to find our way out or navigate the world with the understanding of how thoughtforms shape our reality. For those of us who make it through, it is with the understanding and vantage point on a different level. We are able to see how collective thoughts, fears, emotions, as well as personal thoughts, fears, and emotions, shape the reality we are a part of. We are able to see the previous layers of conditioned reality in ourselves, in others, and the world. Once we take responsibility for our own thoughts and no longer distance ourselves from any of our thoughts we are able to release the charge, the emotion that is causing us to want to separate. We can then come back into the world with full knowledge and responsibility for our own thoughts and see them as we interact with others.

Coming back into the world with this understanding is a powerful thing. It is really the first big taste of what freedom is. We can choose to work with these thoughtforms for personal and collective good. Thoughtforms look different to everyone. Some see them as clouds, some see them as threads or lines, insects or animals, and some sense them. We are able to sense on some level how these thoughtforms construct our relationships and our reality. If we are fearful of money and never have enough we can now see how that thought has created our reality. We are able to notice these thoughtforms and change them. If we change our thoughts there is no promise here that any of us will be a millionaire if we only rework our thinking. This is a common misconception that if we think about a BMW every day or that if we make a vision board with a BMW, that we will manifest one. In fact, if we do this and do not get a BMW we must have done something wrong. The universe is not quite as simplistic as this. What we receive in life is a result of many forces coming together. If we progress from this point we will find that thoughts can manifest if applied with a sense of doing (yes, you might need to think about and get a job to get a car) as well as divine will.

When we are in the stage of awakening where we are able to reweave thoughtforms we realize that things are how they are supposed to be. It sounds funny to people who have not reached this stage, but as we progress to being less literal and logical, less materialistic and more spiritual, we need less and less. We begin to realize the grand scheme of things. We desire qualities more than things—peace, love, flow, and to truly know the Self and the divine. This is not to say that we do not appreciate nice things, but the incessant need and focus on manifesting them will be gone, and the realization that we have enough, or even too much, will set in. Even the endless discovery of new spiritual teachers, workshops, healing methods, and other forms of spiritual consumerism ceases. We discover that once we are in line with ourselves that we are in the perfect spiritual state and always have been. In fact, we have always been awake. The seeker state ceases and we are able to look within, allowing the perfect outer materials, teachers, students, and others to come to us by synchronicity. We lose the spiritual competitiveness and with humility realize that we can never know everything and no longer pretend to.

This is the final stage to reach cosmic understanding. In this stage we surrender our brains (this is, of course, not literal) and open up to true faith, beginning a new period of letting go of the rest of our needs, fears, and doubts to enter into illumination. This is different for every person. When we reach this stage we flicker between feeling oneness and then coming back to the logical brain, the need to know, and doubt. Notice the sensation of both logical and divine. Then give your logical brain to the divine. All of your complex thoughts, doubts, just surrender them to the divine. Feel white light pouring through your head, into your brain, filling you with divinity. Your ego will resist this, telling you that you need logic, doubt, and to know everything. For some, the imagery appears of going through a gateway or jumping off of a cliff into the unknown.

This surrender, this jump over the cliff or through the doorway will allow you to fully realize your divine nature and the entirety of divine flow. If you are ready, let go. Let go many times if necessary. Surrender. Realize that your brain will always be there, you are just surrendering the part of yourself that constantly is chattering, that needs to know, that tells you that you are not good enough. Fully allow yourself to give up the rest of your "I" and immerse yourself in divine flow, completely surrendering anything that is left of yourself. If you choose to surrender to this state, feel the fear and do it anyway.

When we fully enter divine flow and surrender our logical brains we will feel silence. No more talking, chattering—just oneness and light. If this is not felt, surrender again and again over time until it is. Eventually our logical brains, our ego, our selves are dissolved into oneness fully and at even a deeper level than before. Our brains, our thoughts will return, but the endless chatter will not. This surrender will allow us to come to the cosmic consciousness stage of awakening.

Cosmic Consciousness

At some point we begin to interface with cosmic consciousness, where we begin to expand and unfold into oneness. Many people catch glimpses of this before this state. For example, drug-induced cosmic consciousness is actually quite common but not sustainable without working through the other layers of conditioning. When we are able to come to the understanding that we are not only the world but the Universe and begin to feel divine flow and grace, this stage has begun. It is in this stage that we can begin to interact consciously with global energies. We are no longer in the passenger seat of having to deal with larger flows and global energies but can be a conscious helper and developer of these energies. As one of my teachers used to say, we move from being the dreamed to the dreamer in this stage.

At this stage there are other layers that form the outer layers of conditioned reality that will appear before cosmic consciousness is a permanent, nonflickering state. Mythic and Archetypal Influences and The Destroyer are the last aspects of conditioned reality to be worked with to turn cosmic consciousness into a permanent state. Otherwise, we continue to flicker between cosmic consciousness and lower levels of conditioned reality. At this stage we will also begin to view the geometric patterns of the universe, ourselves with wings, our inner stars and constellations, and interface with other dimensions, universes, and timelines.

Wings

The constant presence of wings occurs during the awakening process. They begin as the understandings of divine origins set in, but flicker until the physical body (specifically the back, but the physical body as a whole) is clear enough for them to fully grow in. Once they are fully grown they are permanent structures that you will always have awareness of and can utilize as a source of protection or in other spiritual pursuits, such as healing. Sensitives are able to sense, feel, or see them in others. Wings can be rather large or small, vary in color, and others may be able to feel a sense of wind or breeze when the person with wings turns suddenly.

Stars and Constellations

Seeing images of space, specific stars, constellations, and planets happens when a flickering understanding of cosmic consciousness occurs. We each are composed of a specific star or grouping of stars as one of our core energetic structures. This again goes with the understanding that the further inner we explore our depths in our inner landscape the further outer we are in the world. At the point of seeing individual stars it may be simply a glimpse of cosmic consciousness. For those of us further along in the process of awakening it becomes a permanent direct experience. When reaching the cosmic level of consciousness it is understood that we are each originating from stardust; we each have an individual constellation or energetic pattern composed of stars that are from the time of our origins that is a unique signature. This unique signature—a visual of the specific constellation, star, planet, or star group that is at the depths of our core physical structure—allows us to be an individual with a unique energetic signature as well as within divine flow.

DNA

By becoming aware of our own DNA we can deeply become aware of who we are and who we are meant to be in this world. As we come to the later stages of awakening, we view our DNA and can see it changing or becoming more activated. An understanding of DNA as a tapestry that can be energetically shifted and altered as well as a viewing of similar strands and formations of DNA-like shapes in nature can occur.

Although it is common for people to get glimpses of cosmic consciousness and their true nature before processing the influences of archetypes, it will be a flickering understanding until these other layers are processed. In order to remember a permanent state of cosmic consciousness and further awakening we must begin to work through the outer layers of conditioned reality.

Flickering

Flickering occurs when we go between two or more layers of reality. When we begin to remove the layers of conditioned reality we begin to flicker between where we currently are and other layers. Momentarily feeling or understanding concepts like oneness, cosmic energies, world energies, archetypes, and the grids that surround us without being fully at that level of consciousness is flickering. It is a glimpse of things to come and the first (or second or third) introduction to a new state that we are coming into.

Flickering can cause a great deal of depression, Dark Night symptoms, and confusion. When we are able to see ourselves as a constellation or deity during meditation and then we need to go clean up cat barf or pick up our child from the principal's office, it is understandably a difficult transition. When we are at the societal level of understanding and flicker to understanding ourselves to be a deity it can be quite emotional. We go back to our societal level of understanding and see the wrongs of the world, feel isolated, alone, and like we are the only one who is awake and then flicker to feeling complete oneness and compassion for everything and everyone. In flickering states this oneness or memory of who we really are can come through us suddenly like a crashing wave. These memories and experiences are to show us what is to come and to inspire us to continue to carry on. The spiritual journey can be extraordinarily difficult, and many times we are on the verge of giving up. Flickering allows for us to see ahead to advanced spiritual states that if we carry on we can attain. It allows us to see who we were and clean up the previous layers that we still have unprocessed material in. Eventually we have nowhere to flicker to—we are fully who we are—and we know enough to simply surrender and continue to unfold and deepen our experiences of divine flow.

Third Layer:
Archetypal Influences

The archetype and mythic layers of reality are the last layers of collective conditioning. There is quite a bit of discussion of how archetypes inform our existence through modern psychology. During awakening we begin to understand the archetypes we embody. These archetypes, the last defining characteristics of who we are, can be released into divine flow to reach full oneness. Later, archetypes can be picked up again for use as a source of strength and power when we reemerge out of oneness into separation.

Archetypes are labels and patterns of conditioning. They are symbols, personalities, and patterns of thought that come together to make up an image. They are thought to be universally present and are often instantly recognizable. Although philosophers like Plato thought them to be a largely fixed idea, forms that were imprinted on the soul to be played out throughout the lifetime, Jung thought archetypes to be prototypes— universal understandings and collective conditionings that made certain personalities, people, and ideas instantly recognizable to society at large. Another interesting thought concerning archetypes is an Islamic understanding that archetypes are a form of divine destiny—that before birth God has written down all that will happen in our lifetime and we are destined to fit a specific pattern of behavior and way of being because God knows how we will act and what decisions we will choose to make in our lifetime.

In either case, archetypes are a part of our conditioning, whether preconditioned or placed upon us by society. There are many archetypes—Mystic, Warrior, Mother, Judge, Lover, Slave, Student, God, Rebel, Musician, Addict, Child, Man, and Diva are some of many. These archetypes confer a set of expected behaviors and understanding about place and role in society to us when we have been branded with an archetype. We would expect and be comforted by a Student or Child acting one way, but a Mother acting like a Child would be unacceptable.

As we begin to understand these labels we begin to realize that we have been unconsciously labeled with specific archetypes that have caused us to act a specific way. These roles that we have placed on ourselves, or that society has placed upon us to explain and accept our existence, now will feel confining and sterile. If we were to use the tapestry analogy again, specific threads and patterns are woven together to create an archetype, which make us easily and instantly understandable to a society that dislikes anything that creates discomfort or causes questioning.

Breaking free from archetypes requires awareness. If we have been branded as an Artist due to the fact that we paint, does that mean that once we awaken we no longer produce artwork? No, not at all. But the archetype of artist also includes personality characteristics, ways of being in the world, and even appearance that have been placed on us that we can break free from. It is in this stage that we recognize the common archetypes of the world, the common archetypes that we are composed of, and begin to deconstruct what is expected of us from others due to these archetypes.

Once we break free from these archetypes we can discover the truth of whatever we truly are and keep the essence of them. This requires courage. If we are the Mother archetype, and we wish to remain a Mother, but do not wish to maintain the societal constraints of being a Mother, it can understandably be difficult.

The point of releasing archetypes is to surrender the barriers placed upon us by that archetype. The point of awakening is to truly and totally be who we are. Breaking free from the roles and societal expectations of archetypes, the threads that make up the tapestry of "Mother" will allow for us to eventually weave our own tapestry of what Mother or Motherhood should be like.

EXERCISE: Releasing Archetypes

The way to release archetypes is to understand what archetypes you fit into. Develop awareness of what archetypes you may be.

- What do these archetypes mean? How do they look and act and what is expected of them?

- What of this archetype is truly you? What do you wish to keep of it? For example, if you are a mother you may enjoy being the nurturer and spending time with your children. You may not like the rigidity of how you are supposed to act as the Mother archetype.
- Fully claim the aspects of the archetype that you want. Say out loud, "I am a nurturer. I love spending time with my children."
- Begin to notice the constructs of that archetype that others (or even you) place on yourself in that role. Either note these down or simply keep awareness of them. For example, notice that as a mother there is an expectation that you will constantly be tired and overwhelmed, that you and others expect a strict code of behavior at the playground.
- Each time you notice yourself playing into the archetype, develop compassion for yourself for taking on that role.
- Then release yourself from bondage of that role. Imagine a pair of handcuffs coming off, or a tie releasing.
- Return to the aspects of that archetype that you love, or completely free yourself from that archetype for a time until you wish to return to the power that the archetype gives you without the constraints.

In working with archetypes this way you will eventually find the core traits or essence of who you are without the construct and rigidity of the archetype. We are all composed of many archetypes, and when one is released, several more will appear. Patiently work on each one, discovering the essence of it (or what you want to keep), and letting go of the bondage of the role.

It is interesting that when we gain access to the archetype level of existence there is a general clearing of life that occurs and a desire to let go of everything. We may wish to flee our marriage, change our name, move to a different country, quit our jobs, give away all our possessions, and release friendships. We have felt this before, but this time it is all-consuming. We have so little left that confines us that anything that is felt or viewed as a constraint we wish to let go of. But it is not necessary to run away to free ourselves. We are intended to be physical beings with lives, and loves, and even material possessions.

In some ways the clearing of old friendships and even marriages is necessary. It is actually often easier to flee than to consciously work through the spiritual while remaining a physical being who goes to PTA meetings and grocery shopping. It is also understandable to awaken to the realization that we are a consumerist culture and do not need all of the stuff that we are fed to believe that we need in order to survive. Some clearing and consolidating of material possessions is expected as we awaken to who we truly are. It is more difficult, but understanding that the presenting urge to flee is nothing more than an urge for freedom allows for us to understand that we can free ourselves from anywhere while remaining in any situation—in suburbia, in prison, in our job, in the grocery store. It is not necessary to go anywhere to become free. For those of us who feel this urge, know that we can consciously think of the roles we are confined to, the archetypes we embody, and release the bondage of the roles while not releasing our whole existence.

In the Qur'an, it is stated that everything has a likeness in the Divine Treasury. So instead of letting go of the archetype, the suggestion of Pir Vilayat Inayat Khan, a Sufi mystic, is that we go through a process of envisioning and bringing forward the divine archetype rather than a flawed version of it. For example, if we were to envision the archetype of Mother, we would either bring forward the purest energy of "Mother" that is from the Divine Treasury, or we would call through a famous archetype of Mother, like Mother Mary, in her divine, pure state.

EXERCISE: Working with the Divine Treasury

- Connect with the light of the divine through meditation.
- In that light, imagine a treasury where all of images, shapes, and historical figures are congregated.
- Say out loud the archetype you wish to work with, for example "Teacher."
- Your attention will naturally be drawn to the exact pure archetype you need—that of Teacher.
- When you find it, allow for yourself to face it, and then step in to that archetype—physically walk in to the archetype (if it feels appropriate, ask permission first).
- Allow yourself to feel the energy of that archetype permeate every cell of your body.
- Know that as you step into that pure archetype it will begin to inform you as to the divine nature of that archetype, and will shift your previous ideas and blocks concerning what this archetype entails.

By stepping into the pure archetype in the Divine Treasury you no longer are expending energy and feeding the false version of that archetype that you and others around you have created. You can then begin working on mythic influences.

Second Layer:
Mythic Influences

Similar to archetypal forces, we live within the illusion of many myths and mythic deities. We are surrounded by myths as children—fairy tales, Greek and Roman myths, King Arthur, and Aesop's fables are all examples of myths, mythic creatures, and mythic deities. As we get older we are not only under the mythology that we had as children but of many myths from a variety of sources, from religion to television shows to creation myths about our very own lives. This is how we understand our lives—through story and myth.

Myth and archetype are the outer layers of conditioned reality, and they form a grid like societal and global energies do. We also have a tapestry composing each level of reality. There is a Self tapestry, a family tapestry, ancestral, past life, community, country, global, and archetypal tapestries. Every religion has its own tapestry. These tapestries are composed of threads that tell us who we are, where we came from. They confine us to the narrative that has been told. By understanding that these threads, grids, and tapestries are holding us to a particular narrative or myth for our lives, we can begin to move beyond them or shape them as we wish.

There is a striking similarity in people describing this outer layer as a golden grid or net-like structure that encircles the globe. This is a wider and larger grid than the others that have emerged in societal and global conditioning. Mythic and archetypal grids appear to be the same grid as they are composed of the stories that create our conditioned reality.

There is an interesting realization at this stage that our previous experiences were self-created out of ego, thoughts, and the previous layers of reality we have now worked through. This can be upsetting to us that we have constructed most of our own prior experiences of spirit, spirit helpers, and the divine. It can be rather an embarrassing realization that our previous spiritual experiences and knowledge were images and understanding created out of our own needs. This is a layer of disillusionment and understanding that the world is created out of stories—stories we tell ourselves and stories we have been told. There is also a feeling of imprisonment that comes up at this time because we are incredibly close to being free yet still have a few more chains left. This is a similar sensation when flows of energy first came in and the physical body responded by showing exactly where there were blockages and issues in the physical body. We are awakened to the state that this final layer of conditioned reality and its chains are appearing and pointing out what is stopping us from being free.

This results in a Dark Night that is difficult to describe, a flickering between conditioned reality and realization that we are still in chains and the Void, which is what is beyond conditioned reality. Flickering realizations of what is beyond story, what is beyond space and time come through. We also begin to come into contact with real spiritual forces—and new spiritual teachers, forces, and glimpses of freedom will begin to appear to us.

As we begin to awaken to the mythic layer of conditioned reality we begin to come to one of the final states of illusion and one of the significant spiritual tests. This final grid and test is of the God Self. The God Self is a reality, a truth of who we are, but also a part of mythic influences. When we are able to let go of this God Self we are able to fully awaken.

The God Self

There is an important distinction that happens at this stage of real divinity and divine flow vs. simply the creation of more illusion. Although many of us undergoing the awakening process have come into contact with profound spiritual realizations and divine flow and oneness, this is a stage where the direct experience of divinity deepens. The flickering qualities to the previous experiences have lessened. As we approach deeper stages they become more difficult to describe to those who have not had direct experience of these stages. We come into direct experience with divinity, have spiritual experiences unlike anything we have experienced before, and realize that true divinity and spiritual experiences are not under our control.

Many of us on the spiritual path who have not come to this point have created a whole army of angels, deities, animals, plants, rocks, etc., who serve us and tell us what our inner desires and needs are. These are important relationships—it is a very important process to understand what we truly want and to integrate disassociated aspects of Self. But up to this point these spirits and beings are self-created or created from the collective grids. When we come into this stage we integrate these illusory and disassociated aspects of Self and come into contact with real spiritual forces.

Many of us get stuck at this stage. We live in a society where we are never good enough, never smart enough, simply never enough. It is rare that we will want to leave this last layer of conditioned reality. This is the final illusion—the illusion of Self as God.

Self as God/Goddess is an important realization. It is what finally fills us after feeling empty for so long. In this stage, we view ourselves as the God/Goddess. For years or maybe lifetimes we have surrendered and have emptied our proverbial cups. After releasing all of the previous layers of Self and of conditioned reality our cups are empty and we are able to see what is at the bottom. What is at the bottom is the understanding of the Self as God. We finally feel power and our inner divinity fills us. This is understandably a wonderful feeling. But it is still an illusion. Everyone and everything in this illusion still fills the "I"—the concept that the world revolves around us, that we are important, powerful, and that we are creating the whole world singularly. Many of us close ourselves off to awakening to who we truly are because to do so requires moving past this realization. To proceed we need to realize that we are both big and small. To leave this stage requires humility and to realize that although we may be divine we are also nothing.

This state is the disillusion of the idea that we are powerless in this world. Many tell me of becoming an Egyptian priestess, or Jesus, or Vishnu in this stage and seeing themselves with dozens of admirers. It is understandable to not want to leave the place of finally feeling whole, significant, and powerful. But there will be something whispering to us that there is more beyond this place. We will know this as an inner truth, and realize this logically because this state is not a permanent state—it is still flickering.

To go beyond this state is to surrender this power, this feeling of being big and important. It is the last and final surrender. It is a test to see if we can humble ourselves now that we realize our divine selves and are feeling the flow of divinity through us.

Many of us do not leave this state—we stay here and begin to talk as if we are Gods and develop followers. This is an awakened state, but it is one in which we are still creating illusions. What is unfortunate about this is that people who have awakened to this level are working with the threads of reality. They have gotten to a point where they understand some of the grids and how to work with them. Instead of moving beyond them they are contorting them to an illusion that they have wanted of self-importance and of power. They do not understand a fully awakened state because they are still working within the outer confines of conditioned reality. This means that they are still susceptible to the material world, jealousies, and all of the very human emotions and depression that comes with flickering. Inwardly they know that they have not passed the test because they have seen beyond the grid and know it is filled with love and divine flow. But it is comfortable, and it is powerful to be in this state.

CAROL, a woman who came to me to talk about her experiences, described herself as Sita, a Hindu deity. Carol was able to describe Hindu concepts and stories without being Hindu, and she found herself time and again as Sita, sometimes with children, sometimes with other Hindu deities. She thought it miraculous that she was able to describe her experiences and shared them freely with others, developing a relationship with people who could tell her about the myths and stories and who told her how spiritually aware and God-like she was in reality. She loved this attention but was unaware that she was creating this reality for herself out of the mythic consciousness that creates a common veil of illusion over us all. Carol took this opportunity to call herself a teacher, develop followers, and continued to have meditation after meditation about being a deity.

All of this sounds lovely to most. Carol felt wonderful, finally full after struggling with so many feelings of emptiness and despair from her difficult childhood. These feelings of fullness would never last though, and she would find herself constantly meditating and looking for these experiences again and again. Carol was flickering between the high of mythic illusion and the lows of earthly life. Since she saw herself as a Hindu deity and teacher, she refused to humble herself or become small again, and so she still is in a state of flickering between illusions.

As far as I know, she is still there. In her spiritual life she is a deity who is beloved by all. In her daily life she suffers with a difficult marriage, the effects of abuse she suffered as a child, and feelings of wanting to flee the country, change her name, or just simply die so she does not have to deal with having a physical body.

To pass the test of this stage we must surrender. When we surrender and humble ourselves we begin to be filled with humility. We are now both big and small. We are now beyond the grids of collective reality and have begun to truly awaken. We will now come into contact with real spiritual forces, the Void, and the Destroyer.

At this stage we will begin to come into contact with true divinity. The divine (God, light, etc.) is something that is of true love, compassion, and understanding. In that it can be quite fearful and overwhelming. It is unlikely that we have felt the amount of love that comes from being in true contact with the divine. This contact with all-encompassing love will bring everything up in us that is not love for us to deal with. Our fears, shadows, and patterns that remain will come to the surface after we experience true divinity. Many of us flicker after our first experience with the divine because we are not ready—we are not ready to fully surrender and accept the amount of love that is flowing in that space. We then flicker, going back to a space of deep despair or a Dark Night-type experience because we have now known what it feels like to be with the divine, and we have lost it. An immense amount of grief and anger follows until we are finally ready to surrender and feel ourselves worthy of such love.

True spiritual experiences and the power that comes with them that come at this stage are quite different than before for us. What comes through at the God stage of awakening is an understanding of our true self, our true power. It is becoming whole and embodied to all of the power that comes from us. It is realization that we are an eternal being. We are light, we are divine, and we are powerful. But there is a deeper layer that begins to appear for those of us who are close to being fully realized. We come to the realization that these previous journeys and encounters that we have had were not false, but were creations of conditioned layers of reality. We are ready to begin coming into contact with power outside of ourselves.

Real spiritual forces are a much different experience than the created spiritual beings and forces we have come into contact with prior to this point. They are not under our control. It is a common misconception that every spiritual thing that we come into contact with will be of love and light, or that we can simply send them love or change our own emotions to that of love to appease them. This works well for forces of our own invention. While spiritual beings and energies separate from us may be compassionate—they may be love itself—the primary objective is often not us and our needs. We are a very tiny part of the universe and are not that important in the grand scheme of things. Everything is not about us. When we get to a certain point in our spiritual journey, we are simply open and able to see and be seen. We are open to be a channel, to be a tool of the divine but also of the spiritual realms.

Although these energies can have a great degree of love, it is very much a student–teacher relationship. We are told what we need to know instead of what we want to hear. There are often tests, initiations that occur to ensure that we are ready to receive the knowledge they have to offer. These tests are often unpleasant and require a great deal of struggle. Initiations are often dangerous, and sometimes deadly. The end result of these tests is reaching a new knowledge, a new understanding, and a new set of tools for our spiritual toolkit. Often the result is a drastic leap forward in our evolution. This can result in being able to work with a whole new realm of spirit, energy, or dimension.

The first time, or first few times that we come into contact with real spiritual energies they are often overwhelming and cause physical issues. This issue could really be a topic for a whole book, but often energies not created by the Self are of a different vibratory nature entirely, a different dimension, or even a different universe. Higher spiritual energies are composed of energies that are more powerful than our own so it takes a while to entrain, or get used to, the strength or difference in this energy.

At some point we will find ourselves in a space of nothingness, a Void. This is a place where we momentarily feel alone and separate again, out of divine flow. Since we have been in oneness and have let go of our God Self we find ourselves again separated and alone, without a sense of divine or even ourselves, and beyond any of the layers of conditioned reality. This space is the Void—the space between the grids of reality and the Godhead. We may not realize we are here. We feel horrible, suicidal, alone, and in the darkness. We are left with our worst, base instincts. We have found the Destroyer.

First Layer:
The Destroyer

There is an aspect of ourselves that wants to destroy us. It wants to annihilate us. It does not want us to move forward. It will do anything it can so we do not do so. In other layers this will show up as forms of milder self-sabotage—watching TV instead of going to yoga class, never starting that diet that we wanted to. For those who have access or glimpses into deeper parts of themselves the behavior can get more intense—addictions, suicidal thoughts and actions, depressions. The Destroyer wants us to go back to sleep; it wants us to stay how we are.

This is the last showdown with the Destroyer. At some point we will find ourselves out of divine flow and again differentiated as a singular person. We will then meet the shadowy aspects of ourselves we would prefer stay hidden—our baser instincts, the horrible thoughts we have about ourselves, the things we have done in this world that we cannot forgive ourselves for. The Destroyer appears in the Void and tells us that we cannot move forward. It wants us to die, to destroy ourselves. The voice and intensity of the Destroyer is astronomical at this point. There is a force within us that does not want us to awaken, and it gives us a final opportunity to go back to conditioned reality.

The Destroyer will test us, show us our fears, and create issues in our physical, mental, emotional, and spiritual reality to cause us to go back to sleep. The natural thing to do is to be upset about this, to listen to the Destroyer, and to flicker back to the stage we were once in. We may realize that this force is there and name it as depression, shadow, evil, demons, or other names. The Destroyer enjoys getting us angry, being considered evil or dark, and watching us destroy ourselves. If we do so it continues to exist.

What I suggest at this point is likely completely opposite of what you may be inclined to do. If you wish to move forward, stating this intention out loud is certainly applicable, but in order to let the Destroyer go you must learn to love and integrate it. We can no longer disassociate from the base instincts, thoughts, actions, or any other aspects of ourselves. By re-associating ourselves with the Destroyer and our primal emotions and drives we become fully embodied and whole. We no longer are neglecting ourselves in any way—even the actions, thoughts, and experiences in life we truly dislike.

Whether you are in your final showdown or simply noticing yourself having self-sabotaging behaviors, you can love the Destroyer until you recognize it as a part of you:

- Picture the Destroyer as a monster. What does he/she/it look like?
- Give it a name and introduce yourself to it.
- It may begin being difficult, nasty, or upset you in some way. Give it a funny hat when it does.

- Begin sending it love. Tell it you understand why it is afraid.
- Ask it if it needs anything from you.
- Reinforce positive needs it may ask for—if it needs rest, a piece of chocolate, or a movie, say you understand and give it to the monster.
- If it says negative things, again simply smile, give it a funny hat, or send it love. When it brings up instances of self-hatred, experiences you wish to forget, or primal drives (sexual, for example) that you would rather not associate with, acknowledge these as part of you. You do not need to act on them but simply recognize them as yours.
- If it feels right after each encounter, allow for the monster to change how it looks—shape, size, etc.
- Repeat this process each time the Destroyer comes out for you.

Over time, this monster will change with the love and understanding you provide. As long as it wants something small that you can give (as long as it is not self-harming in any way!) offer it that as a gift. When you are ready you will be able to accept more and more love that flows in from the divine. You will let go of the rest of the fear that has come up; the Destroyer and you will recognize that you are in fact worthy of the love that you are receiving. When we wake up from the thrall of the Destroyer, we find ourselves outside of the layers of conditioned reality and in the Void.

The Void

The Void is scary because by this point we have been on the spiritual path for some time and are used to sensing and feeling energies around us. This is a sort of blackout where all of those energies disappear. At first the realization will be that we are out of contact, or feeling off, and that is why we can no longer sense anything. The longer this blackout period remains the more we begin to feel as if we are in a Void, a place where we are out of contact with anything, even the physical. This can lead to a Dark Night of the Soul, where we feel entirely alone and separate. Since we are now beyond conditioned reality we are fully immersed in the Void. We have let go of the idea that we are God and have humbled ourselves to be nothing. We have passed the test of the mythic layer—that of believing the Self to be God and have fully allowed for the ego, our physical selves, brain, emotions, and every last part of ourselves to disappear into nothingness.

When we are able to realize and wake up to the fact that we are in the Void we can explore our surroundings. This Void is the space between layers of reality but is also at the end of conditioned reality. This is the dark Void—a place of darkness and isolation. It is a place of feeling entirely separate from God, from Self, from anyone

THE SPIRITUAL AWAKENING GUIDE

who can help. It can sometimes take quite a bit of time to really understand that we are in this place because we have lost our Self and are dissolved into the Void. Then there is a light Void, a place filled with light and nothingness. Then they merge and we have the big bang of merging with the Godhead.

When we are ready we can work with the Voids. They are where everything is created from. It is a space of pure white or pure dark, depending on the Void you visit. When we have moved beyond the grids that compose our reality we end up here. There is no time or space here—everything is as it was, as it should be. Eventually we discover that the darkness ends and we are faced with the beautiful nothingness of pure light. We then are able to see the dark and light merge into oneness and realize that they are not a place, but a base part of our being.

From this Void and sense of separation is where the true awakened state and illumination begins. If we venture forward we will have an experience with the divine that will change our entire existence. To get beyond the Void we realize that we are there and know that the Void is a part of us, the basis of our dual nature and the yin/yang creation force of the universe.

When we accept this Void as part of us we become illuminated through it and are able to access and fully flow with divine love. We have likely never felt love like this before and are scared to accept it. There is fear and anticipation of what is to come. There also may be aspects of the Destroyer left, telling us not to fully merge into divinity. By realizing we are in the Void we can begin to feel flickerings of divine love. This is love straight to us without having to work through the grids and barriers of conditioned reality. It is pure love and will grow exponentially the more we accept it. The parts left of us that resist this love will dissolve if we let them. It is our choice to allow divine love in and allow it to illuminate and awaken every part of us that is not illumined or awake.

After the Void/Post-Layers

After the Void we may talk directly to the divine as we did before in the forms of familiar guides and teachers or we may choose to be guided solely by the light, the Void, or new teachers who we now know to be aspects of the divine or the archetype or mythic layers of conditioned reality.

The first direct experience with the Divine/God/Goddess/the Universe is strikingly similar for many of us. There is an immense amount of light, there is love unlike anything we have felt, there is a sensation of being totally cared for and held, sometimes there is an intimate encounter like a kiss or making love, and there are waves of bliss. The first time that this experience happens it is beautiful and difficult to describe. For many of us an experience of the divine, such as a peak experience, is the first stage that catapults people into awakening. For many it is also a final stage where we are greeted by the divine and welcomed, never to flicker again to non-awakened states.

JESSIE, a former patient, described his experience. He had been a serious spiritual seeker for twenty years, and the last ten he had been undergoing a Kundalini awakening. He would often feel bliss and orgasmic throughout random times of the day, go into spontaneous yoga-like movements that allowed for his body to process stuck energies, and increasingly felt like light was surrounding him. During meditation one day he felt himself in the middle of a garden in which he was naked and felt a presence beside him. That presence was a beautiful woman who was much larger than him. He felt his smallness and nakedness next to this beautiful and tall woman. As he felt humbled, he went into a bowing position toward her and she started to shrink in size until they were similar sizes.

They then began to make love, but as he entered her he realized that he was now inside of her fully—his entire body was taken up by her and she was again large and he was small and in her heart. He could feel her heart throughout the meditation, and her love for him, and he started weeping, realizing how much he was loved. He then came out of the meditation and felt waves of bliss and love flow through him. This sensation remained for several hours and simply the recall of it later was enough for him to feel waves of bliss move through him.

KATIA was a young woman who was always sensitive. Luckily her parents nurtured those sensitivities, so they remained with her and she had a good relationship with them. She was a natural medium and clairvoyant, which was passed down through her mother's side of the family, and in her late teens she began having visions of a man in a castle. This man would wave at her and say hello. She was never able to reach him though.

Finally, one day she felt welcomed into the castle. She made it past several rooms until she found him. When she eventually found him he was beautiful and he gave her a hug. She felt herself merge with him and then expand until she was filled with the whole world and then galaxies that she had never seen. Each day she would merge again and again with him until she finally held this energy on her own, and she felt the flow of the world consistently through herself.

When this stage begins to finalize, an understanding sets in about the true nature of divinity and our own individual truth. Before this our realizations may have centered around a particular deity or understanding of the universe. But as we reach this stage, we begin to understand that these are but illusions. What this means is that although these deities, gods and goddesses, etc., are real, they are too small to be confined to a single thought. Rather than that, the divine is all those thoughts—it is Rama and Krishna and God and Goddess. It is everything. This thought then filters down to understanding, similar to the first stage of oneness that the divine is in everything—every creature, situation, and person. This realization is different from the first realizations contained in a peak experience or beginning understanding of the spiritual journey because it is more than an understanding—it is now a deep knowledge that the divine is in everything. We can feel, sense, and touch oneness consistently and constantly with this realization. Everything is now an aspect of the divine. And with this knowledge we begin to feel very small and then very large at the same time. We feel small because we realize we are not as significant as we thought. We are again re-individualizing from divine flow and the state of oneness with the relationship to oneness remaining intact. We are now an aspect of divinity, but the vastness of the divine and these new understandings about how the universe flows have allowed us to realize that we are but a drop of water in the stream of divine flow.

At this stage, we begin to fully experience divine unfolding, which is like a stream or flow of which we are an aspect. We begin to understand at a cosmic level, and we begin to recognize that becoming fully awakened is actually the start, not the finishing point, of our journey.

Cosmic Understanding

In this stage we have let go of much of the conditioned layers of reality. Fragments of those layers will and always will remain, even when we get to Cosmic Consciousness. We always have work to do within the layers of conditioned reality and always will as long as we are in our physical body. We still have surrendering left to do, patterns to process, traumas to release, and deeper realizations to understand. This stage is humorous because we begin to see this truth—that even when we contain the knowledge of ourselves as cosmic beings the spiritual literature and conditioned layers of reality that aspire to this state make it seem as if we will no longer have any issues, that we will no longer have to deal with taxes, or trauma, or all of the little things in life that we all have to as humans. Out of oneness we have emerged into being an individual—one that has a daily life, family, neighbors, friends, and a physical self that breaks down and has diseases and dysfunction and eventually will die along with the realizations of a fully awakened state.

It is common for us in this stage to know that our world is totally different. The flickering is minimal here. When thoughts or patterns come up they are recognized as illusions and gently cast aside with compassion. This is a stage of drastically different identification and a wider scope of seeing. We no longer are participating in the loops of expected behavior; we are no longer repeating our patterns again and again like most people do. If we do find ourselves doing so we immediately recognize the loops and patterns we have placed ourselves in. With the awareness we have gathered from the previous stages and shifts we now see things from a cosmic understanding.

Cosmic understanding means seeing and feeling things from a drastically different perspective. Throughout the process we have gradually gained a wider perspective, and we are now able to see that issues are nuanced and contain many opposites, that they have many different layers of meaning, some logical and some incomprehensible. We are able to see the many different patterns and layers of things we previously released and react with compassion instead of anger, fear, or separation when we view them in ourselves and others.

We are now able to interact with people with compassion. More than that, the world seems infinitely humorous. Rather than feeling better than, or needing to prove ourselves, we simply are. This can be a strange sensation as most of us constantly felt the need to compete with others to prove our worth prior to this stage. Things start to become very simple. We either do something or we do not. The past and the future cease to be worries. There is only the right now. There is a sense of lightness, of joy, of humor, that begins to permeate us. At first there are waves that come through of bliss and even orgasms. We no longer go between the depths of despair and darkness to the divine light—our flickering is between being fully realized and a slightly less realized state. We flicker between feeling fully loved and having that love in the background of all we do.

Cosmic understanding comes after we have surrendered our logical brain for a reason. The logical brain wishes to categorize and understand everything. With cosmic understanding there is a realization that we know nothing, and we could never possibly know anything. Then comes the understanding that we know a great deal but we will never know everything in the universe, or everything even about our own lives.

Right before this stage begins there is often an intense fear or rage that comes up. This comes out of nowhere and is not connected to anything. It is the primal emotion of our body releasing. When we recognize and do not shy away from our primal emotions, when we see them as valid, they will simply be a recognized and accepted part of us.

This is a stage of understanding divine will, which is a stage of being okay with not understanding at all. We surrender to the flow of divinity. We have faith that everything will be okay. A certain type of apathy and moving away from being so involved with the drama of our lives occurs at this stage. Many have described this as a stage lacking emotion, but with an undercurrent of bliss and joy. There is a peace here, as we have surrendered to oneness, to flow, and yet are a separate person. The many wars that we have waged on ourselves, the many wars that we have had to participate in from conditioned reality are over. We have peace and understanding. We can now rest after a long journey and much struggle. We are no longer seekers. We have sought.

Plenty of us stay in this state. This is a beautiful place to be but not a place of action. We feel that sense of oneness, of being one with all creation. Many who have reached this state have described just wanting to sleep for long periods of time, or of finally being able to relax for the first time in their lives (or many lives). There still may be struggle, health issues, and the complications that life and living consists of. But they come up and pass like everything does. They do not need to be dramatized. They are what they are, and nothing more. There is no charge from the past, or worry about the future. There is embodiment, a feeling of being fully in our body, and of being fully in the present moment. We still have life happen, struggle, but it is as if we are at the bottom of an ocean watching waves crash above us.

This is the state of flow, of being okay with divine will, of sinking into oneness. We are divine because we are a part of the flow. We love and feel compassion because everything is part of us. We feel anger, sadness, grief, and utilize all of our senses and know the full range of being human. This is all beautiful. At this stage we realize that we are a mirror of the world; we are a mirror of the universe. Everything is an aspect of us, and we are an aspect of everything.

At this stage many health issues cease. The growing pains of spiritual progression, worry, and fear simply go away. Again, this is not to say that we will not have health issues, but they are fewer, and they are without drama. We have an intense connection to the divine because we fully acknowledge that we are divine. We are an aspect of the divine just like the trees, the animals, and everyone else is. Some people just have more layers of sleep over them. We fully remember who we truly are.

After this understanding we begin to treat people like they are all divine but have simply forgotten. We feel compassion or understand their rage, their emptiness, and their lack of self-worth. We begin to feel surrounded by light, and begin to feel our own light emanated from within us. We feel self-love; we feel love and bliss. We love every emotion and our human experience on Earth. We accept the love of the divine, merge with the Godhead, and become fully who we are.

It is understandable to want to stay in this stage. Plenty do. This is the stage of flow, of feeling okay with everything, of letting the divine truly guide and flow through us. But divine flow will continue to unfold and we can choose to move forward—to take the driver's seat of our lives and come out of the state of blissful inaction into a state of conscious and driven action. We are becoming illuminated, fully understanding who and what we are and how we can be of service to the world.

Illumination

Illumination occurs in conjunction with understanding ourselves on a cosmic level and as a cosmic being. After illumination, there is no more flickering. We fully understand ourselves as illuminated, realized beings who are both large and small, part of divine flow and yet also divine flow itself.

The illumination process may occur gradually or all in an instant. Some of us may flicker for long periods of time before fully becoming illuminated. We may subconsciously know and fear that becoming illuminated creates a new life of faith, continual surrender, and discovering the true self.

Illumination is as it sounds: it is light. This light is divine in origin and comes with the experiences of being in divine flow, in divine unfolding, and being in oneness with the universe. It is divine love. It is merging with the Godhead. This light at first comes from the outside—it permeates us. It is a light of love, of bliss. Moments of this will be felt in the semi-awakened states, but during this state we begin to feel this illumination permanently. It constantly surrounds us. We understand that we are loved and cared for. We feel bliss and waves of bliss that can be overwhelming. Gradually we begin to feel light coming from inside of ourselves. When the light comes from both inside and outside of us we are fully illuminated. We now understand divinity as coming through us, the whole world as coming through us and from us. There is no separation of inner and outer—we are both separate and individualized as well as being part of the divine flow, the cosmos, the world, society, our family, and yet a very human being with faults, imbalances, and human difficulties.

Our physical body becomes a gateway, a door, for divinity or other energies to shine through. We are now a direct link, a strong vessel for these energies to work through. We recognize no difference between the physical and spiritual realms—they are one—and we bring forward this light into the world. We may see images of ourselves opening like a door or column.

The sensation of illumination is difficult to describe. Pure joy, bliss, waves of orgasms, looking at mountains and realizing we are breathing with them ... this is the state of dissolution of the belief that we are in any way separate. We are able to look at the world and understand, feel, and taste that we are a part of everything yet separate. Each bite of food, each moment feels truly special and full of joy. This current of bliss and joy is now a permanent fixture in how we approach the world and what we know to be true about ourselves.

Some of us do not understand the nuances of this stage and resent our physical bodies for still having issues. Although this is an awakened state, a state of bliss and being in divine unfolding, there will always be issues in the human form. Our divine self has emerged; we can feel divinity coursing through us. But we are more than that. We have a human container for a reason. Some people have described to me their disappointment at reaching this stage and realizing that they still have physical issues and a person at work who doesn't like them. We are able to feel an underlying bliss, a connection, but our human self still has to interact with the world. We still have to interact with others who are sleeping and interface with the conditioned layers of reality and the collective dream of the world.

This is much different than previous stages and awakened souls who didn't have to interact with the world. In our human forms we have issues, we have things to learn, and we have pains. It is the nature of being human. Learning to notice these things and deal with everyday life is simply a skill that the awakened soul has to learn. Since we are past the point of duality we will discover that we can feel full divine joy and bliss as well as pain, sorrow, and anger at the same time. All of the emotions are divine and are part of us.

At first this may cause a bit of a fracture. There is our divine self, which feels awake and bliss and full of joy, and there is the human self, which is a sensate creature that has to deal with highway traffic and cable guys. But since we are this far along on our path, at some point we will realize that this separation does not need to occur—it is an illusion. There is only our divine self, and then a mirroring, a tapestry of other "selves"— the other layers, the other nesting dolls. We can bring through any of the selves that we wish, or look at our lives through any of those perspectives. Eventually we can bring our energy through fully to that self—but many of us choose to simply bring forward the divine self since everything else is a manifestation of it, or go between the physical self to go to family functions and participate in the illusion and the divine self when it is appropriate. These are all things to individually calibrate and learn.

From this stage we can choose to move forward to a state of action in which we begin to learn who we truly are and what we are intended to do here on the physical plane. This is a full integration of the awakened state into the physical body.

So why would you go on to the next stage? You are awake right now. You realize now that you have always been divine, and you have always been with divine flow. Finally, after years of searching, you have peace, you no longer feel separate. You can separate yourself from the drama, from your logical brain that seeks to know and rationalize everything. There is bliss, and joy, and a sense of your quest being over. There is no more seeking at this stage. You can rest. But there is a state past this, and if you are able to surrender fully, you can achieve it. It is becoming fully human while being awakened.

Awakening

It has been a long journey. There is a part of us that wishes to stay with divine flow, to feel that beautiful oneness and to remain at peace and stillness. Yet we will feel the call to do something again—to be of service. This is the state of realizing who we are. The previous states had everything to do with surrender. We have realized the illusions, the layers of conditioned reality, the threads that make up the tapestry and have gradually lifted these layers, unraveled or rewoven the tapestry, seen through the grids. To reach this next state requires filling up the proverbial empty cup. This is a scary thought, even to those who are awake.

To fill our cup is a choice. In the Bible there are many references to the empty cup. To be filled it must first be emptied—completely emptied. This is what has happened in the previous stages. Total surrender is different for every person; emptying this cup requires tests and initiations to ensure we are ready—testing of our faith, of our emotions, relationships, belongings. For many this is quite literal—we leave our families, let go of our belongings, move, or lose jobs. For some it is a choice to let go, for others bankruptcies, sudden loss of income, near-death experiences, foreclosures, and other experiences have forced us to surrender. These tests are difficult. In the moment of surrender, we can realize that it is a test of faith, of surrender, or we can struggle to maintain who we thought we were. For those of us who have not gone through the surrendering and testing aspects of awakening, it seems scarier than filling the cup. But to be fully filled with divinity, to fully become who we are and actually be who we are—full of our own power, fully awake, with the knowledge of what we are here to do and how to do it—requires fearlessness. It can be easy to stay in an awakened state of not-doing, to stay with the empty cup, finally at peace.

It is a choice to fill the cup. After full surrender, falling into divine flow, jumping off the final cliff of who we thought we were, being at total oneness with the universe, there is fear, especially while jumping. But once fully in divine flow, there is love, and bliss, and understanding. There is joy. There are still human affairs to attend to, emotions that come up, but the flow remains. After a while the bliss seems to be not that big of a deal, it just is. And at some point, total illumination occurs. We are freefalling in divine flow, and we feel the light surround us, we feel our own divine light come from within us, and we feel no difference between outer and inner light.

From this stage of realization we understand now fully that we are divine and we are an aspect of divinity. This light remains with us. Although we must continually surrender that which doesn't serve us when it comes up (and things will still come up), this is a stage of filling. At first it is with light, with understanding. Then it is with a realization of who we truly are: what our individual purpose is here, what our strengths are, how we are an individual yet in divine flow, and what our truth is. This is a much different stage than oneness. With oneness we are a part of everything. This is true here as well. But we are different as well. We still retain the oneness, but the drop that is us in the ocean of divine flow realizes that it is a drop and the ocean at the same time. When differentiation occurs after merging and illumination, we understand how we are supposed to walk in the world, how we can be of service. It is freedom.

We are no longer bound by the past, by the present, by any of the layers that were previously released. We know who we are and act from that place. We are filled with love, have merged fully with the Godhead, the divine, and allowed it to fill us. With this filling comes the energy and capabilities to be who we truly are supposed to be in this world without struggling with the patterns, traumas, and conditioned layers of reality imposed upon us previously. We know what we are here to do, how to be of service to the divine, and simply go do it.

During this stage we realize that we are meant to be a physical being, a sensate being. We are divine but in a physical container. That has meaning. When we start to become individuated from divine flow there is a connection to all of our bodies—physical, mental/emotional, energetic, and spiritual. They are all one. There is a realization that the physical body is necessary—it is not something to be cast aside for spiritual meaning. The spirit, the divine, the physical—all parts of us—become one, and we become fully rooted into our physical body, illuminated into our physical body.

There is an understanding of shadow, of darkness, of ego, that all of the parts of us we disassociated from, neglected, or thought were "bad" are now loved and understood. We take full responsibility for every part of us, every emotion, every experience. We experience the full range of emotions and allow for them to flow through us—rage, anger, sadness, grief, joy—all in their pure states. We fully take pleasure in our bodies and fully experience the power of our sexuality, gender, and history. There is no longer anything to apologize for—we are who we are.

We discover our divine role and how we can be of service to the world here. This may be as a teacher, a millionaire, or a janitor. Instead of staying in a place of inaction we begin to realize that we can be a part of the healing of the world. We do this not through words but through actions. We volunteer, we are activists, we are fully whoever we are and bring that into the world. We deeply care and feel passionate about the world around us; we spiritually, physically, and on all levels participate in the world the best way we are able to. When we get to this stage we have the courage to fully be in our power and to fully be who we are. Our cup has been refilled, and instead of it being filled with our wounds, thoughtforms, and the conditioned layers of reality, it has been refilled with us, and who we truly are.

After Awakening

We recognize with a sense of divine humor after awakening that we have always been awake. Most of the initiations, tests, and path were created by ourselves as a need to work our way logically out of illusions. We know now that awakened is what we always were; we have just remembered it and have cast off the layers that were causing us to forget. There is no path. No illusion. No time. There is only us … and God. And oneness. And us in divine flow merging into oneness and then differentiating into oneness yet separation.

We are now tasked with maintaining this state. It is natural for this state to naturally ebb and flow, for us to continually need to surrender, to continue to fall, to continue to feel the love and light and divinity within and surrounding us. With families, jobs, and ordinary life, this can take some effort.

But after awakening there is no shift back to any of the states of illusion. The deeper we go the more we learn from divine unfolding. The more love we are able to give the more we will receive until we are bursting from it. There is always bliss, and love, although sometimes it will be in the background as we attend to daily matters. There is always life to attend to, but from an awakened state there is no chaos. Things are how they are, and we approach them with simplicity and compassion. Our lives become simple, we are fully embodied, and we are fully in the present moment. There is peace, bliss, and love, as well as all of the other emotions.

We realize that we can begin to work with the tapestry of life. We can become a specific archetype like putting on a hat from our closet. We can fully pull all of our energy into our physical container to compete in a soccer game, or tap into ancestral and family pattern history to inform our decision about what to do with our own family. We have full contact with Spirit here, and are noticed by spiritual beings.

Although we have no desire for control, and realize by this point that things are perfect the way they are, we understand how we can shape our reality. Staying awake requires being of service and understanding how we can benefit humanity. At this stage we understand our place in the world and what we are meant to do. Gone are the selfish understandings, the "me first" attitude that sweeps through many of the other levels. There is an understanding here that we are awakened, and thus must be of service. It is a responsibility to be a part of the realized divine presence on earth. It is a rare gift to be in this space, and to understand that our service may be very simple, such as volunteering at a soup kitchen, or to become a teacher or healer. We are in human form and can accomplish much for humanity at this point. But we are also small, and one person, and we must humble ourselves to realize that being awakened may not mean to be a world-renowned guru or multi-millionaire—it may be simply be to smile at every person we serve in the coffee shop we work at. Many of the fully realized souls on this planet are not famous. They are the ones who realize exactly who they are—whether it be a social worker, a postal worker, or a CEO.

Maintaining our full awakening is easy in some ways at this point. We do what we are supposed to do. We let go of everything else. We are fully in the present. We continually surrender, continually unfold, and continually immerse ourselves in bliss, love, and divinity. We now realize with divine irony that we are actually at the beginning of our journey. We are able to live life the way we choose. We are fully in contact with our own truth and the divine and let it inform us and flow through us. We are free.

PART 2

Types of Awakenings

There are many different types and endless variations of awakenings. The ones listed are the most dominant ones—there are certainly others. We may notice ourselves in more than one category, or have had one type of awakening trigger another. As we go through the levels of awakening there may be a shift in the type of awakening that we are going through. The end result and purpose of all of these types of awakenings is the fully awakened state.

The awakening experience has peaks and valleys, waves where there will be sudden realizations and openings, and periods of stagnation. There are also gradual and sudden types of awakening. When we go through a sudden awakening we may find that our experiences eventually become more gradual. When we go through a gradual awakening we may find ourselves at certain points going through a period of accelerated growth. Some of these awakenings, due to their very nature, such as the Kundalini awakening, are always sudden and known for their drastic shifts and difficulty navigating. Other awakenings, such as the subtle energy awakening, are always gradual.

For the sake of simplicity, we will navigate through the gradual awakening first. This path results in the cast-off of old material and energies at a slow but gradual pace, resulting in the incorporation and integration of new heightened energies.

The Gradual Awakening

We can liken the path of gradual awakening to going up a spiritual elevator one floor at a time and getting out at each floor to explore. Each floor that we find ourselves on is a gradual perspective shift, a different understanding of the universe and Self. These floors are not necessarily easy to incorporate, but the worldview and self-view that comes from them is not so drastically different from the floor before so they can be integrated somewhat smoothly.

During a gradual awakening we may take a long time at each floor, get stuck on a level, or may not know how to get back on the elevator. While the severity of a sudden awakening creates going up many floors in the spiritual elevator at once, the gradual awakening opens the spiritual elevator at every floor. Due to the step-by-step nature of gradual awakenings this process can be a part of the background rather than something that needs attending to, and we can usually place a divide between our spiritual experiences and our daily lives. We can still remain in the job we dislike, remain in the same patterns of sleep and loops that repeat again and again, relegating our spirituality to weekends or peak and momentary experiences. This may be a perfect state of awakening for many of us. But at a certain point we must make a decision. Sometimes this decision is made for us and is out of our control, and sometimes it is a conscious decision that we must make—we can decide to stay on the floor we are on or go back to the elevator.

When we get to the mid-floors of this elevator in the gradual awakening we start to see the patterns and loops of our lives and can no longer deny the path that we are on. There can no longer be a divide. Subconsciously, many of us know this and choose to remain on the floor we are at, or utilize drugs, alcohol, or other numbing agents to stop ourselves from progressing.

MARTHA started attending yoga, meditation classes, and doing nature hikes and began having peak experiences of oneness where she felt bliss flow through her. These experiences left her feeling wonderful, and she started to seek them out more and more, staying in nature for longer periods of time, taking a class on flower arranging, and reading voraciously about different spiritual paths and self-help materials.

She began experiencing memories of abuse as a child and went to counseling to help sort things out. As she worked on the patterns through counseling and continued her meditation practice she began to realize that the patterns that she had endured as a child were playing out in her current life. She was not physically abused, but her husband frequently talked down to her and made fun of her for being interested in meditation and her hobby of knitting. As she gradually became more conscious of this pattern she realized that it originally came from her mother. She then realized that this was a pattern that appeared in all of the women in her family. The thought of this greatly upset her as she could now see a whole line of women who had suffered from this pattern and had passed it down to her.

Martha began drinking more than she regularly did and watching television. Her kids were teenagers at this point and were out of the house most days. When she was sober and not distracted, she could see the pattern of her lineage playing out in her life and she could not deal with it. Although there was a part of her that wanted to deny awakening to this pattern, there was also a strong part of her that wanted to heal it. She went back to counseling, came to see me for energy work and ancestral clearing, and started meditating again. She got back on the proverbial elevator after being stuck for more than a year and was gradually able to clear herself of this pattern and move forward in a healthier way with her marriage.

Gradual awakenings have plenty of blessings. When we go through the process of awakening this way we are deeply invested and aware of each level of surrender, each test that we go through. We are intimately aware of symptoms, happenings, and have some control over the process. When we gradually awaken and want to slow the process down, provided we have only reached a semi-awake state, we can simply stop participating in spiritual activities. When we stop reading, meditating, or being a willing participant in the awakening process while going through a gradual awakening the process will typically stop. We are then able to proceed when we are ready or when we feel called to do so. The patterns and lessons that have appeared will still remain, but when we decide to not do anything about them, or to put ourselves back to sleep, we are able to numb ourselves to our wounds and live with our patterns instead of working through them.

Attaining realization and an awakened state through gradual awakening is ideal. There are stops and starts, but until we reach the middle floors of the elevator of awakening we feel in control of much of the process. We decide what workshops we want to attend, how much to meditate, and what we are able to surrender. With each new floor we are able to gradually change perspective and incorporate the new knowledge and realizations attained.

On the gradual path there are slow periods, faster periods, and complete stops. When we maintain awareness of when we are sabotaging ourselves, when we are stopping ourselves from getting back on that elevator, and when we are numbing ourselves or putting ourselves back to sleep rather than dealing with our wounding, we can work through a gradual awakening in a conscientious manner.

The Sudden Awakening

For some of us there is an abrupt moment or realization that creates a sudden shift in understanding and awareness of Self and the universe. This is a more difficult path and is becoming increasingly more common now that we have incorporated yoga and meditation practices into our lives and workplaces without having a solid understanding of the spiritual precepts behind them. For many of us with a new devotion to a yoga or meditation practice this can result in a sort of "crash," where Kundalini, chakras, or more subtle energy systems are activated and we find ourselves in the midst of a spiritual awakening. Some of us with no spiritual backgrounds find ourselves suddenly thrust into a spiritual awakening and have even greater difficulty because we have no cosmology to support ourselves or prior knowledge of the process.

With sudden awakening, the body then has to get rid of past and present blocks very quickly in order to catch up to the new spiritual state so that mind-body-spirit are once again aligned and balanced. This can be physically, emotionally, and spiritually disorienting—especially when we have no idea what is going on.

SARA was a 25-year-old tech expert who began meditating at the behest of her counselor to help her with anxiety and depression issues. Always sensitive, Sara was drawn to art and nature, enjoyed spending time alone, and felt social anxiety in groups. She began with a meditation she found off the Internet that was supposed to cleanse her chakras. She found the exercises enjoyable and found that they, along with the counseling, began to help with her depression and anxiety symptoms to the point that she was able to interact with others, felt less stress at work, and the TMJ and neck tension that she once had was not a constant source of pain for her. This phase lasted for six months. She reported not really feeling much during the meditations during this time other than a state of relaxation, improved sleep, and improved social aptitude.

When Sara had been meditating for six months she began to notice that she had an increase in fears, her heart began racing at odd times or feeling like it was beating out of her chest, and her anxiety returned to the point that she needed to work from home. She was unable to go outside and started having her groceries delivered to her because she felt overwhelmed when she went outside or was around people. Sara began having twitching in her hands, what she called restless leg issues, and waves of headaches, nausea, and a constant feeling of being queasy or seasick.

She went through medical testing, MRIs, brain scans as well as blood work, all of which had no significant findings. Xanax as well as other medications given to her by her psychiatrist made her anxiety temporarily better but physically made her feel worse. When she came to see me she was pale, was not digesting foods beyond very simple cooked meals well, and was feeling waves of heat and nausea frequently throughout the day.

Although I encouraged her to further explore the Western medical route, it was through listening to her meditation that I was able to find the culprit behind her symptoms. The chakra balancing and awakening she was doing was allowing for her heart, third eye, and crown to open, but since her lower chakras were not open she had become extremely unbalanced.

Sara is a fairly typical example of what a modern-day awakening looks like. It is easy to become out of balance, to not understand that physical symptoms can come from something spiritual like meditation without an appropriate teacher. Through treatment to balance her energy and specific exercises to discharge and ground her energy Sara could become more balanced. Once the blockages of her first, second, and third chakras were lessened, the heat, anxiety, fear, and twitches Sara experienced subsided, and she was able to work through the beginning stages of awakening in a stable and healthy manner.

Some people find it surprising that awakening can happen rather suddenly without a link to any sort of spiritual practice or even without much, if any, spiritual knowledge. This is more rare and most of us who are on the path to awakening already have an interest in some sort of esoteric material, mythology, or religious belief that has guided us. But there are those of us who have a sudden shift, and in an instant our entire world, belief system, and what we understood about ourselves has changed. This sudden change is exacerbated by the fact that spiritual awakenings are not understood or talked about much. It is common for those of us undergoing sudden spiritual awakenings to be hospitalized, given medication, and thought mentally ill by the general populace.

In many cases for sudden awakening, hospitalization and medication may be necessary and helpful because we are unable to take care of our own needs due to the sudden transformation and huge mental, emotional, and physical shifts that occur. When we go through sudden awakenings we also lack the type of friends or loved ones who would be able to understand or adequately assist us in the transition.

MAX was a 35-year-old lawyer with a wife and small child, who was on disability from work due to posttraumatic stress disorder (PTSD) and anxiety. He was on several medications to help with the debilitating depression, fatigue, and anxiety that caused him to be unable to think, read, or watch television. Five years earlier he had an incident at a local beach where he had almost drowned, and while that had seemingly not caused him many issues at the time, four years later he was in the shower and felt water flowing over his head and felt a burst of energy like a lightning bolt go into the top of his head that was so strong he passed out. When he came to, the sensation of lightning was still with him, and he felt as if his body were erupting like a volcano. He got out of the shower, went to bed, but was unable to sleep. He had the profound realization that something major had happened, but he had no idea what it was or what he should do about it. He contemplated going to the hospital, but he told himself that he would see how he felt the next day and that what had happened was not life-threatening.

Over the next month his world fell apart. Max's body began contorting and he felt large surges of energy run through him, all of which he had no control over. He began feeling as if everything was fake, that the world was false, and he could not reconcile the new thoughts and understandings that came to him with his Jewish faith. He could not read and in his vision he began seeing spots and grids surrounding him. At times he thought he could see shapes and people out of the corner of his eye, and he began having visuals of men and women that pleaded with him to help them. When he closed his eyes he could not sleep and was getting increasingly depressed when activities he once enjoyed like watching television, eating expensive meals, and running no longer seemed important to him. His energy would be extremely high for a few hours and then he would suffer debilitating fatigue for days.

At the urgency of his wife he began seeing a psychiatrist who admitted him to inpatient care. When he was well enough to be in an outpatient facility and was medicated to the point that he no longer felt suicidal he began seeing spiritual healers and counselors for assistance. He realized that there may be something beyond brain chemistry issues in his case going on and although reluctant about "woo-woo" practitioners, he searched for and went through many spiritual practitioners in an attempt to find one who could help him.

When Max came to me it was obvious that he was in a great deal of distress. Since he had no basis for the understanding of what was happening to him, he had understandably gone the route of Western Medicine. Western Medicine still separates the physical from the emotional and has no basis in the spiritual. Since his awakening was so sudden and there were no precursors Max had no understanding of what was going on other than the fact that something was obviously very wrong and that it might have something to do with something spiritual because medication, testing, and Western Medicine had little explanation for his physical and mental symptoms.

Working with Max was extremely difficult in that he lacked any sort of framework for real spiritual knowledge, and his resistance to his own transformation and symptoms was what was causing some of the difficulties he was experiencing. Ultimately, Max was hoping that when he came to me that I would tell him that there was nothing going on with him and that the current trajectory of medication and psychotherapy would cure him. Although there was no doubt that talk therapy and medication (at least for the time being) were helpful in his process, the real issue was the resistance and lack of surrender as well as the sheer amount of material coming up to process at the same time. I was able to help Max to stabilize his nervous system and discharge some heat, but when the issue came up of accepting that his life would contain odd yogic movements, jerking sensations, waves of volcanic heat, and disruption of everything he knew, he resisted.

In sessions he would have profound realizations of ancestral patterns, his faith, and his place in the world, but after each session he would reject his new understandings and sense of Self because it was too difficult to realize what he did without changing his marriage, his faith, his career, and his entire life. The last I heard from him he had gone through a difficult divorce and was an inpatient at a local hospital.

In almost all cases, a sudden awakening is like a death—everything we knew about ourselves and the world has died and we are left with the remnants of our former lives. We then are tasked with rebuilding and recreating new lives only for them to be torn down again through another wave of awakening. Understandably in most cases there is extreme resistance and wanting to keep fragments and known patterns and loops of our lives. We experience extreme emotion—anger, hostility, fear—during this process. When an awakening happens so suddenly there is little chance for transition time or physical, mental, and emotional stability. When we awaken suddenly, we can remain in a victim state—blaming the Kundalini, God, the Universe for our awakenings and our lack of control over the process. Our bodies often prove this lack of control with drastic heat, energetic changes, fatigue, and twitching and yoga-like movements that are out of our control. Mentally this process creates brain fog, depression, anxiety, and a fear that accompanies knowing something is terribly out of the ordinary. Spiritually we have deep understandings and knowledge that are out of the depth that we have experienced before and a loss of previous rigid and confining belief systems.

Many of us know that what is happening to us has a spiritual basis but we are unable to approach it through these measures because there is no standard of care for sudden awakenings. When we go through sudden and difficult awakenings we find ourselves in a position where we are experiencing physical and mental symptoms that allopathic medicine cannot figure out. It is easy for health providers to prescribe antipsychotics and antidepressants because the symptoms appear similarly to what those medications are used for or the doctor simply does not know what else to do. When we go through a sudden awakening and come to terms with the fact that we are going through a spiritual sickness there is a lack of real and knowledgeable practitioners who can assist and a great deal of false information. Many practitioners unfortunately who believe they can help with this are out of their depth with the severity of symptoms.

They may create more harm by not understanding or being able to hear what we are saying or do not have knowledge about the very real physical and emotional symptoms that are occurring.

Energetic Transmissions

Experiences such as *shaktipat*—receiving an energetic transmission from an enlightened guru or teacher—can result in a gradual or sudden awakening. Reiki transmissions and attunements or healing sessions with someone of an awakened state can propel us up several floors on the spiritual elevator as well. This path is fairly well known, and individuals who are seeking shaktipat or a Reiki attunement are already on a spiritual path. Much has been written about awakenings from shaktipat, and there are different levels of awakening that come from receiving it.

Most of us who go through a Reiki class or receive *shakti* from a guru or teacher achieve lower-level awakenings. These awakenings are temporary and fill the recipient with feelings of peace and calm while in the presence of the giver. Although these feelings are temporary we have a choice in realizing that the type of peace, calm, or energized flow we have felt can be a part of our existence. It is rare that when we experience this that we understand that this experience is coming from us, and that the teacher is merely allowing for us to access a deeper layer of ourselves. Most of us attribute this experience to the teacher, follow the teacher around to be in their heightened presence, and go home to how our lives were when we left.

It is very common for us to take workshops in order to feel this lower-level type of awakening and consider it a type of vacation—meaning that we are specifically looking for the feelings that heightened vibration, greater flow, or a slightly more awakened state can create for us, but we are unable or unwilling to create a space for this in our daily lives. It is only through the understanding that the feelings that are created through the guru or teacher can be part of our daily lives that this lower-level awakening can be heightened. For the person who has given us shaktipat or whose mere presence allows us to feel heightened flow is giving us a glimpse of our own divine energy and temporarily allowing us to access higher levels of consciousness.

Most of who receive shakti from a guru, *qi* through a Reiki teacher, or go to a spiritual workshop will temporarily go up several floors on the spiritual elevator only to come back down again. This is not a bad thing. Our body, mind, and soul now understand the potential for this to happen again. We have lightened our load some. In some cases we can permanently be changed by energetic transmission by receiving it at a specific junction in our awakening process.

Some gurus and teachers permanently mark the student energetically, providing a link so the student can constantly feel the guru. This will provide the student with some of the understandings and energy of the guru, allowing the student to quickly work through their own material while still being held in safety by someone who has been through the awakening process. Those of us who have reached the final stages of awakening realize our own divinity and no longer need the energy or guidance of the guru and can surrender that relationship, even if we still maintain a relationship or enjoy the company of the guru. But most of us feel the heightened energy with shaktipat, a workshop, or a teacher or guru and come up to that level, going back down a few levels on the elevator once the workshop or event is over.

Why does the shaktipat not last? Achieving awakening involves incorporation into daily life and a level of surrender and lifestyle change that many of us are not willing to do. In my Reiki courses, I would see students have great understandings of life and how their life could flow differently if they surrendered, gave up certain myths and stories about how their lives were supposed to look, and let go of the trauma, fear, sadness, and depression that clouded them. When most of these students left the class, these understandings would be left in the class so they could once again return to the ordinary reality of their existence—and the unhappiness and old life scripts that cloud their newly achieved, momentarily more awakened state.

For these students, should they go home, ditch their husbands, wives, and children to go meditate on a mountain for a year? Give up all of their physical belongings, let go of everything that they thought they knew? For some, the answer to this is yes. Plenty of people have done this—had a profound realization, an awakening that caused them to move to Peru, or leave their job and their lives. But for most, this is not necessary.

What happens when we achieve a temporary moment of awakening is that the feelings are so different from the rest of our existences that we give the credit to the guru, the teacher, or the workshop experience. This is a mistake. The awakening that we have experienced, however momentary it was, has shown us that it is ours to have.

ELIZABETH went to see Amma, the hugging saint, when she came to a town several hours away from her. Elizabeth was a sensitive, Empath, and Clairvoyant who had difficulty with large crowds. Despite these reservations, Elizabeth felt that she had to see Amma, and was willing to go despite knowing how many people were there and her fears of being overwhelmed. Entering the building where it was held, she was at first in a state of panic and partially left her body as a safety mechanism. As she sat down, she began to feel more settled in and felt an enormous amount of love wash over her body until she felt it difficult to sit upright. When she went to touch Amma, she immediately felt a sense of joy come over her. She looked deep into Amma's eyes and could see her own reflection in them, which profoundly moved her for some unknown reason. Leaving the stage she felt the joy, but also a sense of exhaustion, come over her. After she left the event, she started crying. Elizabeth could not place the tears, but she realized that she was processing something that was hers. She allowed the tears to come up and after she felt lighter somehow. Since she was younger she always had a perpetual feeling of sadness and grief surrounding her like a black cloud, and she felt part of it lift after crying.

The experience of joy for Elizabeth faded, as did the feelings of immense love and being held. But the lightness from the release of tears did not, and when Elizabeth pictured the cloud of grief she could now understand what it was and why the rest of it remained. She was able to come in for sessions and we removed the rest of the cloud, freeing her from that energy.

PAULA had a daughter who was autistic and through relentless searching and studying decided to study Reiki. Her daughter Amanda had responded to Reiki well, and after the amount of money that Paula had given doctors, to pharmaceutical companies, occupational therapists, and chiropractors, the fact that Amanda was calm and interactive for several days after her Reiki treatments intrigued her. She signed up for a local Usui Reiki class that her Reiki practitioner recommended and decided to come to the class with an open but skeptical mind. Paula was willing to do whatever it took for her daughter, but as a practicing Catholic she had reservations about Energy Work. The class was lovely, and Paula enjoyed her teacher and classmates. When it came time for the attunement, they all sat in a circle with their eyes closed with soft music. Paula described feeling wonderful, with a deep sense of relaxation that she rarely experienced in her present-day reality.

When she received her attunement Paula felt a sense of warmth flow through her. She went outside after her attunement and sat quietly under a tree, feeling at peace with the sunshine. Ordinarily fatigued, Paula felt energized but also felt like she could sleep for days. When she went home, things with Amanda went well for that entire evening and into the next day. These feelings of warmth and relaxation faded completely a few days later, but Paula was now able to understand how and why Reiki helped her daughter.

The awakenings from energetic transmission are much different in that we have a context for the awakening. We are also likely not going from the bottom of the elevator to the top of the elevator in one ride—we have already had a spiritual interest or path, and have likely done some spiritual work on ourselves already. However, this transmission of energy can propel some of us forward suddenly from a semi-awake state to an awakened state. These instances would be like bringing us five to ten floors up in the elevator. This is typically different from some of the sudden awakenings, such as a Kundalini awakening, where a person is going up twenty or thirty floors suddenly.

Something like shaktipat is not guaranteed to awaken someone. There is a great deal of false information about this fact out there. When we view videos or visit gurus who claim that they can awaken any student it is usually a person who does not understand how awakening works, is going through an ego-type awakening, and is not a fully awakened individual. Receiving shakti or even an attunement from a teacher or guru is actually a fairly simple equation. The level of awakening and access to spiritual power that the teacher has goes into the receiving student. This energy from the teacher will go into the student and through the body of the student the best way it can until it meets restrictions. This energy will try to work with as much of the restrictions in the student as it can before the force lessens until it dissipates.

An important note here is that a lot of this has to do with the teacher. Plenty of people argue that a transmission or attunement, such as a Reiki attunement, is from the divine and does not depend on the vessel of the teacher. This is simply untrue. If the teacher is fully awakened, divine energy can fully flow through them. This full flow can be transmitted to the student. If the teacher is only partially awake, or ego-awakened, this divine energy loses its potency because it is working with the vessel (the teacher) and clearing them before it clears us. It is rare to find a truly awakened teacher who can transmit pure divine energy, but the power and strength of it is something we are not soon to forget.

Spiritual awakening is an inside job. It requires us to work through our material. Having healers, gurus, teachers, and others help us come to the next floor of the elevator or even several floors is wonderful but is only sustainable and permanent if we do the work to remain at that level. Nobody can sell us enlightenment or awaken our Kundalini for us. This same thing is true of all healing and awakening. As an acupuncturist, I saw countless patients with stomach pain. The patients who went home and worked with the appropriate diet in conjunction with the acupuncture got better. The patients who received acupuncture and went home to a diet of Twinkies and steak felt better after acupuncture but then went back to their normal state of pain.

Similar to awakening through energetic transmission is awakening through a place or event. This is one of the most common awakenings, and for most of us it falls into the category of a gradual awakening, but similar to energetic transmissions, there are some places and experiences that are a catalyst to a sudden spiritual awakening.

Awakening through Place or Event

Recall a beach vacation, a trip to Ireland, a mountain, volcano—somewhere in nature where you felt the natural wonders of the world and felt a sense of peace, timelessness, and that you were in exactly the right moment and time to experience what you were experiencing. You likely felt oneness, a sense of flow, synchronicity, a settling, and a release of everyday stresses. For most people this is a place in nature that corresponds to one of the elements—earth, fire, water, air. But for some, this place may be entirely unexpected.

> DARLENE was a woman with a significant trauma history. Several childhood illnesses meant that she was unable to make the appropriate school-age connections that her peers had, and she described feelings of loneliness and grief stemming from that time that she was unable to get rid of. She was successful as an attorney, but constantly felt struggle, even when she was doing well. These feelings were present with her constantly—sadness, grief, loneliness, a feeling of not being a part of the world and that the world did not want her. She appeared withdrawn, sullen, and would draw her legs under her when she talked. This all changed when she described a recent visit to Paris. She had found a café that she described as having exactly the right amount of people. She had her morning coffee and a pastry, and for the time that she was in that café all of her typical feelings disappeared. She felt a part of the world—she described it as feeling like a part of a painting and had the sudden knowledge that she was very much a part of things. She further described the experience as perfect, as if she had been in that café forever, feeling a sense of ease that she had never felt before in her life.
>
> When she described this experience, Darlene had a look of peace and a careful smile on her face that I had never seen before. By teaching her the meditation below, she was able to call up some of that experience she felt in that café to feel a sense of joy and peace in her daily life.

Abraham Maslow first came up with the term *peak experience* to describe feelings of interconnectedness, unity, and joy that come from certain experiences in life. These experiences can come from anything. People have described peak experiences through dancing, music (both playing and listening to), concerts, sporting events, time out in nature, exercise, workshops, and more. The peak experience gives a momentary awakening—a glimpse into what an awakened state is like. It crumbles any feelings of separation and allows for us to feel the divine nature of ourselves and the oneness of the universe.

Peak experiences are fleeting but addictive. For many of us on a spiritual path the flickering of peak experiences keep us going through the struggles of awakening. They are the complete letting go of the rational mind, time, and just allowing ourselves to be. They are wonderful, blissful, and yet full of peace. For those of us who are to fully awaken, they are a signal of what can come. If we utilize them to keep us going through the difficulties of the awakening process, and realize that this is our true state, peak experiences and momentary experiences can be extraordinarily helpful to propel us through the darkness and struggle that comes with the awakening experience.

EXERCISE: Peak Experience Meditation

- Allow yourself to recall it. Remember the place; time; what you saw, sensed, and felt; and who was there.
- See yourself there, filled with the energy and realizations from that experience.
- Allow the self that you see having that experience to merge with you in your current state. Do this by taking in breaths and imagining the surroundings, the experience, and the people to draw closer to you with each inhale.
- Let it merge and become a part of you. Feel the energy settle and become a part of you at this present moment.
- Do this whenever you need to remember this state, a higher state of awakening that you have already witnessed. Gradually this experience may unfold from within you rather than be brought in.

Greater awakenings from peak experiences do occur. Eventually we may begin to receive energy, or energetic transmissions, from places we visit and events we take part in. When we visit a mountain, we may feel the peak experience of being on that mountain, but we also may notice something else begin to occur. A peak experience is transitory—it is a specific moment in time and often event specific. Once that time has passed and we have left that time and place we can get a faint recall of the experience through photographs, memories, or meditation. But sometimes these experiences imprint on us and attune us to their energy, and may become a spiritual teacher to us.

To clarify, every experience we have places an imprint on us. Really negative and positive experiences carry a bigger imprint. Basically, the more charged or the more important the experience is, the bigger the imprint. These imprints can be cleared or recharged. Some of us receive an energetic transmission from a place or event if we are awake and open to the vibrations and energy of them. Our energetic body receives an imprint with the vibration and energy of a place, experience, or event.

We can carry the vibration of a mountain we visited with us, the energy of a sporting event, the joy of a concert experience. These vibrations open us up, awaken us to the energies of the world. They are not temporary or fleeting. As we become more awake, we can begin to allow more and more of these energies in our system, opening to the different manifestations, teachings, and vibrations of the divine, calling on them when we need them. This is an awakening by energetic imprint, and it is a lasting experience as long as we cultivate our relationship with the energy and treat it with respect.

DONALD was a scientist and had always been interested in astronomy. He had gone to Mount Shasta and Sedona to see what power spots were like, and although he didn't consider himself to be that spiritual he thoroughly enjoyed exploring consciousness, philosophy, and was interested in spiritual matters. He felt a buzz in the spots he visited that took over his whole body and a sense of being very small yet an integral part of the universe. He felt joy. He could recall all of these feelings and events fondly, but it was not until he went into the Sonoran Desert that he experienced the lasting imprint and teachings of a place. It was pitch black and he had brought his telescope with him. When he gazed at the constellations and the moon he again felt a sense of unity, peace, and of being very small in a very large place. He put away the telescope and sat, silently staring at the stars.

Without a real understanding of why he was doing this, he suddenly felt drawn to a group of stars and fixated his gaze on them. Breathing slowly, he felt as if he could sense their individual vibration. This vibration came into his body and it felt like a pleasant, tickling feeling. He laughed aloud, feeling like his whole energy body was expanding and filling with the energy of these stars. Although this energy was not particularly intense, for the duration of the transmission he could not avert his gaze from that section of the sky. When the energy began to dissipate, he could again look to the whole sky but something fundamentally about him and his energy had changed. He thought that it was like his previous experiences, but in the later weeks when he remembered that experience he could feel the vibration of those stars in and around his body. Gradually, although he felt a bit crazy at first, those stars began to become spiritual, non-physical teachers for him, and gave him more transmissions when he was ready for them.

Awakening from energetic transmission, imprint, or peak experience can allow for us to understand that there is more to life than the material and worldly pleasures. We can begin to understand the duality and complexity of the world. For many of us it is the first step on the spiritual path, and a memory that we recall fondly when we are going through more intense stages of awakening.

Subtle Energy Awakenings

Subtle energy awakenings are typically the first type of gradual awakening to occur. This is the feeling of *qi* circulating through our bodies. *Qi* and *prana* are terms from different cultures that describe mild currents of energy that circulate through our body as well as through everything in the world. Feelings of mild heat, electric current circulating, and a sensation of a non-physical, energetic process happening are common symptoms. Our energy bodies are beginning to activate and call attention to themselves. This can be anywhere in our body, or just outside or surrounding our physical body.

Some people use the word *prana* or *qi* interchangeably with Kundalini energy. The electrical currents of energy running through the body are actually a lower level force than Kundalini. All of us have *qi* working its way through the channel systems and energetic grids of our bodies and through the world whether we are conscious of it or not. What occurs on the level of a subtle energy awakening is an awareness and ability to feel, touch, or see *qi* or *prana*. Kundalini is a dormant energy, even for people that can consciously feel the *qi* of their bodies. It is typical for this to be misunderstood as most people have wonderful experiences with *qi* through Energy Work or working out—the nice electric charge or buzz, the feeling of energy running through the body freely. Kundalini is much different in terms of intensity, purpose, symptoms, awareness level, and impact on life than a subtle energy awakening.

An interest in Energy Work and spiritual matters begins in this stage. Many of us take Reiki training or start a yoga or meditation class at this stage or begin to question and seek regarding spiritual matters. As a Reiki teacher, it was fascinating to watch people become excited about their hands becoming warm, mild twitching and other subtle energetic phenomena, or their ability to feel/sense energy when scanning the body of a friend or classmate.

This stage is the first glimpse at energy, and the understanding that there is more to the world than just what is commonly accepted by society as reality. This leads to questioning and information seeking. This is still a stage of logic, so the information seeking and questioning is within the paradigm of the seeker. There is not a drastic change in personal path or worldview of the subtle energy awakening. It is a gentle eye opening, a realization that there is energy in the world, and perhaps a personal feeling of energy running through the body.

For some of us this awakening can become a gradual opening to new knowledge, personal understanding, and greater awakening. The interest in yoga, Reiki, meditation, religion, and spirituality becomes a part of everyday life, and we progress further along our spiritual path. Some of us stay at the stage of subtle energy awakening because we are happy with where we are or subconsciously we know that to move forward would require more opening, more time, and more shifts than we are ready or willing to do. Some of us enter this stage and immediately go up several floors on the elevator of awakening—this subtle awakening is an immediate trigger to a larger and more intense awakening that drastically opens and changes us.

When we are in this stage and wish to progress further we can simply take classes that interest us, begin regular meditation or prayer, participate in religious or spiritual activities that feel good to us, or do yoga, tai chi, or other exercises focused on opening and breath. If we do not get stuck in ego and realize that there is always more to learn, further to go, and realize that there are plenty of people who feel and even see energy, we can move forward if we choose to do so. When we begin a daily practice that suits our own, individualized spiritual needs, we can begin to awaken in the manner that best suits us.

EXERCISE: Subtle Energy Meditation

- Allow yourself to come to a quiet place, a restful place and body position. Bring your hands together, palms facing one another. Allow for them to touch. Gently rub them together. Notice any heat that shows up between them. Now rub them more vigorously and separate them from one another slowly. Allow the palms to still be parallel to one another, but see how far you can move your hands apart while still feeling heat and connection between them.

- Now bring your hands together again and rub them. Put your hands palms down over your eyes, your abdomen, your thighs, anywhere that you feel called to do so. Allow yourself to start to get to know your own body— where could you use some energy flow? Put your hands there after rubbing them together. Do you feel anything when you place your hands on the spot you chose? What do you feel locally? What do you feel in the rest of your body?

- If you feel like you can progress further, hold your hands, palms down, slightly off the body. Can you still feel energy or change in the local area? What about the body as a whole? Eventually you can do these exercises without rubbing your hands together. Bring your hands to a spot that you feel called to, palms down, and feel what is happening. Feel what happens if you are slightly off the body—how far can you back away your hands and still feel sensation?

- Now bring your hands together again. Separate them slowly. Imagine a ball of energy between your hands. You can bring your hands together and rub them again and then separate them to create this ball. For some of you this ball of energy will simply happen. Others will have to imagine the ball or will feel heat or the sensation of something there. For those of you who are more visual you may start to see this ball. Bring your hands closer together, further apart, move your hands freely with this ball. If you lose the sensation, start over. Over time, you will be able to feel the ball, grow it to the size that you wish, even see the ball. After you have created this energy ball, you may choose to bring it into your body by again bringing your hands together and feeling it flow through your arms, or you can place your hands anywhere on your body that is calling to you.

Through this meditation we will gradually come to a point where we awaken the meridian/channel systems of the body or the individual chakras. For a few of us, just doing these meditations once will spark an understanding of these systems, and for others it may take months of continual practice. When we consciously and gradually cultivate ourselves, taking things step by step with the knowledge that where we are is perfect, we can achieve mastery at each level of the spiritual elevator before progressing. It is natural to want to go to the top floors of the spiritual elevator right away, or to pretend that we are further along than we are, but that is rarely how things work. By gradually awakening, and going up the elevator floor by floor, we are able to incorporate these energies much more easily than people who go to the top from floor one.

Meridian and Channel Awakenings

The next type of gradual awakening is the opening of the meridians and channels of the body. Meridians are the name for the energetic channels that run through the body and are utilized in Chinese Medicine, acupuncture, and Shiatsu. In Chinese Medicine there are twelve basic meridians that run through the body and a few other meridians that are considered extraordinary due to their power and depth in the body. The most notable of the extraordinary channels are the du and ren, which create the spine and midline of the body.

These channels are responsible for routing energy, fluids, and blood throughout the body, and the energy that flows through them is responsible for creating our physical form and all of its various systems. Channels are present in every human and animal and are even present in plants and through the energetic grids of the earth.

When we begin to be aware that there is such a thing as energy in the body the next step in awareness is noticing that this energy runs through meridians and circuits throughout the body. Many of us first notice this because of pain. I have had count-less patients come to me and point out that their migraines go through their entire Gallbladder channel, or that their leg pain goes exactly through their Liver channel. Similarly, I have placed acupuncture needles in specific channels of the body and had many patients talk about other aspects of the channel light up, or have worked ener-getically or massaged organs in the abdomen and had people describe the release of a whole channel to me that was associated with that organ.

These are common experiences to us when we are beginning to understand energy. This type of awakening means that there is an understanding and often an interest in the new information, but there is not a call or necessity to do anything with the information.

So what does meridian/channel awakening feel like? Our understanding and expe-riences from the subtle energy awakening is taken a step further. We may feel energy running through our bodies, warmth, electrical-type currents, or an awareness of spe-cific areas of the body and their openness of energy flow. We may begin to experience individual fingers or toes vibrate. We may develop awareness that it would feel good to stretch a specific way or feel urges to do so in a conscious manner under our control. The awakening of our meridians and channels brings awareness to our body as one whole functional energetic unit. There are realizations that come in this stage that the body has energy cycling through and around the physical structure. Often there is an increased desire in this stage to learn more about energy, chakras, and a pull toward spiritual pursuits.

During this type of awakening old memories and personal traumas may appear. As we cycle energy through our body and our awareness increases on all levels—physical, mental, emotional, spiritual—it brings up old or stuck energy out of our meridians. At first, this stuck energy is old emotions, experiences, and traumas we have experienced. Eventually when we awaken more the body will cycle through the layers of awaken-ing discussed in the first section and work through our issues, family issues, ancestral issues, etc. But for most of us what first comes up in this awakening are personal emo-tions and issues that were not resolved in the past.

Many people become confused with this awakening because they begin to feel emotions like sadness and grief, pains resurfacing from old injuries or even in areas that had no injury, and other physical and emotional symptoms that are not associ-ated with their current life and circumstances. On the one hand it can be wonderful to have an interest in energy, to feel energy, and to feel the pull toward spirituality that occurs during this awakening. But when the body begins to release at this level it creates discomfort and releasing of old emotions. This is done in a gradual manner but can be puzzling because it is rare that we consciously are aware of why the physical and emotional issues of the past are coming up into consciousness. It can be difficult for us to understand what is going on and fit together the feeling of energy cycling or a new awareness level with some of the discomfort that occurs. At this level we still do not understand how physical the awakening process can be and we look at the spiritual process (if we in fact understand that we are going through an awakening) as separate from our mental and physical bodies.

Basic awareness and processing of the energies coming up in a healthy way is key to maintaining balance and stability during a gradual meridian awakening. This awakening is allowing for energy to cycle through the meridians and channels of our bodies. When it encounters blockage—old emotions, physical pains, and traumas—it will bring them up in order to clear so we can achieve greater energetic flow in our bodies. Allowing for this energy to arise and processing it through the means that is best for us—yoga, meditation, talk therapy, nature, dancing, painting, and so on—will allow for us to work through this energy and release it. There is a tendency for us to dislike any discomfort and to put ourselves back to sleep when the slightest amount of pain arises. This tendency keeps us where we are; it does not allow for us to process the energy arising to release. When we work through the energies that are arising instead of putting ourselves back to sleep we can achieve greater energetic flow in our bodies and move toward wholeness, health, and awakening.

When you experience pain or discomfort, begin to question if the emotion or pain is something that is current or not. Ask yourself if you have any reason to feel angry, or sad, or in pain at the current moment. Are your emotions appropriate for the current moment? Sometimes emotions become heightened. You may get angry because of something that happened at the grocery store but it seems as if it is heightened tenfold. Begin to sort out what is yours, what is current, and what may be coming up for clearing by simply becoming aware of the aches and pains, the emotions of your day, and ask yourself through the meditation below what is yours and is current.

As your awareness of the energetic channels and circuits of the body increases you begin to have increased awareness of your own energy. You can feel where your energy may be stuck, and by noticing this energy it will start to change and move (provided it is not really stuck). If your channels have anything in them that is really stuck you will need to find assistance—a hands-on healer such as a massage therapist, CranioSacral therapist, acupuncturist, or other healer that can work with both energy and structure at the same time. For emotional wounds that are opening, expressing this energy through talking to someone, such as a counselor, can help. You may choose to do the exercise in the previous section cultivating the energy in your hands and then placing your hands on an area of the body that feels stuck or out of balance.

During the meridian awakening is a good time to start this awareness and differentiation because it will get more difficult when you start clearing on a deeper level. With this exercise as a basis, you can begin to sort out who you are in the current moment.

EXERCISE: Meridian Meditation

- Take several breaths in. Come into a comfortable seated position with your feet on the floor.
- Do a scan of your body—starting at the feet, work your way up the legs, front and back of the torso, neck, head, and down the arms and hands.
- Simply notice what you are feeling. Any areas in pain? Any areas light up for you? Any areas you notice more than others?
- Take an area that really seems significant, and notice it even more. Sit with your awareness just on that area for a while.
- How would you describe this area?
- What emotion or emotions are in this area?
- Is this emotion current or is it from another time, place, or person?
- Now let yourself focus on the pain. It is natural to want to not focus on pain and to disassociate from parts of the body that are in pain. Let yourself actually feel the pain and discomfort. Sit with it for a few moments.
- Ask yourself how much of this pain is yours, is yours right here and now?
- It may be that all of the emotion and pain is all from the current moment. If this is true, simply notice and breathe into the pain.
- If it is not from the current moment ask how much is from the current moment. Some people use a percentage here. If you feel into this area, and the pain is 40 percent current pain that your body is experiencing, and 60 percent from the past or from the original injury, breathe into the spot again with this knowledge.
- Give permission for the pain or emotion that is not yours in the current moment to leave.
- With your breath, blow the pain and emotion that is not current out of your body. Take a breath in and breathe out this pain or emotion.
- As you progress you can blow some of your own current pain down the body and out the feet.

You can utilize this meditation in the moment as well. A well-known yoga teacher came to me talking about how one student bothered her so much that she became uncharacteristically irritated and off-center. It affected her entire class. She realized that some of this irritation was because the student was simply truly irritating, and she was able to identify it as 40 percent because of the current moment and the student. While in class she instructed the students to go into a pose and she breathed out the sixty percent that wasn't of the current moment irritation through her legs and feet. This allowed her to come to a neutral space with the student, regain her center, and continue her class. Eventually she was able to consciously understand that the student reminded her of her sister, which was something that she needed to stop recreating in her reality. The student became only a mild annoyance in the class because the teacher eventually cleared the sister pattern.

Another woman used this in board meetings. She found herself nervous and would eventually have an anxiety attack and stomach aches at the thought of presenting. When she actually presented she felt okay, but the anticipatory anxiety attacks and stomach aches drained her energy and disrupted her whole day. She identified the next morning that she had a board meeting that 70 percent of the anxiety was hers and 80 percent of the stomach ache was hers. She did her breathing and felt slightly better. Each time she was able to do this, she discovered more and more that she was a sensitive person who took in the emotions of other people at her office. Other people in her office were feeling anxious as well, and she took that on emotionally and physically. When her awareness grew she was able to identify that most of the emotion was not hers. She does this now each time that she has a meeting and each time identifies what is hers and what is not. Last I spoke to her, only a small portion of the anxiety was hers and she was able to utilize her growing awareness and breath to let go of anything that was not hers prior to the meetings.

Channel awakenings are the start of energetic and spiritual understanding. They allow for us to begin to process our material and come to the realization that we are not only a physical and mental human being but an energetic one as well. It is the opening of this awareness that allows for the start of spiritual understandings and the choice to follow a spiritual path.

When we experience meridian awakenings it is common to become aware of chakras. Due to the influx of Eastern materials into the grid of collective consciousness, the understanding of chakras is often at first mental and logical. We learn where chakras are, their colors, and take courses in how to open them. When individual chakra awakenings occur, similar to meridian awakenings, we move beyond the didactic knowledge into feeling and directly experiencing the chakras.

Individual Chakra Awakenings

We can experience individual chakra awakenings during both gradual and sudden awakenings. During a gradual awakening an awareness of the chakra, the area of the body that the chakra is part of, and emotions frozen or blocked in that area, will begin to come up for processing. During a sudden awakening the individual chakra may release a huge amount of information to process with severe physical and emotional symptoms or multiple chakras may release in conjunction with one another.

Prior to this, the openings in our bodies were mainly of an energetic nature. It is typical for us to not consider how our spiritual process is affecting our physical body or emotions prior to this point. During individual chakra awakenings there will no longer be any doubt that we are an energetic being with a physical body. The knowledge that energy informs, runs through, surrounds, and even creates the physical body is a profound realization when we begin to awaken at this level. This knowledge will only deepen the longer we are on our path, ultimately realizing that there is no separation between our spiritual, emotional, and physical selves.

This type of awakening is the beginning of a deeply spiritual path. We all have spiritual paths, regardless of how awake or asleep we are. Before this time it is easy to question if we are on a spiritual path, or if we are experiencing a spiritual awakening. At this point it is difficult to have much doubt. This realization allows us to consciously process that we are undergoing an awakening and to commit to a spiritual path, purpose, and identity in this world. For those of us going through more gradual awakenings this can be a claiming and choosing to deepen our spiritual path.

Chakras are the storehouses of all of our material, and all of the layers of reality. All of the trauma of Self, family, ancestors, and even all of the grids to the outer edges of conditioned reality are contained within the physical form and the chakra system. Each chakra is on or near the midline and informs the entire section of the body near which it is located. For example, the third chakra, located at our solar plexus, is responsible physically for the Stomach, Liver, Spleen, Pancreas, and all of the nerves and physical structures (like the spine, the skin, and the fluids) that are in that local vicinity. Each chakra has an emotion associated with it, a strength, as well as a job. This job is different for each chakra, and what is stored in each chakra is different and correlates to the emotion and job of the chakra.

Chakras can open individually at first or two or even more chakras may open together. Many of us may have been born with open chakras. A common misconception is that once a chakra opens that it remains open. Our chakras are actually constantly opening and closing like doors. They need to open and close to process material that is constantly coming our way. As we awaken we are more conscious about the sheer volume of materials and stimuli that our chakras process for us.

When a chakra begins to open from a closed state it will release the emotions and traumas that were stored in it. After a certain amount of releasing it will become less active in its release cycle. There is more to release from that chakra but it recedes into the background so that other chakras can open. To fully open a chakra will require other chakras to do some releasing as well. It is not unusual for a chakra to go through cycles of opening ten to twenty times before it has released enough to open and close appropriately and for energy to flow through smoothly.

Chakras differ in terms of number and placement according to the society they were created in. In North America we are used to the seven chakra format, but some cultures have three, some have five, some have ten, some have forty-two, and some people include many of the microchakras, which basically coincide with acupuncture points and number in the hundreds. For our purposes, we will use a chakra system that includes the seven major chakras plus the Earth chakra that is below our feet, the Heaven chakra that is about six to twelve inches above our heads, and the chakras in our palms and bottoms of our feet.

Before we go further, let us get a basic understanding of what a chakra is. Essentially, a chakra is like a whirlpool—it is a cone of vibrating, circulating energy that extends from the spine or midline, moving outward. In the case of the seven major chakras, these cones extend in front of the body as well as in back, except for the first and seventh chakra that only have one side.

Chakras can be blocked, frozen, sluggish, open, or operating normally. A blocked chakra is no longer able to process material. Everything in the local area will be sluggish and dysfunctional and will create physical symptoms. A frozen chakra is a step beyond a blocked chakra. In a blocked chakra there is very little movement and we have disassociated from the area. A frozen chakra means that nothing can pass through—total disassociation from that area as well as severe symptoms occur. A sluggish chakra means that the chakra is operating. It is opening and closing but there is a molasses-like quality to it. Sluggish chakras move slowly as if a great weight were attached to it—there is almost a groaning-type quality to a sluggish chakra. Open chakras are actually stuck open. There is a culture of Energy Workers who want to open all of our chakras. This is because most of them are sluggish, blocked, or even frozen. However, chakras are not intended to be always open. If chakras were always open we would have no filter to the massive amounts of information coming into our bodies. This is an imbalanced state. Hypersensitivity and a lot of physical and emotional symptoms result from permanently open chakras. Normal chakras should be able to open and close on a regular basis to let in the information that they should process without letting too much information affect the physical body and nervous system.

The more awake we are the more that we notice that chakras hook into and penetrate the grids that surround us. They hook into the deepest layers of self and the energetic blueprint that composes our physical body as well as the very outer layers of conditioned reality that compose our universe. There are chakras beyond what we discuss, such as the chakras that extend beyond the Heaven chakra and hook into pure cosmic consciousness and divine flow. These chakras are activated when a person achieves a truly awakened state and goes beyond the grids that make up consensual reality. They create direct connections to the Void, spirit, and divinity. All of this is knowledge that comes later. What is necessary to begin with is a discussion of the first three chakras.

Chakras 1–3

The first three chakras are about the Self. Personal, ancestral, and family histories are stored in these chakras. Ideally we will have these chakras open first so we can deal with our own stuff before moving toward opening the upper chakras that deal with the deeper layers of conditioned reality, psychic abilities, and connection to spirit. This doesn't happen for various reasons, mainly because working through our own stuff is difficult. What results from this is a culture of top-down awakened individuals, where the top chakras (crown and third eye) are open, but the rest of the body is not, resulting in imbalances we will discuss later on.

First Chakra

Our first chakra has to do with grounding, our ancestral history, and hierarchy-of-needs-type issues. Hierarchy of needs has everything to do with fear and survival instincts. Issues with money, fears of having enough food to eat, a place to stay, and day-to-day-type issues are here. This is also a place our ancestral and family issues are stored.

All of our chakras are storehouses of information. They get stuck or blocked because of a subconscious desire not to process the information or energy contained, a lack of understanding of how to process the energy, or simply a huge amount of information that is difficult to process. This information can come from a wide variety of sources. The first three chakras are difficult to clear because they contain most of the trauma we, our ancestors, and families have experienced. It is understandable that we live in a culture of learning how to be psychic in six easy steps and countless books, schools, and workshops on how to work with the top two chakras because that work does not create the discomfort of dealing with our trauma and inner pain. When the upper chakras can awaken with cleared and balanced lower chakras we are able to see clearly without filtering the information through our wounds, emotions, belief systems, and the layers of conditioned reality in the first, second, and third chakras.

Along with being the storehouse for grounding, fear, family, and ancestral issues, the first chakra also contains the dormant Kundalini, which for some will awaken and clear the chakra system quickly. The first chakra also has to do with passion and sexuality. It contains our life force, our fire, our dormant awakening potential. The first chakra also contains all of the information on our physical body, our nervous system, acts as an anchor to earth energies, and is responsible for reproductive energies as well as the physical act of sexual intercourse.

The first chakra is known as the root chakra, or muladhara, a word meaning *root and base*. In a woman, the first chakra is more internal due to pelvic anatomy. In the male, it is more exterior. On most people, it originates in the area of the perineum or the tip of the coccyx (tailbone) and creates a cone of energy that encompasses the pelvic bowl and comes between the legs at approximately a 30- to 45-degree angle.

Many people who come to me for healing have issues with their first chakra. Our views on sexuality, our fears, and our ancestral patterns rule our lives until we are able to process them appropriately. I do not know of many who have a healthy nervous system, passionate sexual life, a zest for life, grounding, and have processed their fears and their ancestral patterns. Many of us who are awakened continue to work with our first chakras.

If our first chakra is out of balance we will feel ungrounded, lack sex drive or passion for sexual intimacy, feel fear (oftentimes irrational to the present moment), and have financial issues or a feeling of constant lack. We will feel constantly in fight or flight—meaning that our nervous system is constantly engaged and in an alarm state. We will feel blocked from moving forward in our lives and feel separate and isolated. We constantly are on alert and feel that anything can happen to us at any time.

Those of us who have significant difficulties with unprocessed materials in our first chakra will typically either be totally disassociated from our physical bodies, especially our lower bodies (lower abdomen to feet). This is evident by physical imbalances—very small legs and pain in the hips, legs, and feet. Pelvic floor pain, itching, heat, difficulties after childbirth, inability to derive pleasure from the genitals, chronic constipation, hemorrhoids, and knee, foot, and leg issues are all signs of an imbalanced first chakra.

Emotionally, feelings of fear, shame, deep anger, and grief are stored here. Traditionally grief and anger are housed in higher chakras, but when we experience a huge amount of grief or anger that is not culturally appropriate for us to express, or we experience it at a very early age, it will be pushed down into this chakra. In-utero experiences and early childhood emotions are stored in the first chakra. It is understandably difficult for us to process trauma and emotions at a young age, and many of us have a deeply emotional healing process when this chakra begins to open.

Memories of sexual abuse at any age, understanding the patterns of our sexual history, and realization of outer societal patterns surrounding sex begin to come up to process when the first chakra opens more. These memories, traumas, and experiences surrounding sex are difficult and confusing. We live in a culture where we disassociate and have a huge cultural shadow surrounding sex. Even the most puritanical forms of sexually relating to one another can inspire shame and other emotions. When the first chakra opens in conjunction with the second there is a call to action to explore our sexual history and ways of relating to another human being sexually. For the first chakra, this will be an exploration of our own sexuality. When the second chakra begins opening, this will be how we sexually relate to others and our openness in doing so.

Other physical symptoms of imbalance include reproductive issues, menstrual cramps and gynecological issues, hormonal imbalances, lower-digestive-tract issues, and weight gain in the lower abdomen, hips, and thighs.

Many women come to me with first chakra issues after childbirth, and both women and men can develop first chakra issues after localized surgeries. Due to giving birth, the physical rearrangement of the pelvic bowl, organs, tissues, and possible tearing, incisions, and surgeries in the lower pelvic region translate into energetic issues. It is necessary in this instance to correct the physical imbalance, release any scar tissue and allow lymph and other fluids to flow, release the emotions of the surgical experience, and then work with the energies of the region to fully correct the imbalance.

When our first chakra is opening we will feel heat. This is especially evident in those of us going through a Kundalini awakening, where the heat from the first chakra can be enough to burn holes through skin or clothing in the pelvic region and sacrum if the second chakra is blocked. When the first chakra opens it will release this heat down through the genitals. If we are experiencing a Kundalini awakening it will also attempt to start moving energy up into our second chakra in an effort to move Kundalini up our spine. Even if we are not experiencing Kundalini the first chakra needs for the second chakra to be open in order to process energy properly. If the second chakra is closed the first chakra has to use whatever force it has to try to work its way to releasing the second chakra. Picture a wave hitting a rock. If our first chakra is open and flowing it will be a huge wave hitting the rock in the second chakra. If our first chakra is barely open it will be a small stream hitting a rock. If our second chakra is a huge boulder (blocked or frozen) then the small stream will take a very long time to work its way through or even a huge wave will have difficulty. When we are able to work through the blockages and traumas of the first chakra this frees up more energy. Our second chakra can now open, allowing for us to process the material there so we will have flow through the first and second chakras and open further to the higher chakras.

When this first center opens we will feel an increase in sexual desire, a feeling of being grounded and physically in our body, increased interest in life, spontaneous orgasms or feelings of localized bliss, and a desire to be physically active and healthy. There is interest in the physical body, in sex, in being alive. Proper elimination will occur, both physically and energetically. Addictions and other disassociations will begin to be naturally worked through.

When the first chakra is in the process of opening, the material it brings up can be difficult to process. Our darkest fears about being alive, birth, death, traumas, sexual history, and ancestral issues will all come up to clear. Thankfully this is often not all at the same time except in the most sudden awakenings. Individual chakra openings will bring up a subject or pattern, like sexuality, and our bodies will attempt to process all of the instances that sexuality was and is an issue for us. It will bring up our patterns around sexuality, and possibly past life or ancestral issues that feed into that pattern. This pattern will make itself known until we are able to understand what is coming up, what we have to learn from it, and begin to act differently or allow for it to release without fear. Our body may then bring up another pattern from the storehouse of the first chakra, or it may need to move to the second chakra or a higher chakra to process other material before returning to process more from the first chakra.

For some of us who are undergoing more sudden awakenings, all of the material from the first chakra will come out at once. This will result in not only emotional upheaval, but very physical symptoms localized in the first chakra as well. Every pattern, every issue will flood the body to be healed. When this happens, or even when the body presents first chakra opening issue by issue, the response is often to resist or participate in numbing behaviors. By choosing to consciously process the material coming up rather than putting ourselves back to sleep we can eventually become lighter, more balanced, and more awake. Our first chakra really responds to the physical realm and physical releases. Developing an exercise routine, spending time in nature, developing healthy sexual habits, and finding passion in life or in a hobby are all excellent releases. Grounding ourselves, such as the tree exercise in a later chapter, is excellent to release and process the first chakra.

Beyond releasing of heat, many people report vibration, energy movement locally and going into the legs, and greater embodiment and interest in life when this chakra begins to balance. This chakra, like most of the others, often flickers when releasing. This means that it will open up and we will feel heat, increased passion, grounding, and embodiment, and then it will shut again. This can lead to a temporary illusion that we are in greater despair, or have all of our first chakra issues back. What is really happening is that our chakra is opening and cycling more than it has before, and then it goes back quickly to a more closed state. This is not the state it was in before, but it feels more drastic to go from a state of passion and orgasm to those feelings diminishing. When we realize that it is natural for this chakra to have to rebalance and try to come to a state of balance where it opens and closes naturally, we can come out of a state of fear and maintain conscious awareness and respect for the fact that our body and chakra system know what they are doing. We simply have to not block or stop the process.

EXERCISE: First Chakra

- If this chakra is opening for you, let yourself focus on the sensation.
- What do you notice? Heat, vibration?

- What else do you notice? Fear, anger, apathy?
- Do you feel separated from the rest of the Earth?
- Are you able to feel the cone shape of the chakra? What do you notice about your chakra? Is it straight between your legs, or is it off to one side? Is it more forward or back? How far does it go out from your body?

If you are ready and have a strong visual and/or felt sense of what is going on with your first chakra, you can continue.

- Notice if you are resisting this chakra opening. Know that if this chakra opens, you can clear significant detrimental patterns in your life.
- Talk to the chakra as if it were a person. Ask what it is trying to tell you, what patterns it is trying to clear. What should you know? Reply back.
- Let it know that you are ready for it to clear, or you understand what it has said to you.
- Ask if there is anything you can do to help it release.
- Realize that many people resist opening this chakra out of fear or discomfort. Surrender your fear, and let your body and your mind know that everything is going to be okay.
- Fear is the basis of all of our other emotions. Know this and feel emotions like rage, anger, and all of those other emotions you have stuffed into this chakra. Let them flow over you. Give them permission to flow for the next five minutes, or next ten.
- Breathe into this area, the discomfort, and whatever visuals, sensations, or patterns that are showing up.
- Let go of control and your need to know the story behind everything coming up. Do not hang onto things because your logical brain wants to figure everything out. Just let it go.

I suggest letting your body vent this area, realizing what is happening. Simply give it permission to release and picture any blocked energy moving down your legs and out your feet. You can close it off by asking it to or resisting the patterns, pain, or emotions coming up, by doing Kegel exercises or drawing the genitals inward, closing the openings of the body. At some point the releasing of this chakra may be out of your control. Be okay with that. Realize that what is coming up is not from the present moment. Let yourself know that it is better to clear these things than have them in your physical body. Resist the urge to numb yourself. During the time of your first chakra opening, realize you need nature, physical activity, and sexual activity. Realize that the patterns coming up are major patterns that make up the basis of who you think you are. Be okay with letting them all go, the stories, the pain, the fear, the desire to feel separate and unconscious. When you rouse this center, energy can move through the first chakra to the second.

Second Chakra

The second chakra, *Svadhisthana*, is located in the pelvic bowl and extends in front approximately halfway between the pubic symphysis and the belly button and in back from the sacrum. In most of us it has no angle and forms an inverted cone shape going into the body from both sides. Many systems of working with chakras treat the first and second chakras as either one chakra, or chakras that must be awoken together. This is because while the first chakra is about our connection to the Earth, to the world, to humanity, to our ancestry, the second chakra is about our connection to our emotions and to individual people.

While the first chakra is about basic, primal sexual instincts, the second chakra is about the acting out of that sexual instinct in a balanced way. Our feelings about our physical body and our relationship to ourselves as sexual beings capable of reproduction are housed in this chakra. Since our society is rather puritanical and closed down in terms of sexuality and it is common for all of us to have a fair amount of self-hatred toward our physical bodies, this chakra is often clogged or frozen. This results in lower abdominal bloating, reproductive issues, sexual issues, intimacy difficulties, dislike of the physical body, lack of passion, and retracting and separating from the physical world. Emotionally this leads to an inability to let go of emotions and traumas that we have experienced—this is the area of our body that many of these emotions are stored due to an inability to release them from our second and then first chakra.

The second chakra is our sensate, physical experience of this world. Art, beauty, sounds, music, movies, and physical exercise are all processed through this chakra. Orgasms and pleasures from the sexual experience, although brought up by the fire of the first chakra, are felt in the second chakra.

In the awakening process it is a common issue to separate from the second chakra and to form an intense dislike for anything grounded, physical, and body-oriented, resulting in an antagonistic relationship with the physical body. When we separate from this center the spiritual experiences we have are always outside of our bodies. When the first and second chakras are balanced we are integrated, embodied, enjoy our sensate experiences, and understand that we have human, physical bodies for a reason.

To work through this chakra it is important to have a relationship with the physical world and our senses. Exercising, doing yoga, going for walks, going out for tea with friends, seeing plays, listening to music, playing a musical instrument, exploring our connection with nature, going to a museum, painting, drawing, and dancing are all ways to do so. Understanding not only our own sexuality but our sexuality in relation to another will balance the second chakra. Most of us have huge sexual issues that are housed in the first and second chakras. Sexual trauma—such as rape, molestation, or other traumatic acts as well as common experiences of teasing about our bodies, breasts, abdomens, losing our virginity in a manner that was different than we would have chosen, and subverting our own sexual desires because they were considered culturally inappropriate—are housed here. There are also family sexuality issues if our family didn't talk about sex, or talked about it too much, or there were sexual issues in our parents' relationship. We may also have past-life, ancestral, and karmic sexual issues. It is not uncommon for people (both men and women) to have past lives or ancestors that died during childbirth. There is also the societal grid that creates a puritanical view and black/white, bad/good version of sexuality that has created a huge shadow and difficult issues for everyone in this center. The obsession with young girls, the illusion of celebrities, the lack of openness in our society about even the most rigid and narrow forms of sex create patterns and layers of patterns in the second and first chakra that are reticent to being worked with consciously.

When we realize what a huge block sexuality has in our own existence we can know that this has had a significant impact on our sexuality and the openness of this center. Deciding to explore this territory in small steps, whatever we are ready to work with, will allow for this center to slowly open and for the blocked, frozen, or rigid aspects of sexual patterning within us to gradually unlock.

This chakra often contains self-hatred for the physical form. Letting go of self-loathing, difficult body image issues, and being okay with our physical self in the present moment is crucial in this chakra being balanced. Self-hatred is understandably a difficult concept to work through, and it may not come up or release until after everything else has been worked through with this chakra, or until the third and fourth chakras process. Since it is such a deep issue, having patience and as much compassion and love for ourselves as we can, as well as understanding that the self-hatred is present on a very conscious level, will allow for it to begin to come up for processing.

The lower abdomen is considered the second brain, and we process thoughts through our digestive systems. We live in a culture where we cannot turn off our brains—all of our thoughts, especially repetitive looping thoughts and harmful thoughts and resulting emotions, get stuck in our lower abdomen. Since we now know that our digestive systems create many of the neurotransmitters and brain chemicals that make us happy, having a second chakra that is functional enough to process our thoughts can quickly make us happier and allow for us to have quieter minds. Learning meditation or cultivating quiet spaces within ourselves will allow for this center to open and process.

Third Chakra

The third chakra is the last of our "I" chakras. In the back, this center typically extends from the junction of the thoracic and lumbar vertebrae outward, and from the front it typically is located halfway between your belly button and your ribcage approximately midline. This is the solar plexus chakra, or *Manipura*.

This chakra is about us—who we are and what we are intended to do here. While the first chakra is about how we were formed (our ancestry) and our second chakra is about our connections, the third chakra is about us and our individual power and gifts.

This is also the chakra that provides us the drive to do something in life. Our ability to make decisions, to move forward, to build a life, and to build our self-esteem are located in this chakra.

The third chakra stores trauma and issues related to lack of self-worth, difficulty with our own power, and imbalances of personal care vs. caring for others. Empaths and other individuals who extend themselves past their own boundaries to care for others frequently have imbalanced third chakras. This chakra also is in charge of our intake of and assimilation of food and other outside energies. When this center begins opening we may find ourselves having difficulty with our food intake.

Once this chakra is processing appropriately there is an ability to make decisions and to be in the driver's seat of our own lives. When we have the first, second, and third chakra functioning well we will have power flowing through us and informing us. This energy or strength can then come from the confidence of the inner Self, from our ancestors, and from the Earth. Once this chakra is balanced, the energy flowing through will provide understanding and access to our unique, individual gifts and powers in this world.

EXERCISE: Accessing Your Power and Gifts

Once the lower chakras no longer have significant boulders, emotions, or issues blocking them you can now access the power and gifts of these chakras. The first chakra's gift is of grounding, feeling a part of the Earth, and connecting to your ancestry. The gift of the second chakra is connecting to your senses, to your sexual drives, to your physical body, and one-on-one relationships with others. The third chakra's gift is about deeply understanding yourself and what power and individual gifts you bring into this lifetime.

You will know when your lower chakras are reasonably clear and processed when you no longer sense any heavy energy from the area of the ribcage down to the feet and do not have any significant physical problems in those areas. If you do have significant health issues either internally or in the outlying musculature of those areas—such as hip pain, back pain, leg pain, or foot pain—it is a sign that more processing work needs to be done. This being said, it is still possible to claim your gifts and individual power while having issues with the first three chakras ... it becomes a stronger process the clearer you are in these areas though. It is also possible to have physical limitations and still have your first three chakras functioning at a high level. One of the most grounded and awake individuals I have ever met was wheelchair-bound.

- To begin to claim your gifts, sit in a comfortable place with no distractions. Allow for your hands to rest gently where you feel like your third chakra is. For ease, you may wish to have your hands resting on your physical body rather than in front of your body in the air.
- Feel energy flow through your lower body, front and back. What does this feel like? Is the current strong? Is it weak, wide, chaotic, choppy, electric? Describe it the best you are able to.
- Now, close your eyes and imagine that you are entering a museum. Gradually you will come to a hallway that is all white with many doors. Allow yourself to become naturally drawn to the door that is yours. When you see this door and know that it is yours (this should be a gut, natural instinct or a sense of ease or discovery) go through the door.
- In this room will be a gallery of all of the gifts, powers, and memories that make you an individual. Ask out loud or internally to be shown where your power is. If you work with a guide they can assist you. This power can be anything—any shape, light, color, texture. Allow yourself to be shown or to find this power. If you do not find it you may not be ready yet for this meditation. That is fine—just try again in a few days, a few weeks, or a few months. If you do find it, allow yourself to see the beauty of your power. Allow for yourself to hold this power in your hands and guide it with your hands into your physical body where your third chakra is. Allow yourself to feel the sensation of this. You can return and come back to this place to receive your power as many times as you wish.
- If you feel like continuing, again find yourself in your room of the museum. Ask for your gifts. Ask your guide to show you this or simply follow your gut instinct to show you. This will be an object encased in glass. Look at the object. If you do not find one simply come back to this exercise at another time. Either ask your guide or ask for a museum guide to tell you about this gift. This is a gift you bring to the world, and it should feel right to you when you hear about it. At first, you may wish to just hear about the gift. If you are ready to move forward you can hold the object in your hands and ask it directly what it is to be used for. Ask if it is willing to come home with you

and be integrated into your body. If the answer is "no," simply put it back in
the case. If the answer is "yes," bring it into your body to your third chakra
or anywhere that feels right.

When you have learned about and incorporated your gift into your body, remember
the object or the energy of the object. Ask that energy about that gift, how to utilize it,
where it comes from, what it means, and how you can bring it into your physical, daily
life. Listen, and over time the gift will come to fruition. You may visit the museum
again to find other gifts, such as ancestral or past-life gifts, or to view aspects of your
life. It is a powerful place, a viewing room, and a place that is solely yours. Be respectful
of this place, and it will show you everything you could want to know about yourself.

Fourth Chakra

In a fully awakened state, we see through our hearts, our fourth chakra. The heart is
where we branch away from our lower chakras that are about our own issues and needs.
It is a pivot point, an intermediary between the higher chakras of the throat, third eye,
and crown that connect us to energies of spirit and divinity, and the lower chakras that
connect us to energies of the Earth and allow us to become embodied.

In Chinese Medicine the heart is where the spirit resides within the body. It is also
the place in the body where we store some of our deepest wounds. When the heart begins to awaken, these wounds appear to be processed. Physical pain in the chest, breathing issues, heart palpitations, and feelings of joy, bliss, and love for humanity flicker in
the early stages of heart chakra awakening. If there is a more significant awakening, this
process can be more physical, such as heart pain, feelings of the heart cracking open,
and even heart attacks. It is extremely important with this chakra to get the physical
elements taken care of. Simply because we are having heart pain and are experiencing
an awakening does not mean that our experience is only spiritual and we do not need
physical intervention. If anything, at this point, there should be a realization that mind-
body-spirit are the same thing, and physical issues should be taken care of on a physical
level, and then the consideration of emotional and spiritual causes can be realized,
especially when symptoms are emerging from a vital organ such as the heart.

At first when this chakra awakens it is a glimmer of what is to come. Love and bliss
wash over us and we begin to see from a place of the heart rather than from the eyes.
The lower chakras as well as the upper chakras are awakened before the heart can be
fully balanced. This is due to the pivot functioning of the heart. The heart is the central
command of the chakra system and any large boulder, wound, or energy not flowing
properly through the body through the chakras and the midline creates a space of fear
and anxiety that results in the heart not being balanced.

It is common for the first awakening of this chakra to be brief and minimal, our awareness and processing quickly moving to another chakra, such as the throat or back down to the solar plexus. All of our chakras, but especially the heart, may need to awaken several times before it has cleared out layers and layers of trauma and blockages. Since this is such a core place, such a wounded place for most of us, we tread carefully in the processing of this space. It is rare, even in a sudden awakening, for all of the stored material in this chakra to come up at once. Since it is a pivot point, the more that we are able to process in this chakra the more we are able to relate to both the first three chakras as well as the upper three chakras. This allows for us to be balanced and connected to both Earth, ourselves, and the Divine.

When this chakra is fully open we are able to see through this space. Seeing from our heart means that we are able to actually sense seeing from the heart space and a sort of glow falls around people and places that becomes increasingly permanent. An ability to understand and have compassion for people, a letting go of the Self and individual experiences and the entering into divine flow begins. This is often a large switch for us. We are so used to our own truth, our own understandings of the world that anything outside of that is wrong or scary. When the heart chakra opens we are able to understand others with dissimilar opinions without finding them threatening. We are able to understand that each person has a truth. From this heart space we begin to understand how much we have struggled, how much others struggle, and how wounded other people are.

Through seeing from the heart space we begin to not only get glimpses of the grids, masks, and tapestries (this capacity is fully awakened through the third eye and crown) but are able to have understanding and compassion for how each individual person or group is formed. There is a loss of judgment and instead a sense of discernment forms. Once in this space it is easy to see how most of the spirituality, most of the people in this world are beginners or child-like, playing with spiritual concepts and ascribing meanings to things without the understandings that we now have. But with this chakra opening this understanding is met with compassion for people who remain in spiritual immaturity or ego awakening.

One of the more intense aspects of individual chakra awakenings is when chakras open in conjunction with one another. The first, second, and third chakras at some point will open with the heart to allow for healing of any self-hatred or Destroyer tendencies. The ability to not only not want to destroy or harbor hatred for ourselves but the journey to self-love and kindness for ourselves leads to a sense of beauty, peace, and stillness in what can be a chaotic world. The outer chaos that once was reflected by our internal self-hatred quiets, and when the first four chakras are flowing (open enough to exchange energy up the spine and between one another) an indescribable background bliss and acceptance of life as it is develops.

The heart has two "parts" to it energetically. There is the physical, energetic heart and also the covering or pericardium. The pericardium has the job of protecting the heart and often needs to soften before the heart can be opened. The meditation "Softening the Pericardium" may need to be done several times. Be patient and wait for your body to surrender this covering. It has been on guard, rigid, stiff, and protective for a reason. Thank it for protecting you the best way it knew how.

EXERCISE: Softening the Pericardium Meditation

- Feel the area where your heart is. Sit with it for a few moments.
- Now, look for or feel for the covering of your heart, the pericardium. Sit with this covering for a bit.
- Bring into your awareness the texture, color, or any imagery that comes to mind from the space of the pericardium.
- Ask your pericardium what would happen if it softened, let go, and stopped being on guard to the extent it is now.
- One of the main reasons that the pericardium does not want to stop being on guard is because the heart contains painful emotions. If this is true, acknowledge this.
- If you are ready, ask your pericardium to soften or change, even if it is just slightly. Be prepared for emotions or experiences to come up for processing.
- Sit in the space of feeling the pericardium shifting. If there are emotions or energy coming up, let yourself know that these are not current experiences and let them pass out of you.
- If it feels appropriate, say "thank you" to the pericardium.

EXERCISE: Seeing from the Heart

Once we have awakened the first three lower chakras and the upper chakras so that they have achieved a reasonably flowing and balanced state we can see from our hearts. If you have not already done so, some work with the upper chakras (specifically the throat) may be necessary to bring energy into the heart center. This is a very simple awareness exercise that will increase in strength the more that these centers are awakened. This is a similar exercise to the clairvoyant opening of the third eye discussed in the 'Psychic Awakenings' chapter, and you may need to open the channels surrounding your third eye before doing this exercise.

- First, allow for yourself to focus on the area between your eyebrows (your third eye).
- Now, allow for your focus to shift to your physical eyes and your third eye.

Feel or see a triangle begin to form.

- Allow for your focus to go to the visual cortex of your brain (near your occiput or the back of your head).
- Feel your whole head light up with as much energy as it naturally wishes to form. You do not need to push this, let it occur naturally. Pushing more energy to form can cause headaches and other issues.
- Allow for this energy to flow down to the front and back of your heart.
- Now let your focus shift to your heart.
- If you would like to continue, view from this heart space something that you truly love. This can be your child, a pet, a loved one.
- If you are ready, look at something that you ordinarily would find judgment with from this space. See if your perspective has changed.
- Find someone that you ordinarily dislike or hate and think or look at a photo of them. See if your perspective has changed.

Eventually seeing from this heart space is a permanent thing. When fully awakened we see from our physical eyes, our heart, and through our third eye. This does not mean that people will no longer be jerks or that we will be in a permanent dazed hippy sort of love fest for the world. Rather, it will be a place of compassion, understanding, and discernment. The more that the world is seen through this space certain people, places, and objects will hold a sort of glow. Once the heart is balanced and we have flow through the first four chakras life becomes embodied, simple, and we have compassion toward ourselves and the world around us.

Chakras 5–7

The top three chakras allow for us to make spiritual connections, open our sensitivities, and allow us to see the patterns and energies that comprise the universe. We process and understand larger and more spiritual energies such as archetypes, past lives, karma, global patterns, and grids through these chakras.

It is very common for the crown or third eye energies to open without embodiment or the processing of the first three chakras. The first three chakras have to do with us. The upper chakras, while dealing with us, have to deal with the lighter or more distant aspects of Self. For many of us they are opened through energy work, genetics, trauma, previous lifetime experiences, karma, or through going through the previous types of awakenings (meridian, subtle/pranic) without having knowledge of grounding or working on the first three chakras. The first three chakras are difficult to get to a place of balance and most of us prefer the excitement of learning about the higher chakras than the work required to be centered in our lower chakras.

These are the chakras of spirit, and the connection of spirit to our own human consciousness. These are the subtler senses, the "clairs" and other extrasensory information. This information then is intended to filter through our physical bodies from the crown down into the abdomen, meeting the energy of the first three chakras and finally processing out the feet, through the aura, or through the three spirit gates which are in the spine at the sacrum, back of the heart, and back of the neck. Without having the lower chakras open this does not happen and we are left with physical, emotional, and spiritual repercussions. When we have balanced our first four chakras and the fifth, sixth, and seventh chakras open naturally, we can have energy flow through our entire midline and out into the Earth and the Heavens in a balanced manner.

Fifth Chakra

The throat chakra is notoriously known for being a bottle-neck of blocked energy due to its location as well as what information it stores. It is responsible for the difficult patterns of expressing oneself truthfully, communication from that space of being in our truth, and living a life of integrity and honesty. It is also responsible for understanding truth, creativity, and seeking. The throat chakra, or *Vissudha*, is also considered the space of personal records. All past lives are stored here, although they also involve other areas of the physical body as well. This is also the space where the grids that surround us are held—if we are able to open our throat chakras and third eye we are able to sense the geometry of the universe and the grids of conditioned reality.

It is also worth noting that many people have suffered a great deal of trauma to the neck area. In the birth process infants can have the cord wrapped around their necks, and in other lives it is not rare to have deaths by hanging, strangling, or being murdered with blunt force to the throat area. A difficult pattern within many of our lifetimes is being unable to express ourselves honestly and authentically due to societal and family restrictions. This inability to express ourselves, be authentic, or express ourselves creatively creates blockage in the throat.

The throat chakra may need some bodywork or therapy to release and balance. SomatoEmotional Release by an experienced CranioSacral therapist can be extraordinarily helpful, as can basic massage of the neck musculature, particularly if the therapist is experienced enough to know how to work with anterior throat musculature. Internal mouthwork, done by an experienced CranioSacral therapist to release the throat musculature so you begin to find your voice, can be life-changing. Talk therapy to release pent-up emotions and to express in a safe place emotions and experiences can be helpful in opening this center. Yoga positions that involve stretches and movement of the tongue, such as in Lion Pose, and meditations involving chanting and mantras can open up this center. Creative pursuits and being honest in your dealings in life as well as not stifling feelings or thoughts will continue to open the throat.

In order to maintain a balanced throat chakra it is important to remain honest and pursue your creative path. At some point in our spiritual journey honesty is no longer a choice—it is something that we are compelled to be and do. When we have energy flowing through the first four chakras we begin to experience self-love and the truth of who we are. When we open our fifth center, our throat, we begin to express to the world who we are. It is no longer an option to hide, to wear a mask, or to lie.

When this center opens we also experience a difference in terms of flow of emotions and tastes. The tongue is tied in with the throat center, and when it opens we get waves of bliss and orgasmic tasting—a peach never tasted so good! Subtlety and distinction in tastes, appreciation of food, and the opening of the digestive tract to accept foods that previously we may have been sensitive to or unable to eat comes with a balanced throat chakra. With balance there is also a free flow of emotions, an inability to hold back emotions, and an understanding that there is no need to be anyone other than who we are.

Sixth Chakra

The sixth chakra, the third eye, or *ajna*, is the center of perception. It is rather well known for its ability of opening clairvoyant abilities (seeing beyond the normal capacities of others). It is also the center of clear thoughts and guidance from both inner and outer sources. Discernment, or ability to see clearly what thoughts, advice, literature, and teachers are providing wisdom relevant to us, is cultivated here. We move from mimicking the wisdom of others to seeing and knowing clearly our own wisdom when this center opens.

This center is fairly easy to open but difficult to open in a balanced way. The upper chakras, particularly the sixth and seventh, often open long before the lower chakras do. This leads to the symptoms of being able to see beyond conditioned reality, dimensions, or simply seeing more than the average person but with a lack of grounding, discernment, and mental balance. This center opened in a mentally imbalanced, ungrounded, or disassociated individual can lead to an inability to function properly in society. We may lack the ability to discern the everyday reality that we need to function in with the amount of stimulus that is coming in. This can lead to a wide variety of physical and mental symptoms that are difficult to care for properly.

When this center is open we begin to see what is going on with ourselves as well as others surrounding us. In a balanced way this information would lead to a sort of sanity, embodiment, and rationality that is a true gift. In an imbalanced way this center can open and lead to a tendency to see everything but the Self, mental imbalances, psychosis, ego awakenings, and the creation of further layers of illusion and delusions that take us further away from real understanding.

Further Layering of Conditioned Reality

Although we have discussed previously reality being twelve distinct layers, many of us begin to discover when we open our third eyes that we, as well as those surrounding us, have many more than twelve. These further layers are more trauma and wounding patterns, issues around sexuality, race, gender, money, and many more. Most of these layers are thoughtforms—thoughts that we, our community, or our world have called into being. Other layers are grids created from schools and education, religion, television and movies, books, gurus and teachers, and the many other sources we interact with. We conform our identity and shape our reality around our experiences and teachers. At some point in the awakening process we free ourselves from all of our layers—and can be around gurus, teachers, read books, go to school, participate in religious activities ... all without changing who we are or adding on layers.

Removal of Masks

One of the larger aspects of awakening is the removal of masks—typically many of them. Each time that we learn to conform, to change ourselves, to put a further layer of illusion up that is different than who we truly are it is a mask. Some of these masks are removed as soon as we leave a particular situation. Others remain permanent. Although these masks are separate in a way from the layers of conditioned reality, they do stop us from seeing who we truly are. If at our core we are still a hurt five-year-old who has put mask after mask on to hide that fact, at some point we will be tasked with unmasking her and processing her wounds. If we have put on a mask of being "spiritual" or "enlightened" at some point we must remove that mask to actually become enlightened. If we are wearing a mask of being functional and happy and inside we are angry and depressed, taking off the mask and getting to know our inner emotional selves, who we truly are, may seem frightening. But removing the masks that we wear allows for us to process the wounds that we carry and to understand who we truly are.

By the time that we are experiencing the third eye awakening it can be easy to see the masks of others. We also may be able to look beyond them. At this point we have access to understand each person as divine. The person we are looking at may have no idea—they in fact may be the person who flicked you off in traffic or someone who is the first to judge and gossip about everyone. When we look at their masking we can see their wounds—what has caused them to put on masks in the first place. When we look past the masks to the inner light that fills each person we will lose our sense of judgment and can come to the important realization that everyone is awake; some people just have many layers and masks that they have no chance of remembering.

To look inward and remove our own masks is more difficult but is necessary to be who we authentically are. Sit in a comfortable place with no distractions. Close your eyes, take some breaths in and out. Allow yourself to settle. Imagine a cave in front of you. Walk into this cave. If you would like to bring along a spiritual guide, you are welcome to. When you walk into this cave you will see several tunnels. Walk to the tunnel on the left. This tunnel will lead you further and further back. Eventually you will come to a dimly lit room. This is the room of the masks you wear. Sit down and simply ask to be shown your masks. Acknowledge each one and sit with it for a while. Try the mask on. Feel how it changes your behavior, your mood, who you are. Do this with as many masks as you are shown. If you are willing, you can thank the mask for protecting you. Ask for it to diminish, change, or dissolve. This is a powerful journey, so you do not have to change or remove them if you are not ready to. Even acknowledging a mask will change your life.

If you do not see any masks do not be upset. It simply may not be the right day or time to do this. When you are ready, go out of the tunnel and come back outside. This journey can be repeated as much as you wish. Each time simply view the masks, try them on, and see how they feel. When you come into awareness of the masks they will begin to change. When you ask the masks directly to change they will as well. Even the most minute change will have a large ripple effect. There is no need to force anything in this journey.

The third eye will open in its own right timing. Chakra exercises, meditations to open the third eye, or whatever the trend is these days is not necessary. When we meditate on a regular basis and consciously work through the lower chakras, this chakra will open in a balanced manner on its own. We then work with whatever material is coming up for us to process. The clearer we are—the fewer layers of conditioned reality and masks we have—the more the third eye awakens. We are then able to see further and with more clarity. With this ability comes the tendency to see outer and focus on what we see in others. Allow for this sight to focus inward and it will blossom.

It is quite dangerous to force this center open due to the mental imbalances it can create, and those of us who naturally have this center open are often not able to psychologically or physically deal with the amount of stimuli coming in. Even for the most balanced or awakened soul the information and truths that come from having this center truly open are quite difficult to process. By working through the other centers and our issues with personal awareness we can see from this center in a balanced way.

Seventh Chakra

The crown chakra, or *Sahasrara*, allows for us to receive divine input. Since the crown chakra is still part of our physical body (at the crown of the head) this divine input is filtered through our wounds and the conditioned layers of reality. The crown chakra allows for us to taste flickering oneness and be able to experience awareness outside of ourselves. It is the pivot point between the Self in physical form and the divine.

The crown chakra is a door, a gateway. This gateway allows for us to leave the confines of conditioned reality and experience larger spiritual realities, such as oneness and the Void. The crown chakra is an initiation for us, a junction where we can decide if we would like to experience freedom and let go of the chains that remain around us. In a balanced state in which all of the other chakras have flow and are balanced, this gateway leads to progression of the awakened self, other dimensions, realities, universes, and more.

In an imbalanced state the crown chakra is a release hatch, a way for us to disassociate or be partially embodied. This leads to ungrounded spirituality, or an escapist tendency where we feel as if spirituality is always somewhere else, and a preoccupation with rigid rules, ego, going home, and other mental imbalances that make it difficult to function in daily life. This center can be worked with through grounding and consciously having physical, sensate experiences, exercising, spending time in nature, appreciating our physical body, and working through whatever patterns of wounding are causing us to want to leave our body and the Earth.

In a balanced state this chakra opens to large spiritual experiences, access to currents of energy, and seeing and experiencing things beyond the conditioned layers of reality. The crown chakra once opened leads to the eighth chakra, or Heaven chakra, which is the first chakra that is more about the divine than us. This crown chakra can be passed through by reaching for and going through the doorway when it is presented to us. If a doorway or gateway is not presented to us in our meditations we can imagine a doorway opening at the top of our head. When done at the right time in our path there will be an energy flow from the first chakra through and above the crown. When our seven chakras are functional and balanced we can feel this flow of energy through the spine going up, as well as spiritual energy coming through our crown down. We then can begin to feel other energies from the Earth coming up into our root, and energy flowing out of our arms and hands. These chakras in the hands and feet are important to properly cycle energy through our bodies. When we are awakening we have huge amounts of energy cycling through us. Without the proper ability to release, these energies reside within us, causing us energetic, emotional, and very real physical pain.

Hand and Foot Chakras

The chakras in the hands and feet are smaller chakras that are responsible for fully awakening the entirety of the human body. The hand chakras awaken with feelings of heat, itching, coldness, trembling, shaking, and other symptoms. This can be a flickering thing, such as the twitches after a Reiki attunement, or can be more permanent. The chakras in the hands can range from a mild feeling of *qi*, *prana*, or electrical feeling to fully opened with strong currents of energy running through them. When the upper two chakras (crown and third eye) are open as well as the throat being reasonably open, energy is able to flow through from spirit into the head and down the arms. When our crown, third eye, or throat is closed, this energy is then subtler in the palms or is pulled from our own personal energetic reserves. If we are utilizing our personal reserves of energy we will feel buzzing or heat in our hands but no sensation of flow or current going up or down our arms. There will also be more global feelings of fatigue and a lessened ability to discern outside energy and emotions from personal energy and emotions.

The chakras in the soles of the feet correspond to Kidney 1, an important acupuncture point associated with grounding as well as the water element. The opening of these centers is important for the proper processing of energy. Feelings of stepping through the Earth, growing stems or roots, and being able to feel vibrations and connections in the Earth itself are felt when these centers are balanced. Being able to see our whole body, from feet to head, as well as full embodiment (being fully in our body with no disassociation or feeling like part of our body is missing) is facilitated through these chakras.

Proper cycling of energy coming in, especially for sensitives who are inundated with constant stimuli, is done through the chakras in the feet. Most sensitives take in energy and it gets stuck in the head or the digestive tract. By opening the energy circuits and the chakras in the soles of the feet, this energy can easily and readily flow out of us rather than get stuck. This can be done through the tree meditation exercises near the end of this book.

Grounding deeply into the Earth and having full flows of energy through our bodies allows for us to access higher and stronger currents of energy above us as well. The Heaven chakra, the first chakra above the head that deals with pure divine energy, is one of those.

The Heaven Chakra

There are several chakras above our heads, but the Heaven chakra is the first from our physical body (after the crown) and the last that is about us in our physical body. The chakras beyond it are about pure divine energy and are no longer concerned with our individual experiences or our experience on this Earth. Once we are aware and opened to the chakras above the Heaven chakra the experience of spiritual energies and understandings far outside the realm of anything that can be logically written about or discussed increases exponentially.

The Heaven chakra is approximately two feet above our crown chakra. It is the first truly "spiritual" chakra, meaning that it is not concerned with our day-to-day existence. This chakra contains the blueprints of our existence, our karma, and at death all of the energy from our other chakras pulls up into it. When we are able to access this chakra we are able to fully experience oneness and are able to understand much of our karma and other global patterns. After accessing this chakra we begin to have understandings beyond the constructs of conditioned reality, specifically time and space. We may encounter our future selves, patterns that are outside a linear timeline, and understandings of other dimensions, realities, and beings.

This chakra is about the ocean of divine flow. Once it reaches our crown, it is again about us, the drop. This chakra is the first interface with the massive ocean of oneness, the letting go of "I" in order to expand into something much greater than the Self. In death, all of our energy rolls up into this eighth center to take our individual Self, our drop, back into the state of oneness. In spiritual awakenings the awareness and opening of this center allows for the states of ego death, oneness, and a release of our own fears surrounding death. In further states of spiritual awakening we are able to access further chakras that are no longer about the Self or the individual experience—they are about pure spirit, the Void, divinity, and understandings that most of us would not be able to fathom until we have direct experience of them.

The further that we are able to access above ourselves we are also able to nurture beneath ourselves as well. The Earth chakra is not only about grounding and embodiment but also of a deep sense of awakening to the spiritual unfolding of the Earth. Primal instincts and realizations of ourselves as emotional, sexual beings with instinctual rhythms develops.

The Earth Chakra

The Earth chakra is approximately one to three feet below the physical feet into the Earth. Like the Heaven chakra, it is a gateway between the concept of individual Self and Earth energies. Earth energy is not just simply about grounding but is very spiritual, sensual, and embodied, leading to feelings of deep rootedness, caring for the physical earth, and love for nature. A deep opening of the lower chakras occurs in conjunction with the Earth chakra opening, leading to a release of sexual inhibitions and patterns, a reclaiming of sexuality, an understanding and integration of the "dark" or shadow aspects of Self, and an ability to just be who we are, a fully sensate, sexual, physical being with complete awareness of the darkness and light that we carry.

A connection to the animal or primal instincts beyond sexual also appears with this chakra—a realization of primal, deep emotions such as rage. A loss of separation between the "higher" nature of the human and the "lower" nature of the animal or Earth is achieved. We become earthly, we become wild, we understand our shadow and are comfortable working with and even playing with it. We fully understand the impermanence of our bodies. A sense of humor, a certain darkness, and a deep settling into our physical body happens through opening the Earth chakra. The ability to process larger energies and connection to larger spiritual energies of the Earth, such as the elements and elementals, can occur.

When this chakra opens we no longer understand ourselves as separate, rather puritanical creatures. We are in touch with the rhythms of our bodies and the Earth. We no longer feel shame or fear around our darker instincts, and understand that dark and light are simply a continuum. There are other chakras below this that connect us to every single plant, animal, and layer of Earth. Connecting deeply to these chakras allows for us to integrate our shadows and our primal emotions. Emotions are no longer something to fear or avoid. There is an understanding that comes through that we are meant to have emotions—all of them. Rage, anger, fear, joy, happiness, sadness—they all have their own rhythm, their own flow, and are all equally beautiful. When we are fully grounded through the Earth chakra and below we can fully experience these flows of emotion, and discover that a flow of sadness may be exquisite, the flow of rage may be orgasmic, and the flow of everything that we experience as humans, both pain and pleasure, we can take responsibility for. There is no more shying away from full embodiment, our shadow, our emotions, or any other part of us.

PART 3

Sudden Awakenings

Sudden awakenings drastically change our functioning level, thought processes, and our concepts about reality in a short period of time. These awakenings are often dramatic and require a great deal of proper understanding to venture through intact.

Unlike many of the more gradual awakenings, sudden awakenings are often a sort of calling—meaning that they are not typically brought on by conscious desire or choice. Experiencers of sudden awakenings often just wish for the symptoms and issues that come up to simply go away. Many of us are confused about the drastic physical, mental, and emotional transformations that sudden awakenings entail. For those of us who can see a sudden awakening fully through, the awakenings allow the clearing of all layers of conditioned reality, deep understandings and remembrances about ourselves and the world, true connection to the divine, and a fully realized and awakened state.

Top-Down Awakenings

A top-down awakening is by far the most common of the more significant awakenings. This type of awakening in simple terms means that our crown chakra and third eye are open. Due to genetics, spiritual pursuits, or other reasons we have opened ourselves to the divine, to spirit, and to the different layers of reality. It is actually fairly easy to open to spirit and to start to open our third eye and crown to sense or see energies that are not normally visible or felt. The focus on psychic abilities in our culture makes it so that opening the third eye and crown are done before the root or first three chakras are opened.

Many of us end up with a top-down awakening because we became interested in spiritual pursuits, started attending classes, doing drugs, reading literature, and finding gurus and other teachers who show us how to seek outside of ourselves. This externalization of spiritual pursuits leads to advanced work without the basics of spiritual work being done. We live in a culture where we want to be advanced—more awakened, more spiritual, and above everyone who surrounds us yesterday. When we go through this sort of spiritual kindergarten, where spirituality is a commodity and has a materialistic nature, we look for what can separate us from one another. This spiritual materialism allows us to consume endless books, gurus, and teachers that center around

133

the upper chakras and participate in the competitive spirituality that is so pervasive in the modern spiritual community. By looking internally and being able to look at our own wounding, and sit with the patterns and traumas that we carry in our first three chakras, we are able to surrender the illusion of awakening as told to us by others and discover awakening ourselves in a balanced, grounded, and embodied manner.

Some of us begin life with a top-down awakening due to family history of psychic abilities or previous-life abilities carried forward into this one. When this happens it is difficult to process the stimuli coming through, maintain balance, and maintain functionality in the world. Without being in a state of balance it is difficult to discern what is ours and what is not energetically. When our third eye is open without processing the lower chakras we are not seeing clearly—we see everything through our wounds and needs as well as the layers of conditioned reality. Everything we channel or see may be pure messages from divine flow but become distorted through the wounds and layers of conditioned reality we have not worked through.

The issue with this type of awakening is that it is not grounded in anything. It is not required to open our first three chakras to have a top-down awakening. It is not necessary to work on any of our own issues to open these chakras. So we begin to separate from the Earth, from this reality. This type of awakening creates the illusion that spirituality is something "up there" and we divide our spiritual nature and our physical nature and end up disassociating, remaining partially or fully out of our bodies until we are able to and willing to receive significant healing work.

Undergoing a top-down awakening we will have immense energy circulating into our crown, third eye, and whole head, but without having the throat open it will create a bottleneck, resulting in headaches, neck pain, disassociation, ego issues, and over time significant mental health issues, hip, back, and leg pain. The throat will only open with the heart being open in order to express itself fully and honestly, and the heart will not fully open until the wounds and patterns of the lower three chakras are processed.

When we receive information through our crown and third eye only we become energetically imbalanced. Often we are partially out of our bodies and prefer to remain this way. We feel different and separate from everyone else, and some of us remain in elaborately set up illusions of our own creation through having the abilities that come with our third eye and crown open. Significant mental illness can result—hospitals are filled with the top-down awakened. This group more than others can easily become ego-awakened. We have not done the personal work to open our lower bodies and gone through the layers of awakening to understand that we are not special (or that everyone is special). Some of us utilize our top-down awakenings to isolate ourselves from the physical world and to look down on others who are not as "spiritual" as we are. Some of us have permanently stuck open third eyes and crowns without filters, resulting in an immense amount of spiritual energy coming in that we are unable to process.

Other symptoms of a top-down awakening include being open to spiritual guidance; psychic abilities; mediumship and channeling capabilities; understanding of patterns and concepts from a different vantage point (this is due to many of us being halfway out our body so we really do have a different perspective); headaches; sinus pain; closed-off feeling in the throat; disassociation; problems with pain in lower body; thin or emaciated lower body; cravings for meat, chocolate, carbohydrates, or other grounding foods; feelings of separation or like not a part of the Earth; delusions; paranoia; ego issues (either feeling like you are better than everyone, or that you are worthless, or both); mental imbalances; and feelings of heaviness or stuck feelings in shoulders, upper back, heart, neck, and head.

A top-down awakening can be extremely beneficial to tap into psychic abilities. It gives us the ability to connect with spirit, with the different layers of reality, and the ability ultimately to connect with true divinity. It is wonderful to have our crown and third eye awakened—it gives us the ability to have a whole new perspective of our lives. Being able to see the patterns of the universe and having the capability to access spiritual energies can inspire profound understandings and realizations that can be used for our own healing process. But more commonly the focus is on gaining access to spirit, or gaining psychic abilities rather than becoming whole. Integrating spirituality into our bodies, becoming whole and embodied in our bodies on all levels, is what true awakening is. Without this outlook we become severely imbalanced and cannot fully awaken to our true potential.

The difficulty of top-down awakenings is that it is by far the most common awakening to get stuck in. It also can be one of the most dangerous because it creates energetically an environment where we are not quite a part of any reality. With our ability to easily shift through dimensions, times, perspectives, and being fully or partially energetically out of our bodies it also creates opportunity for other energies to attach. Without any support from Earth we can become dysfunctional and without a filter. Many severe mental imbalances such as schizophrenia, disassociative identity disorder, bipolar, and depressive issues are partially or fully a result of top-down awakenings. The more our lower chakras are blocked in comparison to extremely opened top chakras, generally the more issues we have.

So what to do about a top-down awakening? Ultimately the answer is grounding. It is about consciously choosing to be part of the Earth. It is also about the start of an inner journey rather than an external one. It is about working through the layers of conditioned reality and our own issues. Top-down awakenings allows us to get in touch with many things outside of ourselves—they do not require us to be embodied, to work on our own layers of issues, to look inside of ourselves. So to solve this imbalance requires working with the first, second, and third chakras, allowing them to open. It is only through working with the lower chakras that the heart will open as well as the throat, easing the bottleneck of energy that has been created.

CARLA was a 22-year-old woman who proudly told me that she was clairvoyant and recited her long list of accomplishments as a spiritual counselor. She had gone through most healers in town and questioned me thoroughly before coming in as to my accomplishments. Carla told me during the session that she could not handle anyone touching her legs, and even when I was doing energy work a foot away from her lower body she expressed anger and said I was causing her pain. Although Carla was thin, her legs were emaciated and lacked color. As I gently worked with her low back, energy started filling her lower body and abdomen. I felt her entire energy system retract and go back into her head. Very clearly I heard her scream "NO" without words.

When Carla came in all of her energy was at the top of her head and energetically she was standing on top of her body (it looked like her feet were at her third eye and she was standing on herself). She complained of headaches, of constant body pain, of being sensitive and reacting to world events, complained about mercury retrograde, weather, and her classmates. When I told her that she was out of her body and that we could do some work to get her back in her body, she got upset and repeated how sensitive she was and her list of accomplishments and again questioned mine.

I told her that her body was calling out to be physical, to have sensate experiences, for nature, for inner work, and to think about allowing herself back in her body. She said that she would allow that, but her body was still resistant to any sort of embodiment. She mentioned to me at the end of the session that if she were back in her body she believed she wouldn't be as sensitive. I told her that she was wrong, and if anything sensitivity increases with becoming embodied, but I could tell she was not ready to hear that.

MATT was a 16-year-old high school student who was genetically sensitive. His family had gone through a great deal of tragedy ancestrally and he had moved from Hawaii to Chicago at the age of 10, two years after his younger brother passed away. Although he was in therapy, Matt's mother sent him to me because she realized that what Matt was going through was likely spiritual in nature.

When Matt came to see me he didn't want to talk or meet my eye. This changed when I noticed that he had an energy attached to him that was speaking to him, telling him not to say anything. I asked who it was. Matt seemed surprised and said that it was his brother. Matt and his brother knew that at age 16 (but really at any age) if you mention speaking to or sensing a spirit you would be labeled as crazy. So Matt started withdrawing, spending a lot of alone time in his room and stopped going out with friends.

The death of Matt's brother was a catalyst for his spiritual awakening. Matt had always had empathic abilities, but these exploded with his brother dying. He started to develop mediumship capabilities, at first with his brother and then others, clauraudient and to some degree clairvoyant abilities. Matt hid these capabilities and they began causing him physical and psychological pain. He was placed in talk therapy, which he enjoyed.

The first thing I noticed about Matt was that although he was somewhat grounded, his abilities were unskilled (he lacked the tools to know how to work with them) and the amount of information coming at him through his crown and third eye was immense. The large amount of information coming at him was causing him to be out of balance, and he lacked the ability to properly process the amount of information coming through him and the tools to work with his psychic abilities.

By teaching Matt how to ground properly he began rooting into the Earth utilizing a simple tree meditation. At my instruction he began to exercise regularly as well. We then worked on clearing blocks in his heart and solar plexus. He then noticed how restricted his throat was, and began painting as an outlet for that center because he did not yet want to reveal his truth of being awake and his psychic abilities.

Gradually everything in his body opened beautifully and he began being able to take the energy coming in through his crown, third eye, and field, and process it properly through his body and out of his feet. He was able to feel Kundalini in his body properly cycle from his root chakra up and throughout every cell in his body. His abilities began increasing exponentially and when he graduated high school he went to massage school, trained in Holotropic Breathwork, became interested in Shamanism, and is now an exceptional healer.

Clinically, I have worked with many people undergoing top-down awakenings. It is extremely common and can be a beautiful way to realize you are connected to something greater than yourself. As these two examples show, it can either entirely separate you into a world of pain and illusion, or be the start of a full awakening in which you learn to process energies appropriately.

If you are experiencing a top-down awakening, the choice is yours if you want to be embodied and do the work required to be more balanced. Although not everyone is meant to be fully awakened, the top-down awakened can make a conscious decision to work on clearing the lower chakras and ground themselves into the Earth and physical reality to become more balanced individuals.

- If you are experiencing a top-down awakening, feel the energy in your body. Are you fully in your body? Where do you start? Do you start at the waist, the abdomen, the neck, the head? Are you completely out of your body?
- Frequently people undergoing top-down awakenings feel really separate— like they are really different or not a part of the Earth. If you feel this way, what would happen if you became a part of the Earth? Let Earth energy in? Are you resisting feeling embodied?
- Many people have explained to me that they are afraid of losing their psychic abilities if they are in their body. Know that this is not true. Know that if you are informed and feel energy from both Earth and Sky that you will increase your abilities and they will stabilize. The amount of physical, emotional, and spiritual pain you feel will decrease.
- Most of all, know that your body has started the process of awakening if you are experiencing this. There is nothing you have to do but surrender and stop resisting your body opening. Your other chakras, the rest of your body wants to let go; it wants to release. Let it happen. Consciously decide to work on yourself through meditation, grounding, therapy, artistic pursuits, and holistic healers to become more balanced.
- Understand that if you are severely out of your body, are mentally out of balance, have severe mental or physical issues, are non-functional or barely functional, or begin to have trauma or other significant issues come up with starting an inner journey that reaching out to receive help is often neces- sary. People going through awakenings often do not receive help because they do not think that others know what they are experiencing, or that other people will think they are crazy. Realize that you can describe your experiences in a way where you can receive help and support from others even if they do not know what you are going through. Simply tell friends, family, holistic practitioners that you are feeling ungrounded, sad, have insomnia. Describe your symptoms.

- Know that there are others out there experiencing what you are. There are some healers that know enough to assist you. If you are ready to work on yourself on a deep level you can find them.
- Use of your physical body and your physical senses is extremely important for this type of awakening. Physical activity, walks in nature, being around beautiful art, images, smells, etc. open up your physical body and ground you in the sensate experience. Your senses are one of the true benefits of having a human form. Any type of dancing is especially beneficial. Five Rhythms, a movement practice, is extraordinarily balancing and allows for us to feel the flows of divinity through the upper chakras as well as release the lower chakras.
- Meditation, yoga, and other experiences which promote discovery of your inner landscape are crucial. By working through a meditation practice focused on grounding and your own internal landscape (rather than the development of psychic abilities, angels, or other outer aspects) you can find balance.

Psychic Awakenings

Top-down awakenings and psychic awakenings have a great deal of overlap. Top-down awakenings are an energetic phenomena—they result from having massive amounts of energy come through the crown and third eye without proper grounding or opening of the lower chakras. Psychic awakenings have to do with the specific development of psychic abilities. For some, psychic abilities dramatically opening up can be somewhat removed from the awakening process. For most, the development or increase in psychic abilities happens during the course of fully awakening.

Although this is not a full-length book on psychic abilities we will touch on each one and how they present. It is common for us to start with a dominant psychic ability. As long as we are open, our dominant ability will grow stronger until it reaches a certain plateau. When our dominant ability reaches a plateau it will kick-start another psychic ability. This will then allow for our dominant ability to grow in strength as well as the other abilities to further blossom. Eventually we will have a few different abilities all varying in strength. These abilities will then intertwine. For some this creates a sort of synesthesia, where we might experience sound and color intertwine and provide a unique expression for us. Others find that all of our abilities intertwine, and we begin to experience psychic phenomena through multiple senses. This can lead to feelings of actually being present while sensing or viewing psychic stimuli or being able to relate psychic stimuli through multiple senses.

After senses begin intertwining they will often become stronger until they reach a plateau again. At this point, many of us have a sort of blackout experience in which all of our abilities disappear for a period of time. The conclusion of full psychic awakening is all of our abilities intertwining and becoming one—meaning that the differentiation between being clairvoyant, or clairaudient, or an Empath is no longer something to be separated. We are simply at this point psychically open to the extent that whatever needs to come across to us through whatever sense will.

Clairvoyance

Clairvoyance means "clear seeing." It is our visual capabilities. This ability comes from our physical eyes, our third eye (between our brows) as well as the pineal gland, which is behind the third eye. Often this ability crosses with other abilities—we may sense how energy may visually look rather than outwardly see it. For example, we may not see a person as if we would see a person sitting on the bus across from us but we are able to describe a 40-year-old male wearing a blue hat and khaki pants looking sad through our energetic sensitivities.

Clairvoyance is an ability that is often genetic, caused by trauma, or created by another psychic ability gaining strength. There is a common thought that everyone is psychic, and that we can develop clairvoyance. Although we certainly can become more clairvoyant or sensitive than we are, most of us who are highly psychic have the ability come through as a genetic trait or due to a strong psychic awakening. Many genetic and awakened clairvoyants find the ability difficult to navigate and to learn the right tools to work with it. Since most of the literature and movies about clairvoyant individuals is about how wonderful this ability is or would be if we could only acquire it, this leaves those of us dealing with actual clairvoyant capabilities struggling.

Clairvoyance varies in strength but is considered one of the dominant psychic abilities due to it awakening with the sixth chakra. For some of us this ability manifests as seeing energy, spirits, colors of the aura, or even ability to see disease or dysfunction in the body (such as in Medical Intuition). It is somewhat easy to learn how to begin to see energy, and many of us can work our way up to seeing energy fields, colors, and other energies.

Some of us with this ability will have intense dreams, visions like flashes of light or mini-movies, sudden downloads or understandings of things to happen, and spatial understandings (such as ability to easily redecorate our living room). These are either natural gifts or develop over time through a psychic awakening. We may develop the ability to see imprints, dimensions, backwards and forwards in time, and through the conditioned layers of reality.

When a clairvoyant psychic ability awakens it gathers strength. We have intense dreams, see imprints (visuals surrounding people like stamps that give information about their life), health information, past lives, karma, full spirits (instead of clouds, smoke, orbs, or through a crossed ability such as empathic impressions), mediumship abilities, ability to see through dimensions, times, patterns, and layers of reality. Our ability may change from internal (meaning we sense something and can construct a visual from it) to external—actually seeing things as we would in our normal physical reality. We will begin to see what layer of reality people are living at—meaning how awakened they are and what their most pressing concerns are. When this ability fully opens up, the ability to see whatever someone is currently dealing with and what they most need noticed occurs. This may be health information, imprints, a past life, childhood trauma, or even energies or spirits surrounding or attached to someone.

When our clairvoyant abilities have fully awakened it is likely that another ability or two has started to open up. We are also likely overwhelmed or just want our experiences to slow down or stop. We also start to get noticed. This means that we are awakened to the extent that other energies and spirits notice us. Strange experiences start to occur and our dreams and waking life will be disrupted until we develop boundaries with this ability.

The good aspect of being strongly clairvoyant is that we can powerfully see—through people, situations, timelines, even dimensions. Seeing when people are lying or what the inner motivations of people are can be extraordinarily helpful. But with that knowledge often comes a sense of overwhelm, emotions such as anger or fear, and feelings of separation that come from knowing that we view the world differently than most other people. The ability to see the masks, the hidden selves and motivations of the people surrounding us, is difficult to process. For many of us this can result in dissolution of friendships and marriages, and tendencies to isolate. Going into the world with powerful psychic abilities, such as clairvoyance, where we are able to see so much hidden material can be difficult.

The emotions and feelings of separation especially run high with those of us who were born with strong clairvoyant capabilities, or when we suddenly develop clairvoyance. Clairvoyants are one of the most likely groups to go through periods of depression, anger, and experience thoughts of suicide or suicide attempts. The highly psychic clairvoyant no matter how sane they are is always left questioning their sanity, how much of what they experience is true. This continues until we are able to fully awaken, but even then we may choose to separate ourselves because our knowledge base and understandings of deep inner truths can make it difficult to interact with others. When we learn how to develop the appropriate tools and boundaries to stand in our abilities, when we know who we truly are, we will rarely be bothered by questions of sanity or the feelings of being out of control or overwhelmed by clairvoyant capabilities.

Once clairvoyance has fully awakened it can be difficult for us to be in the normal world and we may become hermits or choose to only be around certain people. This can be difficult to understand but it is often necessary for the clairvoyant to function. Once we fully learn how to work with our abilities we can go wherever we choose and be around whomever we want. We learn to block material coming at us or process it by simply noticing things and allowing them to flow through us. We may simply choose to remain alone because it is more peaceful and our preferred way of being.

If you are mildly clairvoyant, that is wonderful. Continue to develop yourself through meditation, clearing, and realize that where you are with your psychic abilities is perfect.

If you are experiencing a strong, sudden clairvoyant awakening, realize that you can work with your clairvoyance so it is a gift to your life. Know that although you are different than others, and your ability to see deeply is rare, you are not separate. Understand that any resistance to your abilities and emotions like anger and fear are causing your ability to partially block. This is likely creating emotional and physical pain. Surrender to the fact that you are clairvoyant. Know that if you grow your abilities and learn to work with them instead of denying, fearing, or closing them down that this ability will fully awaken. Fully awakening the psychic ability of clairvoyance will allow for you to come to a place of peace and understanding with this ability and learn how to work with it properly.

EXERCISE: Unclogging Your Third Eye

- Feel your physical eyes, your third eye, and your occiput (the back of your head).
- Take a breath in. Fill up your body and your chest.
- As you breathe out, breathe out through your physical eyes. This will seem strange at first.
- Do this several times—breathing in and filling up your torso, your diaphragm, your abdomen ... even your legs. Breathe out and imagine the breath leaving through your physical eyes.
- Picture a triangle connecting your physical eyes to your third eye. Sit with it until you can see or feel this triangle.
- Breathe in and breathe out through that triangle.
- Notice any restrictions, pain, or emotions that come up.
- Now feel your pineal gland, which is approximately midway between your third eye and the back of your head.
- Imagine a straight line from your third eye through your pineal gland exiting the back of the head. You will physically feel an indent in this space where it exits.
- Breathe in out into that line, imagining the line lighting up and connecting into one solid line of energy.

- Now breathe in and out through the whole thing—physical eyes, third-eye triangle, and the line through to the occiput.
- Feel these structures connect, clear, and begin to glow.
- At the top of your head (your crown) imagine a small circular door opening. Feel it open.
- Draw in golden light through the crown into these structures.
- Picture light not only flowing into and out of these structures but through them—through the back of your head, through your eyes, through your third eye, and through the center of your head where your pineal gland is located.
- Surrender and tell these structures you are ready for them to open.
- Repeat until you feel as if this entire circuit is clear, or on a regular basis to clear out any blocked, chaotic, or disruptive energies as a result of clairvoyant stimuli coming at you.

When your third eye is fully opened you will no longer notice pain, discomfort, or emotions coming up in the above exercise. You will feel energy fully flowing through and around your whole head like a giant halo or sphere. You will notice that your perception of the world has changed. There will be a constant flow of energy without any concentration or breathing techniques required. You will be able to work with this circuit and close either the back door (the occiput area door) or the front door (the crown chakra) by imagining the door shutting. Eventually if you come to a fully awakened state this circuit will incorporate with other circuits and other energies of the body to circulate through your whole body, up and down your spine, through your palms and soles of the feet, and can be "vented" out of you through the pores of your skin.

Many people ask why they should open up the third eye when they are naturally clairvoyant and having difficulties. They already see too much and are afraid of feeling further separated from others or knowing even more than they already do. They close down this ability due to fear or do not know how to process energy coming in so they end up with migraines, eye pain, fatigue, and other issues. It is natural to fear that symptoms would get worse, not better, if this ability were to become stronger. However, this is only the case if the person continues becoming stronger while having emotional or physical blockages in their body. This is only the case if the person is not grounded, is not physically in their bodies, or is experiencing a top-down awakening without opening of their first few chakras. By breathing and clearing out through the exercise above the circuit that is responsible for working with these energies becomes clear. A clear circuit means less physical pain and less emotional pain. This circuit being blocked results in pain.

By working on the Self (the work of the first chakra), becoming physically embodied such as through exercise and walks in nature, and allowing this energy circuit to come to a clear, ideal state clairvoyance becomes a state of constant, buzzing energy. This constant, buzzing energy can flow through the head without restriction creating a light around the head. Once this is achieved the amount of pain and discomfort greatly lessens. It is by opening, surrendering, and learning about clairvoyance that we can have it be an asset to our existence.

The simplest explanation why to open this ability rather than shut it down if you are experiencing issues with clairvoyance is that this open circuit creates flow and deep spiritual insights and knowledge. A blocked or closed-off circuit creates pain and emotional issues. Only when the circuit is fully open can the clairvoyant have control over the circuit and close and open it at will with no repercussions.

Empathy

Empathy is one of the most common psychic abilities. Empathy can be created by genetics, trauma, and can to some extent be learned. The Empath is the scanner of rooms and people. We are able to sense energies around us and are often constantly in a state of reaction or resonance to them. As Empaths we often know we are sensitive, but we are overwhelmed by our degree of sensitivity and the amount of information coming at us.

Common Empath abilities include being able to sense what is going on in a room emotionally, mentally, and often physically, an understanding of people, and a strong capability to tell when others are lying. We are often artists or attracted to creativity, expression, and utilizing our imaginations. We are excellent listeners and others feel as if we understand them deeply. Due to our unique ability to see deeply and understand truth behind the scenes and the hidden qualities of people and places we have a unique view of the world. Sensitive to global, local, and communal events, as Empaths we often take the chaos, violence, and extreme emotions of the world into our own bodies.

As Empaths we may struggle with depression and yo-yo between emotional states quickly because we take on the emotions and feelings of others around us, as well as take on energies from land, buildings, animals, global and community energies such as weather and chaos from political and social events such as school shootings and riots. When we do not understand that we are taking on these emotions and energies this is understandably confusing, overwhelming, and exhausting.

As an Empath the world frequently seems too violent, too loud, and has too much stimulus. We cycle emotions through our own bodies and being around too much stimulus or extreme emotions can be difficult. Television and movies can put us into a state of trauma and distress because we will need to process the extremes of emotion and violence that these mediums contain.

Subconsciously we use this ability to resonate with people, places, animals, plants, and the world to our advantage and detriment. We all have a resonance—a vibratory quality, an energy that is uniquely ours. As an Empath when we enter the energetic field of a room or talk with an individual person or group we will change our own resonance to meet the energy of the room, group, or person. In many ways we all do this, Empath or not—we calibrate our energy to make it appropriate for the situation. We would not want to be really high energy at a funeral, or really low energy for a rock concert. But as Empaths we take this to the extreme and are energetic chameleons, constantly recalibrating our energy to match the resonance of the person we are with or the situation we are in.

This constant recalibration has some very good qualities. If we are matching the resonance of a person, animal, or group we blend in well. We are immediately liked by those around us, and we quickly are able to gain insight into the emotions and inner life of whatever we are interacting with. But this constant recalibration causes issues. It is exhausting to constantly readjust our energy. In calibrating our energies we take on the emotional, mental, and sometimes physical symptoms of that which we are calibrating with. Constantly on alert and in fight or flight mode, constantly scanning and processing means that we are aware of any disturbances or potential for issues going on in the space we are in. We are always in a state of overwhelm and reaction. Although all sensitives and psychics must deal with a great amount of material coming at them, as Empaths we have the added stress of changing our energy to attune or match the energy that is coming at us.

It can be difficult to explain this quality to others, and we are frequently called too sensitive by friends and family. Depending on how strong this ability is and how "unskilled" or lacking tools, awareness, and understanding of this ability we are it can create severe physical, mental, and emotional issues.

One of the best explanations for how an Empath, or what any psychic has to deal with, can be explained simply. Imagine that a "normal" person walks into a room. He or she might notice anywhere between 10-60 items in that room depending on sensitivity levels. When a "sensitive" or psychic walks into that same room he or she might notice between 60-2,000 items in that room. In addition, the Empath then takes in that information and changes his or her energy to match the largest energetic currents in that room. Whether it be 60 items or 2,000 items, this is a large amount of material to process.

When we take in stimuli it is processed through our energetic and physical bodies. Energetically and physically it is first processed through our digestive system and nervous system. The digestive system is responsible for digesting not only physical food but emotions and energies that surround us. If we have not learned or are unable to process these energies appropriately there are digestive issues, food intolerances and allergies, fatigue, emotional ups and downs, immune issues such as autoimmunity, hormonal issues, and nervous system issues such as disruption of the sleep-wake cycle, insomnia, constantly feeling "on" or that small stimuli provokes a severe reaction, and weird "mystery" diseases not attributable or solvable by modern allopathic medicine.

At this point it is good to point out that a visit to an allopathic doctor or holistic doctor such as an acupuncturist is ideal if you are having moderate to severe physical symptoms. However, for the Empath, it is frequent that there is shown to be nothing wrong or an autoimmune or functional disorder such as IBS that modern medicine lacks the ability to properly care for. The symptom suppression that modern medicine offers for functional disorders, fatigue, anxiety, and emotional issues that come with being a sensitive can be much needed in the face of severe symptoms. However, until we learn to properly process the amount of stimulus coming in and understand our sensitivity level and how to work with it we will consistently have issues that are difficult if not impossible to treat with modern medicine.

The biggest issue that we have to face as an Empath is an inability to truly know who we are. Because we constantly process energies and shift our own energy in reaction to those surrounding us, it is difficult to have a sense of our true self, our core identity. Our chameleon-like qualities allow for us to be ideal counselors, artists, writers, and friends, but the constant changing state creates a lack of core identity, or an inability to gauge who we truly are and what we want out of life.

If you are an Empath, realize that this is how you operate in the world. There is a big difference between a skilled and an unskilled Empath. A skilled Empath is someone who realizes that he or she is an Empath, has made peace with that fact, and utilizes this ability to his or her advantage. An unskilled Empath is someone who doesn't realize what is happening to him or her, is often in a state of overwhelm, and feels that he or she is too sensitive for the world.

So how to become a skilled Empath? The first step is realization. Realize that you are an Empath, that you take on the emotions and experiences of others, that you are constantly recalibrating your energy, that you are constantly on alert. Start noticing and reading individual people, places, animals, and plants. What do you notice about their energy? How are you calibrating to it?

After awareness and noticing comes actively using your ability. When you talk with a person do you want to resonate with them? Maybe you are in a job interview and shifting your energy to match theirs would be a great idea. Maybe you are speaking to a person at a party who is constantly complaining and you notice your energy starts to resonate—getting lower and darker. You are actively taking on the depression and negative outlook on life from someone else. Realize you are doing this and imagine you are either cutting off your energy to them or place a sheet of imaginary plexiglass between the two of you. Then tell yourself that this energy is not yours, thank it for the information, but the energy can now leave. As you do this more you will begin to understand what is not yours.

As you work with your empathy you will begin to have more control over it. You will never not notice the things around you but this state can go from having to process everything—emotions, energy, mental states, physical states of everything around you—to simply noticing the information without taking it on. Eventually you can read people, read the room, read situations or places, and simply take in the information without it physically or energetically affecting you. You will come to a place where you can decide to resonate or not. This takes practice, and even the most capable Empaths I know do not go into situations that they know they will have issues with.

Empaths lose their identities or never formulate identities because they are so sensitive. Think about who you are, what your unique vibration and resonance is. Allow yourself to sit with it daily. By truly knowing yourself, how you react to things, and what emotions you hold, you can understand when you are taking on something that is not yours. Then when you are in a situation where you are speaking to a depressed woman and you begin to feel depressed, have shoulder pain, and feel digestive issues, you can truly know that those traits are not you. When you realize "you," you can realize "not you" and let go of it.

So how to let go? When you realize that something is not yours, you can ask for it to leave. You can blow it out of your mouth and imagine it leaving through a window. If you have your lower chakras open you can imagine it running out the bottom of your feet into the earth so the earth can take care of it. You can then regain your center by firmly feeling your feet on the ground and recalling your own unique vibration. Say inwardly who you truly are—your characteristics and unique qualities. If you have a sound, a scent, a vibration, a felt sense that feels truly "you," allow yourself to feel it. When the stimulus around you is too strong, recall that sound or vibration that is truly you and allow anything that is not that sound or vibration to leave.

Gradually when you develop who you are most things that are not you will automatically process or simply bounce off of you. It is a natural tendency for Empaths to create shields or disassociate to block stimulus coming in. This is true of both skilled and unskilled Empaths. It can be scary to be in your body with the amount of stimulus coming at you. It can be natural to put up an energetic barrier when you are overwhelmed. However, the energetic barrier that Empaths put up is from their own energetic resources. This means that it is sucking out energy from the Empath to keep it up and working. It also means that others may see you as being shy, hidden, blank, or even rude. They will not understand that you are shielding yourself. When you erect an energetic shield like this it keeps out all of the energy that might come your way—both good and bad. By learning to work with empathic abilities rather than shielding you can learn how to process the energies instead of keeping everything out of your space.

Full embodiment, being in the areas of our body that are feeling discomfort, can be difficult for us. There is a disassociation from body parts that are struggling with the amount of information coming at us but also sometimes total disassociation where we will feel as if we are standing above or beside our bodies. By gradually and slowly coming back into our bodies we will be able to process the energies coming at us and deal with the physical fallout of dealing with so much energy that is not ours. As long as we are disassociated or frozen in parts of our body we will be unable to fully process energy. Fully processing energy means taking energy in through the digestive system and processing it through varying systems and energetic channels of the body—either out through the digestive system, the pores, the bottoms of the feet, or the palms.

If our system does not have these channels clear and we are not embodied in the systems that are supposed to process, our body will find the best way it can to process it. This can result in vomiting, nausea, sweating, chills, heat, headaches, dizziness, and other ways that do not feel very good. By embodying—fully being in areas of our body and working to clear them—we can process the energies coming through us naturally through the digestive system and through the bottoms of our feet.

Receiving acupuncture and other holistic care like CranioSacral Therapy, Reiki, Zero Balancing, Visceral Manipulation (for digestive issues), and Healing Touch can be helpful. Meditation and exercising regularly to process these energies is crucial. When we are starting from a position of weakness and fatigue, which is quite common in unskilled Empaths, simply going for short walks, connecting with nature, and sitting with your back to a tree trunk can be a good way to start. Overall, learning that you are an Empath, understanding what that means, and learning how to work with it with the appropriate tools can be life changing.

Clairsentience

Clairsentience and empathy differ in that the Empath takes on the emotions, physical characteristics, and resonance of everything around them, and the Clairsentient is highly sensitive to their surroundings but will not resonate or become a chameleon in order to change themselves to meet a stimulus.

The Clairsentient picks up energy not by resonance but by sensing energies of a place. This is often one of the most common psychic abilities, and one of the easiest to develop. As Clairsentients we are able to walk into a room or place and understand if it is negative or positive. This is usually the first trait to develop, and is how we start to open up our psychic abilities if we wish to do so. This is our gut instinct, our mothers' intuition, the little voice inside that tells us to switch lanes in traffic, that someone is not the appropriate person to date, or that we should apply for a job that we saw online.

Advanced clairsentient abilities include being able to discriminate between feelings and energies, such as understanding that what we feel as a negative environment might have been a place where a murder took place, or feeling that the person we are talking to has an angel or guardian spirit that is very positive with them. Discerning between these energies and where they might come from is a natural ability that gradually presents for the Clairsentient. Through noticing our own gut instinct we are able to further distinguish between energies that we might come across.

When clairsentient abilities begin to open it is common to experience energetic phenomena—such as energy surges, waves of emotion, and pain such as headaches or stomach pain. These are a result of our physical senses being overloaded with information. With this ability there are typical places in our body that often feel the impact of sensory and energetic overload. For some of us this is headaches, but for many of us it is some form of digestive issue like nausea or solar plexus/upper abdomen pain. This is different than empathic abilities in that we might always feel something about our child in our solar plexus or a headache when something bad is happening but our child could have any experience or physical happening in any area of their body. As Empaths we would have a child having a headache and we would have a headache, or a friend having a difficult pregnancy with nausea might cause us to have nausea. In clairsentience this is more of a general sense where we will always feel specific areas of our body hurt or react to "bad" or "negative" or "good" things. As Clairsentients we are able to sense. We may sense spirits, other dimensions, other beings, emotions, energy, or anything else that is beyond the normal realms of sensing. We may be able to sense beyond conditioned reality. This may or may not be crossed with visual (clairvoyant), empathic, or auditory capabilities. In its pure form, Clairsentients are able to sense beyond.

We will know if our clairsentient abilities are opening up when we are able to feel more about our surroundings and the people within it. Discernment is key here. At the beginning clairsentience begins with the simple gut instinct—the feeling of something being wrong, shortness of breath, punched in the stomach or butterflies in the stomach, headaches, or more positive things such as happiness, joy in the heart, and buzzing feelings in the body. If worked with, this ability can deepen, and the noticing and discerning of what our body is telling us can provide excellent information about our surroundings and the people we are interacting with. For example, if you feel pain in your solar plexus when a bad event is happening, noticing that is wonderful. Taking a step further and noticing the severity of the pain, what the pain might be coming from, and how this pain differs from the last pain in our solar plexus will give us a library to choose from in the future of what different types and qualities of pain might mean to you. A headache is not simply a headache. The quality, severity, and other symptoms of the headache can give you information about types of energies you are dealing with. Gradually you can build up an understanding that the stabbing headache going into our eye means that a person is dangerous, that our mild occipital headache means that the house we entered had some mildly bad things go on in it, and the headache that puts us in bed for three days means that something huge is happening on a worldwide, global, or cosmic scale.

Clairsentients often deeply sense the rhythms, emotions, and feelings of people, places, and things. We will likely experience mood swings without understanding the source of them, abhor violence and charged environments, and simply wish for peace and quiet. With this ability we have deep feelings toward those we are close to. We may feel when someone will call us on the telephone, when a friend is hurt, or when there is a spirit around us.

This ability is difficult to accept for those of us who are experiencing it since it is a "feeling" sense rather than the more concrete visual, auditory, or even the chameleon-like empathic quality. We live in a concrete society that rejects our feeling states, so those of us who have this capability learn to dismiss it rather than learning to engender it. Since clairsentience is sensing but in an unskilled manner and we may be unable or unwilling to link the energy of a house we entered to our physical headache, it can take a while to accept and learn to work with. For those of us who are Clairsentients, learning to honor and develop this ability will allow for us to work with it.

If you are a Clairsentient, begin to build up your abilities by first impressions. Feel what a room feels like. Is it positive or negative? Then you can move on to deeper noticing. Why is this space positive or negative? Go into a really charged space, such as a hospital, clinic, or other medical facility and feel the amount of energy coming at you. It is difficult for even skilled Clairsentients to visit these spaces. What do you notice physically when you are in a really charged space? Now visit a place that is quite calm and has a good sense of flow, like a spot in nature. What do you feel in this space? What do you notice physically when you are in a place that properly cycles its charges? This means that nothing is stuck or dark and it is in a state of flow.

For those of you in a place of overwhelm with your clairsentience, the above activities may help. It is important to know that what you are feeling from your environment affects you physically. You may also try the empathic realizations of saying "thank you" to the information and asking it to leave. This works for some stimulus. If you are in a really charged environment I suggest leaving. Until you are able to properly process negative or charged spaces and people, places like hospitals are likely to cause you physical pain.

So how to properly process? Beyond leaving a highly charged environment, I suggest working with grounding and clearing your body so the information, feelings, and vibrations coming at you can flow through you instead of getting stuck. Know that even experienced Clairsentients have issues with pain when huge amounts of stimuli come their way. That full moon, when your company is going through layoffs, when your daughter is sick, or if there were three shootings in your town might cause you to become non-functional. Instead of fighting it in these situations, go with it. Treat yourself to an Epsom salts bath, take the day off work if you can, or go to bed. Do not feel bad about it or beat yourself up. Do what you need to do and do not force yourself any further. These things happen.

This ability is powerful in that the more it opens up, the more information you are a magnet for and are able to process. At first it starts with individual or specific situations that you are in, but as this ability opens you begin feeling and cycling family, community, Earth, weather, and planetary energies. When you get to the point of cycling weather, world, and planetary energies, know that although you may occasionally be in pain, the amount of understanding it offers and ability to be a vessel of healing that occur with it. You may feel bombings or violence across the planet through head pain, or feel nauseated when a school shooting happens even before the actual event occurs. When clairsentience fully opens, you are able to feel everything in the world and pass it through you.

So what to do with this ability at this point? At this point, clairsentience often intertwines with other abilities so you know what to do with the information you are receiving. Clairsentients make exceptional healers and artists. Through meditation, clearing, and allowing for yourself to become a vessel for feeling and cycling the energies of the world you can come to peace with this ability.

Clairaudience

Clairaudience is extra-sensory healing capabilities and is not a very common dominant psychic ability. Clairaudience is rarely the first psychic ability to open, and it is not particularly linked to genetics like abilities such as clairvoyance tends to be.

Clairaudience can present in a number of ways. In its less prominent states it can appear as muffled sounds, chimes, tones, or even hearing messages in daily life. Many people have described psychic openings in which they started hearing the perfect song on the radio, or heard the exact message they needed to while flipping channels on the television, or sat by someone at lunch who was saying exactly what they needed to hear. On some level, these are all synchronicities that show that we are in the flow, or basically that we are where we are supposed to be and doing what we should be doing. On another level, these beginning experiences are training our auditory capabilities and allowing for us to pick up spiritual information.

For many of us, clairaudience begins with sensitive hearing—being able to pick up physical sounds from longer distances. Some of us may begin hearing tones, chimes, music, muffled talking, or experience ringing in our ears. In significant awakenings such as top-down awakenings and Kundalini awakenings, whole choirs, gospels, and even spoken poetry or verse in various languages can occur.

Because our physical ears are extremely important to not only hearing but physical balance, any ringing in the ears, pain, or discomfort should be looked at by a doctor to rule out any physical issues.

Clairaudience is often a source of interest for many. Because it is not often the first psychic ability to open, and only in rare cases is dominant, this ability can create a great deal of chaos for us because hearing things in our culture is always associated with being mentally ill. Even the most experienced and book-learned person who develops this ability can question their sanity if they start to hear choirs. As this ability grows we may notice specific tones linked with chakras opening; specific music associated with certain guides, energies, or spirits; or even our own song or theme music. Each of us has a song that is usually fairly simple that provides insight into our core personality and power. We can then sing it to feel more in our power.

Clairaudience that comes on suddenly can be extremely uncomfortable or painful. When we begin to open our clairaudient capabilities, we will be noticed by other energies that wish to communicate with us. They will then try to tune in and communicate with us, causing pain because of the intensity of their frequency. We may even find ourselves in the position of constantly being tuned like a radio by different energies that wish to communicate. Since some of these energies are so dissimilar to our own, this creates pain, often in our physical ears. The best thing to do in this situation is to acknowledge that it is happening and communicate through a middle man—a guide or spirit we are already familiar with to either shut down whomever is contacting us or act as a liaison so that we do not have to experience being tuned. Others simply acknowledge this is occurring and meditate, asking for whomever is contacting us to speed up the process of tuning. This way is more painful but much briefer in duration. Gradually, we will be tuned and capable of interacting and listening to many different vibrations or energies and the experience will be less painful, at least until we are contacted by something with an even higher frequency.

It is easy to get out of balance with this ability. When it begins opening we suddenly get much more auditory input than we are used to and it can be difficult to differentiate between physical and spiritual hearing. This differentiation is important to ground us in this reality and to be aware of what may be crossing our boundaries. It is very important because of cultural associations with mental illness and hearing things to remain grounded and functional in reality with this psychic opening. Mental hospitals are filled with people who hear things and who may or may not be going through a spiritual awakening.

Symptoms of clairaudience are simple—hearing things that are out of the normal range of hearing. Sensitive hearing, chimes, bells, buzzing, music, tones and notes, synchronicities of sound, buzzing around the head, headaches, and ear aches are all symptoms of this ability opening. The appreciation for music blossoms with this ability—we may feel or experience sound in a new manner. Sound can be extraordinarily healing and we may find ourselves gravitating toward healing through sound, listening to music to find healing, and eventually hearing the sounds that comprise our very selves and the world. We may find everything too loud and discover an aversion to television, radio, music we once listened to, and even loud talking. At this stage we may find silence difficult to come by and very healing for us.

For some of us this ability is full of joy and vibrations that run through the body. Hearing of choirs in meditation, feeling tones and music throughout the body, and learning how to be tuned to higher and higher vibrations and "radio stations" is an interesting and powerful experience. Many of us who have reached this point later in our spiritual journey will have the ability to deeply surrender to keep the pain from being tuned to a minimum.

The experience of clairaudience can be a great sea of music, an ocean of sounds and understandings of the vibratory nature of the universe that is astonishing. Feelings of oneness, interspecies communication, and hearing the music of divinity are part of clairaudient capabilities. This ability allows us when it is fully open to feel the music and be a part of the flow of the divine in a unique way that is difficult to put into words. We discover in fact that there is a current of music that makes up divine flow and that each animal, person, being, plant, and everything else that makes up our world has its own current of sound. The world will have newly rich sounds, tones, and be experienced in a flow that creates heightened states of joy and bliss that flow in and out of the fully awakened Clairaudient. The access to understandings from a variety of sources allows for great creative potential and deepening understanding of the Self and relation to the universe.

If you are undergoing this type of psychic opening and are experiencing any pain, please go see a doctor to rule out physical trauma or other issues. Your ears are sensitive, and any physical problems such as infections, tinnitus, or nerve issues can create severe problems in physical balance, headaches, and other issues.

EXERCISE: Understanding Clairaudience

- If you have this ability, how strong is it? If you are noticing mild symptoms that are curiosities, start bringing awareness to them.
- Do they happen in certain situations?
- How often do they happen?
- Can you link them to anything? Situations, events, people, meditative states, animals, nature?
- Some people hear or are more sensitive with one ear. Which ear is more open?
- Many people hear music associated with divinity, heavenly choirs, angels, guides, and deities. Let yourself open to this music.
- If you can hear it faintly, say so, and breathe in through your mouth and slowly out.
- Now breathe in and picture yourself breathing out through your ears.
- Feel if there are any blocks. Sometimes we subconsciously block this capability off because it is overwhelming or we fear being crazy. What would happen if you opened this ability fully?
- If you want to, say out loud that you are ready for this ability to fully open.
- Again, breathe in through the mouth and out through the ears. You do not have to blow hard or hold your nose. Imagine a line or a funnel going in through your mouth and going from ear to ear.
- Now, breathe softly in through your ears and out through your ears.
- While breathing in and out through your ears, imagine the crown/top of your head opening as well as the back of your occiput (the third eye circuit).
- Breathe in and out through the ears with the crown and occiput open and bringing in sound and light.
- The world, the divine, each animal has its own music. Focus on an aspect you would really like to hear and ask for it to reveal its song.
- We each have our own "power song"—tones or a song, usually fairly simple, that is who we truly are. Ask for it to reveal itself. Begin humming it when it is appropriate—when we feel depressed, lethargic, or simply need that connection to ourselves.

If you are in a state of overwhelm, pain, or having other issues with your clairaudient abilities, realize that this can come from blocking this ability. If you are doing this recognize what you are doing and realize that you are causing yourself pain. Clairaudience is an ability that can create overwhelm and it is natural to subconsciously block this ability either out of cultural fears of being crazy or because we simply live in a very loud culture and do not want or are not prepared for more noise stimulus. If you are overwhelmed, finding a quiet place to process as mentioned above and to tune into the subtle noises of clairaudience may be all you need to do.

Overwhelm and pain can also come from being tuned by strong energies that likely do not realize you are in pain and are trying so hard to communicate that they are up-setting your physical ears. You can choose to either shut down an energy that wishes to communicate, open more or be tuned more readily, or completely open this capability through using a spiritual intermediary.

Ear ringing is a common complaint of people who are undergoing clauradient awakenings. This often feels like buzzing or vibrating. Again, this can also be tinnitus or Ménière's disease, both physical manifestations, or can have both physical and spir-itual causative root factors.

When this ability opens up more, some people begin to hear talking, singing, or other sounds like chimes or gongs. Crystal, a 19-year-old college student, heard crystal bowls. She then heard low whispering and began to have dreams of light beings talking with her. Hers was a natural progression and opening with no resistance, and she had no issues other than a curiosity about what was going on and an openness to her newly acquired abilities.

For others this process can be more painful, especially in the case of beings from other dimensions or parts of the universe. Todd had a loud screeching noise in his ear for two months when he visited me. He had been to doctors, a therapist, and another acupuncturist in that time. Todd was not particularly spiritual, or following a spiritual path, but he had gone to a Gong bath the previous week to impress a girl. He was somewhat open and had gone to meditation class a few times and did yoga because he was a marathon runner and his coach told him yoga would be good for him. The doctors had found nothing, the therapist suggested it was stress, and the acupuncturist found some energetic blockages and drained energy in the appropriate channel, which helped some. After the acupuncture appointment, the screeching turned into a sort of tuning, where he felt different tones of screeching. After evaluation, I found that he, like many others who develop this ability, was being tuned like a radio. He wanted to stop rather than open this ability, and so I intermediated with what was causing it to shut it down and stop the pain.

Ear ringing in spiritual awakenings is an opening, but it is also a recalibration, a tuning of our energy to whomever wants to speak with us. Most commonly we will develop this to hear spirits of humans that have passed—their vibration is similar to ours. In other cases, it is a being or energy that is much different energy than ours. These beings do not usually understand that they are causing us pain. They have found that we can hear them, or are close to being able to hear them, and are trying to tune us to their radio station, their frequency. This becomes more painful with higher-level beings or simply energies that are much different than ours. Two vibrations must merge, and ours must be raised or changed. For non-human energies, they do not seem to understand that they are harming us. It is like turning up a radio too loud—they are tuning up and down the radio dial and playing with the volume so we can hear them. Often they try too hard and we are left in pain.

For those of you with pleasant sensations—ringing, chimes, choirs, etc., just acknowledging them and accepting them is enough. We don't really need to do anything. Just accept and tell the energy that we are open to communication (if we are). If it is an opening that is painful, caustic, or we sense a presence that we are not comfortable communicating with, there are several things you can do.

EXERCISE: Recalibrating Clairaudience

- The first is to focus on the sensation. Put all of your focus on it. Yes, I realize it is likely uncomfortable.
- If you can, get a sense of what is trying to communicate with you.
- Ask them directly to make the opening more gradual, say that you are in pain, or that you are not ready to communicate with them. Often this will not work, but it is worth a try. It is likely if you are in pain that you are not able to communicate with them any better than they are with you.
- Utilize an intermediary. An intermediary is a spirit that you trust, an energy in spirit form that is already a teacher, guide, or protector that you feel safe with. Ask this intermediary for help. If it says "yes," you can ask the intermediary to shut it down. You can also ask if you should shut it down.
- If you wish to open to the energy attempting to communicate and recalibrate you, use the intermediary as a go-between. Let the intermediary communicate that this energy is causing you physical pain. Communicate whatever else you wish through the intermediary. This should immediately cut down on physical symptoms, because the energy will not have to try so hard.
- Eventually, you will not need the intermediary and will directly hear the energy.

During the clairaudience and the tuning process please realize that not all energy is benevolent or loving. Be safe and use an intermediary to go between you, to instruct you, or to block energies if needed. It is common new-age understanding that everything that is spiritual is filled with love and light. This is not true. Even the most loving and light-filled angel can also be fierce, and may not care about our personal health and safety.

Once you have been tuned to a specific energy, a specific frequency or "dial" on the radio, other energies will notice and communicate with you. This can be overwhelming. Use the intermediary until you are more comfortable with this ability. You do not have to listen to everything that comes to you. If a telemarketer calls you on the phone, you likely have no issue hanging up. Apply the same logic here. With all sensitivities, if you work with them long enough, they open enough so that they no longer cause you pain and merge with other abilities so that it is easier and less painful to notice and be noticed by the spirit world.

Claircoersion

Claircoersion is a little-known psychic ability. It is the ability to energetically affect the outcome or inclinations of people and places. Often this is a subconscious capability and is quite natural for many leaders, gurus, and teachers. People with this psychic capability understand people and situations like an Empath or Clairsentient, but they manipulate the situation for their own benefit. They are able to subconsciously get others to change their opinions, stances, and even core concepts of Self by their abilities. This can be an interesting ability to have, and it is not easily developed if we do not naturally have claircoersive tendencies. An awakened human being would rarely have interest in coercing others, and when we go through any type of awakening we will have a certain sort of magnetism that draws the appropriate people to us naturally.

The people who have this ability often do it subconsciously. They are great orators, teachers, and leaders. Others work to develop this ability, and many great alchemists, magicians, and energy workers consciously choose to pursue this ability to have control over others.

If you have this ability, be aware of it. When you notice yourself utilizing it, stop yourself. If you are naturally good at claircoersion, you already likely have other sensitivities and psychic abilities. Open your other abilities, focus on developing yourself through a daily spiritual practice and you will develop a magnetism that will naturally inspire people.

Claircognizance

Claircognizance is clear knowing. It is a fairly common psychic ability, but it is underutilized and underdeveloped by many of us because we do not listen to the information because it does not come from a logical place. This ability causes us to know information without necessarily knowing where it came from. Claircognizance can be information about the past, present, future, and about ourselves, our family, or even society. With this ability we will know that we should not go out to our mailbox right now (and will later discover that our neighbors were arguing just then), or will take a different route to work or school than usual, later discovering that there was an accident or heavy traffic that morning on our usual route.

This ability also allows us to know about the past and future. The Claircognizant can look at someone and realize that they cheated on their spouse without knowing any other information about them. They may meet someone and instinctively know that they will be a well-known author one day.

This is an excellent ability to have, and it is rarely overwhelming. The only issue that comes up with this ability is the weirdness about knowing information about someone that you wish you didn't, and the self-doubt that comes from not understanding this ability. In rare cases, some Claircognizants know information that they rather wouldn't, such as knowing when people are going to die. This can understandably be difficult knowledge, and many Claircognizants struggle with knowledge and if they should tell the people the information they know. In other cases the Claircognizant may simply know useful and beneficial information, such as when a family member is going to get a raise or when they are in danger of some sort.

If you are Claircognizant, realize that it can provide great benefit for you and your life. Recognize when you receive information that comes from this ability and fully listen to it. You do not need to necessarily act on it, but recognize that it is valuable information and is coming to you for a reason. If you are receiving information about others it is rarely ethical to tell them. Even if you are looking at someone and you know they have cancer it is not your responsibility to tell them. All information we receive is through the lens of our own experience, and it is unethical as well as egocentric to think that we may always be right or that the person we know information about is supposed to learn this information from us. This is a valuable understanding for all psychic abilities. It is difficult for even the most experienced psychic to know what information is coming from their own ego and wounding patterns and what is pure psychic and spiritual information. As we awaken we understand that all of us have wounds, spirits that surround us, and information that we probably should know. Most of us do not want to know this information. If we did, we would go to a healer, a psychic, or a physician to learn about it.

Clairalience

Clairalience is the ability to smell beyond the physical senses. It is a less common ability, but one that can naturally develop and opens with other abilities. I have only met one person who has had this as a dominant ability—he created perfumes and essential oils as a profession. This ability commonly begins with being able to smell things from distances, like a patient who described being distracted by smelling the steak house that was a mile away from his work. Some of us with this ability can distinguish subtle differences in scents in a particular dish, perfume, soap, or other material. Most common of the spiritual smelling is particular scents not associated with any physical reason such as spirits, guides, or deities. The most common report of this is smells associated with deceased loved ones that signify their presence, such as smelling your father's cologne, grandmother's cookies, or tobacco smoke from a cousin.

As this ability opens, it either develops into specific smells for certain types of spirits—such as lavender or rose for light beings and smoke, sulphur, or burning smell for dark energies, or smells associated with a specific spirit, such as smelling roses with the presence of Mother Mary or an incense smell with Kuan Yin. Others have reported smelling different dimensions, layers of reality, and even angelic realms. This ability naturally opens, and can be accentuated by associating different smells with different experiences you may have.

Clairgustance

This is one of the least common abilities to open. This is clear tasting, and it is an ability that seems to only show up when tied to the other senses. This is also an ability that creates synesthesia, meaning that people have reported tasting air, smells, or even visuals.

This ability has never been reported as dominant, and tends to come and go. Beyond feeling temporarily overwhelmed or gagging on a taste, there are rarely any difficulties with this ability. This ability will open naturally with other abilities if it opens at all.

Mediumship and Channeling

Mediumship is a unique psychic ability and can either develop on its own or with other abilities. Mediums are connectors to spirits, beings, and other energies. Some Mediums are also Channels who knowingly or unknowingly will allow energies into their bodies. It is common for Mediums to also be Empaths, Clairvoyants, or have other psychic abilities. Mediumship is a strong psychic awakening. It can to some degree be developed through the opening of other abilities such as empathy, but it largely is passed down through family lineage.

This is an ability that can be extremely overwhelming for those of us who are natural Mediums and do not know or have the proper tools to develop boundaries with it, and is the most common ability by natural psychics to want shut down. Conscious Mediums are aware of their abilities, how to utilize them, and even can form the ability to draw specific spirits, energies, and beings into themselves. Unconscious Mediums may have some idea of their abilities, but they are taken over by whatever they are bringing in to their body for periods of time. Unconscious Mediums have no recollection of events that transpired during the time they took on the energy, and may be aware of losing time or have great fatigue from the experience.

There are also other types of mediumship including plastic (or physical) Mediums, whose physical features will change. A famous plastic medium is John of God, whose facial features will change considerably while channeling energies. There are also mental Mediums, who are able to communicate through thoughts or take on the thoughts of others, and emotional Mediums, who communicate and take on the emotions of spirits.

Many use the terms Medium and Channel interchangeably, but there are some differences between the two. The most important differentiation is goals and natural tendencies of the Medium or Channel. Mediums mostly work with spirits of deceased humans or beings that are going through the death process. Many Mediums are natural psychopomps, which means that they assist in guiding souls to the appropriate afterlife. Channels work with spiritual teachers, beings, Ascended Masters, angels, and deities. Channels are focused on spiritual growth and often bring messages. Channels may work with one being (such as Jane Roberts channeling Seth) or will be a messenger for a group or collective, such as the channelings of Abraham or the Ascended Masters. Some channels also work with darker, demonic, or deceased human energies, carrying on their messages to the world.

The method of taking on energy may vary from the Medium and the Channel as well. Many Mediums take on the energy of the spirit or will partially merge with one, taking the energy into their physical body. When Mediums become stronger they can develop boundaries and choose to only partially merge, fully take on the spirit or deity, or keep themselves completely separate and just relay information. Although mediumship is typically with spirits of deceased humans, once skilled we can draw down energy into ourselves of deities, elementals, and other spiritual beings.

A Channel works by receiving information and energy through their crown chakra and third eye. Although some Channels merge similar to Mediums, many Channels are simply a vessel for information coming through. This information and energy coming through can be quite strong and overwhelming. The Channel will relay the information and energy they receive through writing, speaking, painting, dance, or other forms of expression. The information of the Channel is always colored by the experience of the human it is being channeled through. This means that although the information may come from a high vibration or highly spiritual being, the vessel it is coming through (the human) may be angry, or may be in the throes of an ego-awakening. This will have an impact on the information being relayed.

Downloading

Downloading is the taking in of energies outside of the self. This can be done through channeling—meaning resonating and taking in energies from a particular spirit, entity, or energy group. This can also be done through accessing global and cosmic energies and allowing for their heightened energy to run through us. The taking in of global and cosmic energies can be very unconscious, such as in the case of feeling heightened energy during a full moon, or can be entirely conscious, such as working with a specific deity and calling them into the physical body. Downloads can also occur simply when we are ready for them to through divine timing. This happens when we have transcended a specific layer of conditioned reality or are ready to move forward in our spiritual path and we will get a burst of energy from an outside source.

Downloads contain not only energy from a specific source, but they also carry with them understandings and knowledge from that source. If it is in the case of channeling an individual, it may be a specific message. If it is calling a deity in, it may be a message or body memory of the power of that deity that can be carried forward in daily life. If it is a download from global or cosmic sources, it can create an experience of transcending several floors of the spiritual elevator in a short period of time.

This will result in greater understandings and huge shifts within a very short period. This is also known as "upgrading" the spiritual system. We now have the opportunity to process and release energy from whatever layer of conditioned reality we were in previously to upgrade to the layer and floor we are at now. It is then our responsibility to stabilize this experience. The fear of massive downloads or rising up suddenly a few floors on the spiritual elevator can be deeply disconcerting, as the understandings and experiences we had of Self, family, and the world can be drastically different from the way they were before the upgrade. This can result in emotional and physical upheaval. It is our responsibility to surrender to these experiences if they are out of our control, or to get the physical help and resources (counseling, for example) to restabilize.

Being a Channel or Medium is often overwhelming and can prove to be difficult to find out how to work with it in a society that would normally put Mediums or Channels in a psychiatric hospital. There is also the difficulty of having a real and strong psychic capability in a society where there are thousands of aspirational Channels and Mediums—people with no capabilities who are either pretending or aspire to be the next John of God or Medium on television. It is difficult to get help and the appropriate tools when we are struggling with psychic abilities when there are countless fakes and most of the material out there is for aspirational Mediums who have little to no psychic abilities.

Many of us close off our abilities at the age of six or seven when we find out that our "imaginary friends" are no longer appropriate and that our abilities make us strange or weird. This ability then will reemerge anywhere from the teenage years to early thirties powerfully. With the ability of mediumship often comes a great deal of fear—of death, of spirits attracted to us, of being so fundamentally different than others who do not have this ability. With both the Medium and Channel, there is a strong fear of being found out and needing to hide this ability. Many turn to drugs, alcohol, or other addictions in an effort to stop this ability.

Symptoms of sleep issues, fear and anxiety, loss of identity, anger at abilities, headache, and other body pains are common for this group. The more resistant we are to these abilities, the more painful mentally and physically the symptoms are. Without boundaries, many of us who are natural Mediums and Channels are overrun by opportunistic energies who wish to use us as a vessel or wish to have us help them. Although this ability can be extremely powerful and take us far in our awakening process, without the proper tools a wide variety of very real physical, emotional, and spiritual repercussions may occur.

These abilities are not something that can be shut down. What will stop many of the physical symptoms is to stop resisting your abilities. Make peace and accept that you are a Channel or Medium. Let go of your emotional baggage, the anger and fear that come with having strong abilities, and focus on clearing yourself so you can be a "hollow bone" or empty vessel for these energies. This way they will not affect you as much, will flow through you, and may even become a source of wonder and joy for you.

Most importantly, develop boundaries with your abilities. Many spirits and energies take advantage of the medium/channel, disrupting their sleep, work, and coming at all hours of the day or night. Do not be bullied. Enlist help from spiritual helpers or through prayer to give protection and form a boundary around you until spirits and beings know that you mean business. Do this especially before you go to sleep.

For a Medium or Channel, working with an experienced, knowledgeable, and understanding mentor is crucial. There are many things to learn with strong psychic abilities, and many of them cannot be related in a book. Individual guidance through a true medium is often imperative in learning how to operate in a world where you see too much and are overwhelmed by spiritual experiences. Although I suggest a physical teacher, they can be difficult to find. Although some spiritual teachers provide guidance over the Internet, another choice may be to have a spiritual, non-physical teacher. For most of you who are truly struggling you can do the following while you are looking for a physical teacher:

EXERCISE: Establishing a Spiritual Teacher

We all have many non-physical spiritual teachers. You are looking for one to specifically instruct you in how to establish boundaries and teach you about your mediumship and channeling capabilities:

- If you have a form of spiritual support already that you trust and can access (guide, deity, the Universe, angels, etc.) you can call them in.
- If you do not, you can create an internal symbol (any shape, color, sound, texture, etc.) that will come up when the right teacher comes through.
- If you like, you can use both 1 and 2, as well as your gut intuition.

Once you have established calling in spiritual support or creating an internal symbol, proceed.

- Simply ask for the appropriate teacher to come through. Sometimes there can be many things that we get a sense of that may be a teacher, sometimes there are none. If there are none, try again on a day that you are feeling strong and confident. We often do not recognize our teachers out of fear or anxiety.
- It is likely that an energy has come through that you either sense or see. Check to make sure if you feel comfortable with this energy. If you do not, ask them nicely to leave.
- When you get an energy or being that feels right to you, the symbol should show up. If you are checking with spiritual support, ask your spiritual support if this is the right spiritual teacher for you. If they say "yes," proceed. If you do not see the symbol or something in you says "no," ask again for your spiritual teacher to show up.
- When you get to "yes" from your internal sense, the symbol, or spiritual support, you can proceed. Ask for the energy or being to come through as clearly as it can for you right now. Ask it directly if it is the right spiritual teacher to teach you about mediumship and channeling. If it says "yes," ask if it will teach you.
- If it says "yes" to teaching you, introduce yourself and explain your situation. See if the teacher has anything to say back.
- Once you have done so, say "thank you."
- Each day call up this teacher by simply asking them to come through. Ask them what you should know, what you should do. Use your gut intuition as well as their advice to begin developing boundaries and developing your abilities.

Like any developing relationship, it is important to know that receiving knowledge may take time. We may also not fully understand what the teacher is saying. In that case simply write it down. We may also not agree with what the teacher says. In that case, use your gut instinct. You do not have to do anything that goes against your natural instincts. Some days the teacher may not come through, or you may need a physical or different spiritual teacher to instruct you in your life. Go through this process again to access other teachers. It is common in awakenings to construct teachers out of aspects from archetypes and disassociated aspects of Self. We may eventually grow out of that and develop spiritual teachers outside of ourselves.

Kundalini Awakening

True Kundalini awakenings are actually fairly rare. Recently the term Kundalini has been appropriated by the mainstream and anyone going through any type of awakening or spiritual experience considers it a Kundalini awakening. With the advent of Kundalini yoga and Kundalini Reiki and the appropriation of the word Kundalini into popular culture, there is a huge amount of information that is misinformed or uncertain of what a true Kundalini awakening is. Some of us who have had momentary experiences of Kundalini, such as Kundalini stirring or a brief Kundalini experience, rarely understand that a Kundalini awakening is much different. Likewise, those of us who have had a spiritual experience—whether it be simply feeling energy for the first time as in some of the gradual awakenings, having a top-down awakening, or going through an ego awakening—are likely to call what we are going through a Kundalini awakening because we simply do not know any better or the term Kundalini is considered exotic, deep, or important enough that we wish to be going through the experience. The irony of this is that those of us actually going through Kundalini awakenings know that they are extraordinarily difficult and most would not wish the experience on anyone due to the tremendous issues that come with this experience.

Classically, a Kundalini awakening would be considered a "bottom-up" type of awakening. This type of awakening is extremely intense and difficult to navigate through. If we were to use the spiritual elevator metaphor, a Kundalini awakening would be as if we were going from close to ground level or mid-level to near top level within an extremely short period of time. This results in drastic shifts in consciousness, extreme physical symptoms, mental and emotional instability, and an inability to function that can last for months, years, or decades.

When we go through a Kundalini awakening it results in the processing of huge amounts of physical and emotional material in a very short period of time. The conditioned layers of reality that are covering the realized, awakened Self are suddenly ripped off and we have to integrate this abrupt change and deal with the fact that our views of the world have drastically changed. This is not easy on the physical body—which has to not only deal with physically processing both the traumas and blockages within the body from all of the layers that have been removed, but also with Kundalini itself—a divine force that runs through the body like a volcano, moving through blockages as quickly as it can.

For most of us Kundalini lays dormant at the end of the spine like a coiled-up snake. Some of us have varying Kundalini experiences, and a few of us have full-blown Kundalini awakenings. There is a clear differentiation to be had between Kundalini stirrings, Kundalini experiences, and Kundalini awakenings.

Kundalini Stirring

Kundalini stirring is an encounter with Kundalini energy that is mild in nature and short in duration. It allows us to feel consciously our connection to the divine and to have greater understandings that are out of our current realm of experience—such as great amounts of love, feelings of interconnectedness, and realizations about our true nature.

Kundalini stirrings also allow us to temporarily feel the strong current of energy that is Kundalini rise up the spine. Kundalini energy typically stays fairly dormant at the end of the sacrum, and when it stirs, a wave of heat, bliss, orgasms, and deep insight occurs. The experience of Kundalini stirring is momentary. That momentary experience can happen many times over the course of a lifetime, but if it does not go beyond the symptoms described or does not become a permanent experience in our life it is not a Kundalini experience or a Kundalini awakening. However, stirrings can signal Kundalini beginning to awaken. A Kundalini stirring can be a life-changing experience and can deepen our spiritual understandings and our experience of this world from even the momentary access and wisdom we acquire.

Kundalini Experience

A Kundalini experience is a more intense experience of Kundalini. Like the stirring, it is typically momentary although its implications for our life can be long-lasting. A Kundalini experience can happen as part of a Kundalini awakening or it can be a singular experience. It is more intense than a simple feeling, or stirring, of Kundalini energy, which may rise up your back and give you some momentary bliss and then go back into dormancy.

A Kundalini experience is a full-body experience that is quite intense. There would be no hiding this experience. Shaking, crying, moving into full body and hand postures (kriyas and mudras), extreme amounts of energy running through us, feeling of earth energies and the whole world, pain, drastic increases of psychic abilities, profound spiritual realizations, communion with God or other powerful beings, temporary blindness, and extreme overwhelm happen—typically all at the same time.

A Kundalini experience is extremely overwhelming and can last anywhere from a few minutes to a few weeks. During the duration of this experience we are not able to function or act normally to the world. Luckily for most of us this experience only lasts for minutes rather than hours. The Kundalini experience can be a natural part of a Kundalini awakening or can happen without a full Kundalini awakening. Typically, most of us who experience a Kundalini experience without a full awakening have had it occur through energetic transmission from a powerful guru or through attending an intense spiritual workshop, although it can occur from energetic transmission from a place as well.

Although this experience is momentary, it has far-reaching implications for the rest of our lives. We will never be the same after. The experience of such profound energy has changed us—our outlook, our beliefs, our understanding of the world. Since this energy has moved through us, it has quickly opened up channels and destroyed old beliefs, blocks, and baggage we have carried. It also suggests that we are likely to open to a full Kundalini awakening, if we have not already.

Kundalini Awakenings

The main thing that differentiates the Kundalini awakening from the experience or stirring is the intensity and the permanence. A Kundalini awakening is permanent and refers to the permanent experience of the energy flowing through our bodies. It is not a momentary experience, or a few experiences. A true Kundalini awakening is a process that never ends. It does not go back to a dormant state. When we experience a Kundalini awakening it is a force that is constantly felt in the body and we are forever going through the experience.

Kundalini awakening is like a wave, constantly bringing up new material to process. It leads us deeper and deeper down the proverbial rabbit hole until it is able to run up to our brain and form a fully completed circuit through our center and incorporate every organ, every cell, and every part of our body. Kundalini energy works its way the best it can through us to clear out blockages so it can run fully through us without resistance. It begins to do this by ascending up the spine, releasing the material that is stored within the chakra system. Once it has ascended to the brain it can both meet the flow of the chakras above the head as well as go through the entire body.

There are less active stages of Kundalini, but it is always with us and can always be sensed. It does not go away. Many people report having a Kundalini awakening in 1978 and 1995 and then two days ago. These are stirrings or experiences of Kundalini, not an awakening. A Kundalini awakening is a permanent awakening of the energy. It acts like a wave—and can be as intense as Kundalini experiences or more dormant and gentle. It will work its way through our blockages and drastically change everything about ourselves and our world. With a Kundalini awakening the energy is always with us and is always doing something. It is a permanent spiritual process that has been started and will never stop.

A Kundalini awakening is like a full volcanic eruption. When we undergo this type of awakening we will feel immense intense amounts of heat throughout our bodies, especially in the spine. Some of us experience Kundalini awakenings as cold, but this is in the minority. This heat or cold of Kundalini has to do with the channels that it cycles through.

Kundalini Channels

There are three types of Kundalini awakenings: Sushumna, Ida, and Pingala. Kundalini as a force can actually arise out of one (or more) of these channels and will determine many of the symptoms and issues that arise during the course of our awakening.

Sushumna is the central channel (it runs through our spine). Sushumna begins in the first chakra—specifically in the sexual organs and the area between the end of the coccyx (the pointy end of the tailbone) and your anus and goes out through the seventh chakra (the top of your head). When Kundalini is flowing through the Sushumna correctly we will feel constant energy flow, like a wave going through from the tip of our coccyx to the top of our head. We will also eventually feel energy like a vertical column extending from the top of the head and through our genitals toward our feet. Energy will flow like a current not only through this vertical column but through Ida, Pingala, and through all of our organs and cells when it is fully activated. This is the ideal state for Kundalini—free flow.

However, energy can be blocked in the Sushumna by one of the chakras or unconscious information not yet processed (past lives, emotions, ancestral history, family, etc.). The force of Kundalini will rise up until it hits a barrier. When it hits that barrier it will rise again and again, hitting that barrier until the barrier releases. Picture waves on the beach hitting a rock. The larger the waves and the bigger the rock, the more force and the more violent the symptoms can be. This is especially true if the lower chakras are blocked or partially blocked. Since Kundalini is such a large and dynamic force it will rise with power, and the lower the blockage the less chance it has to dissipate. When there is room to partially go through the blockage (picture a smaller rock) the symptoms are not as dramatic.

Kundalini is often not activated in the Sushumna first—it is activated in Pingala instead. Pingala is a current of energy on the right side of the body. It begins in the second chakra and goes up into the nostril, meeting Sushumna and Ida at the third eye. Pingala is fire and represented by the sun. This energy gives us our mental processes/conscious thought.

If Kundalini originated in this channel the symptoms are typically severe and heat oriented. Ideally, Kundalini will flow through Sushumna, and not only the central channel but also balanced flow through Ida and Pingala. If Kundalini energy is focused on Pingala, there will be a lack of energy in Ida, and the full circuit of energy flow in the Sushumna, going from first to seventh chakra, will not happen. When this occurs we will primarily have energy circulating from our second chakra to our third eye without the benefit of release through our first chakra or seventh (crown and root). We will have a tendency to overthink, and there will be a huge amount of heat and some dysfunction in the first chakra since energy is not properly circulating there. If we have a Pingala-type Kundalini awakening, we have an immense amount of heat circulating from our own issues and wounds trying to release as well as the heat and force of Kundalini itself. This force and processing cannot cycle properly and is trapped within the body. Only through proper redirection of energy and working with the first chakra will this energy begin ascending through the proper channels.

Ida is on the left side of our bodies. It circles around Sushumna, going up into our nostril and meets Pingala and Sushumna at the third eye. This is moon energy. It is cold or cool energy. This energy gives us joy and desire. It is about emotions and conscious desires or wishes. This type of Kundalini awakening is rare to have first, and will be a cold type of awakening, with chills and feelings of cold or alternating cold and heat.

If Ida is out of balance, or if Kundalini is activated through Ida, there will be an extreme of emotions, a flickering between joy and bliss and isolation/depression and despair. There will also be more sensations of energetic circulation and physical issues on the left side of the body. In this type of awakening we must surrender to our emotional selves and the force of Kundalini, allowing for our first and second chakras to open. This will allow for Kundalini to properly cycle through the Sushumna.

Eventually Kundalini will ascend not only through the Sushumna but through Ida and Pingala, as well as through the front and back of the body. In the beginning we are likely to experience Kundalini just in the spinal column moving upward. When it reaches the brain it will meet with top-down energies. This is when we begin to experience energy moving both up and down. We are then able to experience energy from the "heavens"—spiritual energy from the eighth chakra and above pouring through us, as well as from energy coming from the Earth into our first chakra. We then can experience this flow of divine energy, the activation of microchakras in our hands and feet, and the clearing out and flowing of Kundalini through our organs, meridians, and every cell in our bodies. When Kundalini is fully activated we feel this energy flow through our entire body as well as the field surrounding us.

In the previous section we talked about more gradual openings where either individual chakras, or specific life experiences, would open one by one, or a few at a time. A Kundalini awakening will open up all of the chakras and all of the stored wounds and patterns in those chakras and that region of the body. For some of us, this will involve our first chakra opening, and we will experience everything—fears, ancestral patterns, family issues, and extreme emotions—that were being held in that chakra. All of this is coming up for the purpose of processing and clearing out that area of our body. If the first chakra is blocked, symptoms like intense local pain (such as in low back, genitals, lower digestive tract, and legs), burning, and energetic symptoms moving through the local as well as whole body will occur. If the first chakra only is opened, the Kundalini fire will be extremely intense. Patients have reported burning through seats of their pants, intense orgasms and huge variances in sex drive, and overwhelming fears coming up if this area only opens.

Kundalini rises like a thermometer up the spine until it meets restriction. There are waves that come with Kundalini awakenings, meaning that the Kundalini will rise like a wave up the spine, releasing as much as it can in the chakras it has risen to meet. When it hits a significant block (for example, rising through the first, second, and to the third chakra) it will increase activity at the third chakra to open it up. Kundalini will also be activated and continue to process patterns and issues in the first and second chakra as well, but the focus of this energy is clearing blockage so it can ascend. In this way, it focuses on the highest chakra it can ascend to.

We can look at the specific chakra openings to see possible symptoms, but for most of us they include pain that is localized. So if the activity was rising to a blocked third chakra we would experience physical symptoms in our stomach, liver, spleen, pancreas, and diaphragm, as well as immense amounts of heat and energy flow going through our first through third chakras. As the block that the Kundalini runs across is released, it will then proceed up the body until it finds another block, or will rise fully up the spine to the top of the head.

Kundalini has more active and dormant cycles. During the active phase we can liken it to the crest or peak of a wave—it is strong energy that is aggressive and forceful, ramming through the chakra system and in the same manner quickly releasing physical and emotional issues as well as the conditioned layers of reality. In the more subtle waves this energy can be calmer like the energy of water after a storm. This energy is still felt and working, but it is doing so in a less forceful manner. The subtler waves can be difficult, as when the Kundalini is really active it can make its way up the spine through sheer force, but when it is calmer or more dormant it is likely to stay within a localized area, creating lower-level symptoms that will be not as dramatic or possibly life-threatening as the more active stages, but will be constant, dull, and annoying.

What are the symptoms of a Kundalini awakening? Beyond the volcanic heat, we are likely to experience awareness and sensation with energy going through our bodies. This energy is divine energy and is much different than a concept of "qi" or "prana."

Qi, Prana, Shakti, and Kundalini

Kundalini is divine force, divine will within the body. It contains the connection to our own divine nature but also the entirety of divine flow. It is a force within us that is not of us, a force that has created us yet remains dormant in most of us. This means that there is no manipulation to be had of this force—we are not in control of it. We will either surrender to it or we will not. Kundalini is how divinity fills us up, and it is a much greater power than the Self. It is the entire power of the cosmos, divinity, differentiated for us as an individual, complete with divine understandings and the full ability to awaken. In a Kundalini awakening it will work to awaken us fully and to clear everything that is blocked within us until we are a clear vessel in which divinity can flow unrestricted. Kundalini is the basic force that formulates our human bodies. It does this through creating a unique grid, a blueprint of energy when we are formed embryologically. Kundalini is an extension of Shakti, the force and blueprint of the cosmos.

Shakti is divine force flowing through the Universe as a whole. It is considered the feminine force of the Universe along with its mate, Shiva, which is the male counterpart. Shakti becomes Kundalini within the human form. When Kundalini awakens fully (meaning that every cell of our body is awakened) we are now a part of Shiva and Shakti, and the power that is not only Kundalini energy that has individually formed us but the pure form of energy that infiltrates the Universe and cosmos. When we are able to fully recognize Kundalini and Shakti as no longer being separate forces we can feel the connection and oneness to the divine as well as having the direct experience of our basic energetic formation.

Everyone has had the flows and energetic organization of Shiva, Shakti, and Kundalini. Most of us do not experience these forces due to our stage of awakening and they lie dormant in us as simply potential. Shiva and Shakti become Kundalini within the body. Kundalini then becomes the milder forces of qi or prana within the body and flows through the energetic channels (also referred to as nadis or meridians) of the body.

Qi or prana make up our energetic and material world and are more easily accessible and first noticed on the journey of awakening. They are accessed through the elements—air, earth, fire, water, our experiences, and the food that we take in. Everything in this world that we can experience is composed of qi. Everyone can experience qi if they are willing to, even if we are not ready to admit or acknowledge our spiritual nature—the air we breathe, the food we eat, the exchange of emotions and energy during sexual intercourse are all qi. Everything in the Universe is made up of qi/prana. It is life force, and it runs through everything.

Qi is readily accessible for those of us who are interested in working with it. Martial artists, yogis, and healers such as Reiki practitioners and acupuncturists all work with qi effectively to allow for a state of flow and balance in the human body. Anyone can access qi if they are beyond the sleeper state. Accessing Kundalini even for a moment places us on a spiritual path if we were not on one already. Qi is our everyday reality— it is what we eat, what we wear, the air we breathe. Kundalini is a primordial force of divinity and divine organization. Depending on who we are we will have some if not quite a bit of control over qi through diet, emotional regulation, exercise, and moderation in our lives. Kundalini is a force that is of pure divinity and is not something that can be reasoned with or controlled. The only way to work with Kundalini is to surrender.

Symptoms of a Kundalini Awakening

Sudden realizations, knowledge, and circulating energy through the chakras, acupuncture meridians, and a feeling of energy circulating the spine are the most common feature of Kundalini awakenings. Kriyas and mudras (spontaneous finger, hand, and yogic body postures) will occur. Body twitches and spontaneous movement of all sorts will happen during a Kundalini awakening due to the immense amount of energy circulating the body and the body releasing blocks and trauma through movement. Individual chakra-related dysfunctions and bandhas (body locks in a specific area to move energy through) also occur. Kundalini awakenings involve immense amounts of energy cycling—our hands, fingers, and body will need to dance and move. Qi moving through the body results in mild twitching or release of heat with smaller currents of electrical-type feelings. Kundalini is like a volcano erupting and we will have no control over the movements, and there will be very specific postures and hand positions our bodies go into.

Other symptoms including extreme physical symptoms and near-death experiences are typical. A near-death experience can be a trigger for Kundalini and other spiritual awakenings, but significant illness that is unexplainable is very common in Kundalini awakenings. During a Kundalini awakening our bodies are flooded with material to process—individual experiences, family, societal, ancestral, past lives, and all of the conditioned layers of reality. These experiences contain past illness and death. The system of someone undergoing a Kundalini awakening is often depleted, overwhelmed, and the immune system cannot keep up so we may contract an illness that our body is no longer able to fight or we may be processing a past illness or trauma that we were not able to process at the time it occurred.

The near-death experience is also unfortunately a necessary breakthrough and initiation for us when we are undergoing a Kundalini awakening. This experience allows for us to rapidly gain perspective, spiritual understanding, and stop identifying with our physical bodies. The fear of death, which is one of our greatest fears that keep us within the confines of conditioned reality, is processed and released. On some level many of us experiencing Kundalini awakenings realize that we asked for the near-death experience either because we were extremely suffering or understood that it was necessary for our process (or both).

During a Kundalini awakening we have huge spiritual shifts within a short period of time. Increasing psychic abilities, seeing grids, patterns, snakes, and other spiritual understandings will shift quickly and dramatically our view of ourselves and the world. Huge physical shifts, extreme personality changes, and mental imbalances are also typical. It is common for us when we go through a Kundalini awakening to get divorces, separate from friends and family, move, feel waves of depression as well as bliss, and in general feel fear about what is going on. A total personality and life change is not uncommon. Who we were and who we are now are totally different things, which can cause a lot of confusion, grief, and fear in ourselves and our loved ones.

We disassociate or feel separate from ourselves, feeling that there is so much going on mentally, physically, and emotionally for us to comprehend, so we distance ourselves or leave our bodies in an attempt to slow down or leave the process. This is a trauma response and at times is necessary for survival during this type of awakening. Kundalini awakenings are the most likely to result in drug abuse (with Shamanic and psychic awakenings coming in a close second).

Along with pain associated with specific chakras opening, pain in the spine and headaches will occur. Other physical symptoms including nausea and vomiting, inability to eat anything but very simple or bland foods, needing to eat on a regular schedule, or needing to fast or slow intake of food. Insomnia, somnolence, energy fluctuations from feeling extremely energized, almost manic with insomniac tendencies to extreme exhaustion, body heaviness, and depression symptoms, cognitive issues including brain fog, inability to process anything spiritual, and concentration issues come and go. Hormonal imbalances, slowing and speeding of heart rate, and muscle and joint pain are consistently reported.

Feelings of oneness, waves of bliss, and spontaneous orgasms are also part of Kundalini awakenings. A Kundalini awakening allows for us to see through the illusion of separateness and to feel divine flow of energy. Joy and bliss flood the body in waves. Eventually the symptoms of clearing, chakra symptoms, and related issues give way as we are able to process the material. What we are left with are the spontaneous movements, heat circulation, feelings of oneness and spiritual realization, and the feelings of oneness yet differentiation and a return to a sense of new normalcy if the process is seen through. When we consciously process the material that is left we can work in concert with Kundalini. The greater flow that Kundalini has, the wider and longer pathways it can work through, the less physical, emotional, mental, and spiritual imbalances remain. We are left with a fully awakened state, great waves of energy through us, and the creative force of the Universe running through us. There are still times of difficulty—new patterns, experiences, and processing that need to occur—but these can be approached through understanding rather than fear.

How do we get from the difficulties of having to process layers and layers of material to full cycling of Kundalini energies? The first thing that often calms us down is to have a name to what we are experiencing. When we are able to realize that we are going through a Kundalini awakening some of the fear may abate. Once you realize what you are going through, stop resisting. This is fairly simple advice but can be life saving. Many of us going through Kundalini awakenings are full of fear and try to stop the flow because we are afraid of the extreme nature of our situation. We feel out of control, and that is understandable. When we realize that we never were in control it may be funny to look back and see how desperately we were hanging on to the illusion that we were in control, but for now we feel fear, anger, and likely physically and mentally unwell.

So let go. Let things flow. Realize what is happening and consciously release whatever is coming up. Go see an Ayurvedic practitioner, CranioSacral Therapist, acupuncturist, Shaman, or Advanced Energy Worker that knows what a Kundalini awakening is. Test them to see how extensive their knowledge is. If they do not know the intricacies of what is happening or what a Kundalini awakening entails but are interested in helping, explain the situation and see how they react to it. Explain that you are vulnerable, reactive, and ask for extra time at your first appointment so they can properly evaluate you. Bring them this book or other material about Kundalini so they can figure out how to recognize this in their other patients. Practitioners like these can be life saving. They can help you to release, balance energy, and increase your functioning level.

If you are experiencing severe symptoms, stop spiritual activities such as reading, meditating, or yoga. Ground yourself through nature. If needed, medication such as anti-depressants will temporarily halt some of the experiences and process of Kundalini awakening. If you are completely non-functional know that many people experiencing Kundalini choose to take medication, during which time they educate themselves about Kundalini, receive counseling, and go see holistic practitioners to process what has already come up. When you are ready, you can titrate off your medication and will be in a new place to process the energies.

Many of us choose to see Kundalini awakenings through because there is an understanding that the only way out is through. We surrender whatever is coming up, each time lightening the amount of material our bodies carry until Kundalini can flow more readily through our bodies. We surrender to the times that Kundalini is bringing up symptoms and experiences that are difficult or make us feel unwell.

Kundalini awakenings come in waves, and the more we clear out of our bodies, the less physically taxing Kundalini awakenings become on a day-to-day basis. Being gentle with ourselves, regulating our diets to eat a small amount on a consistent basis, and getting healing if needed can all help us through the process. The time between the peaks of the waves of Kundalini is time to immerse ourselves in solitude, seek refuge in nature, and let our bodies come out of overwhelm.

The peak waves of Kundalini are intense. They come with intense clearing, dramatic heat, cold, chills, and dramatic energy circulation through the body. Do not block this from happening. Let your body move and dance like it wishes to. Give it time to do so. Turn on music and dance, go through the motions that your body desires to, release the energy it needs to, and fully experience its divine nature. Surrender to the process. If you are fairly stable, find a 5 Rhythms teacher and explain your situation—he or she may be able to help. Know that the intense experiences of Kundalini ebb and flow over time and that the more you resist the more painful your experiences will be.

Do not focus on the negative experiences but allow for them to release—better out than in. You are clearing massive amounts of material—energies that often take many lifetimes to clear. Yes, there will be physical and mental symptoms. Notice them. Do not feed the fear. Realize this is happening so you can reach full realization. Notice the joy, the bliss, the orgasms of energy, and the feelings of oneness. Know that who you were and who you are becoming are two very different things. Give yourself love; make your home as peaceful as possible.

If there is one word that will help you while having a Kundalini journey it is *surrender*, to let go and let God. Know that you are not in control; you are a vessel of the divine and feeling divine energies. Let them guide you. Let them help you discover who you truly are and who you are meant to be in this world. Realize you are in a unique situation that not many have truly experienced. Your views of the world, your understandings, your depth of emotions, and your light will be a beacon to others if you see the process through. Surrender.

After Kundalini

Since Kundalini is such a dramatic and intense process, I often get asked if there is an "after Kundalini." This question does not understand that Kundalini is a constant process even in the most awakened individual. The real question is likely, "What happens after all of the suffering?"

During a Kundalini awakening energy rises until it reaches the brain. There will often be a spouting of energy at this point out of the top of the head into the eighth chakra, which can lead to disorientation and illness for some time. When there is a clear flow of energy to the head and through the crown to the upper chakras, the understanding of the many chakras above the head occurs. The chakras above connect you through the different layers of reality and into the Void. After the Void, the cosmic chakra—the chakra that connects you to pure constant divine energy and divine flow—is established. This flow like a waterfall flows through you through the top of the head and down. Most people undergoing a top-down awakening are doing so through the societal, world, or collective archetype layers of conditioned reality and are not experiencing this top cosmic chakra. The cosmic chakra allows for a direct flow of divinity to flow through the top of the head and down the body. Eventually Kundalini will awaken energy from the Earth and lower chakras (below your feet) to transmit energy up. These two energies meet in your abdomen and transmit out to every cell of your physical body, through your arms and legs, and through all of your energy bodies. This energy surrounds and encases you in light and divine flow. The energetic grids surrounding you are lit up and you are able to see clearly as well as connect to others energetically who are going through similar experiences.

Once Kundalini has found its way full circuit, there is a constant flowing back and forth of energy and a constant working of the energy through the chakra system, channels, organs, and every cell of your body. This energy may be like a gentle wave flowing, or it may be a constant crash and power surge through the body. Although it has made it through its constant circuit, life still happens, and more trauma, issues, and experiences may create blockage in your system that needs to be worked through. It is natural for people even with fully awakened Kundalini to go through crashes of energy and of health. It is also natural for people with fully awakened Kundalini to be highly energized, creative, and full of a power that is difficult to describe in mere words.

After Kundalini has made its full cycle there is a feeling of peace and an understanding of the process—a knowledge that it is better to surrender to it. There is often a resting period in which we feel like we have been through many years or even many lifetimes of war and struggle. We go from seeker to sought. After that, there is a call to action, a choice that each Kundalini-awakened person must make to do something with the energy. By this point, there is an understanding of how to do this and who to be in this world. There are no more illusions, and things simply are as they are. Like all fully awakened individuals, there is an ability to see struggles, emotions, and pain that come up as if seeing it from afar or looking at it from the bottom of the ocean and seeing waves at the top. This is not a disassociated state, or a refusal to see or participate in the difficulties and chaos of life but a discernment that engaging in these energies and wrapping ourselves into the chaotic and looped patterns is of little use. This then changes into a state of action, where we fully embody all emotions and experiences on Earth and are called to be of service to humanity. Life is never easy for the person with fully awakened Kundalini, but the understandings and pure periods of bliss are enough to shine through even the most difficult waves.

Shamanic Awakening

A Shamanic awakening is a call to be a Shaman and is a fairly rare and severe type of awakening. Shamans are intermediaries between the spiritual realms and the world. They are considered "spirit lawyers," and when we have this ability we are able to broker deals with spirits to improve communities, the world, or individual people.

A Shaman is called by a death experience. This experience of death or near death, typically occurring somewhere between early childhood and early adolescence, will mark the child as a Shaman, and will give them the ability to communicate with spirit. This mark of death gives the Shaman a unique vibration as well as the ability to traverse worlds. Traditionally the Shaman would then be put into apprenticeship, where they would study with a Shaman for many years and go through many initiations before they would become a full Shaman and operate separately in the village from their teacher Shaman.

In modern society this does not often happen. There has also been an explosion of interest in Shamanism, which has made it difficult for someone who is called to be a Shaman in modern society to find peers, an appropriate teacher, and an understanding of their abilities. Many of the tools, journeys, and exercises presented in Shamanism courses can lead to subtle awakenings, deeper understandings of Self and world, and the ability to temporarily view our lives from a different and more expansive vantage point. Many people who are interested in Shamanism will take classes, utilize the techniques, and develop themselves through them. They may call themselves a Shaman, or Shamanic Healer, or more likely Shamanic Practitioner, and start a business helping others with their methods. This is obviously wonderful due to the amount of people that require help and understanding of their spiritual nature and a general spiritual emptiness that has become a part of modern culture. Any way that people can explore who they are and become more whole and embodied human beings is wonderful and desperately needed.

That being said, what many of these people who develop interest in Shamanism or Spiritual Healing in modern day do not realize is that being a Shaman is an awakening, a calling, and it is difficult and dangerous to be a Shaman. Although many people not called to be a Shaman do help others as well as themselves feel powerful and connected to nature, the utilization of techniques without a call to be a Shaman or direct experiences and initiations by the spirits has led to a culture of ego-awakened "Shamans" who do not understand that they are self-creating most of their experiences and that they are more in the realm of mental and psychological constructs than spiritual. This has left the modern generation of Shamans and spiritual healers being truly called with little material or resources to truly help them understand and work with their overwhelming experiences.

There is a saying that if people knew what being called to be a Shaman really entailed they would run screaming in the other direction. The Shaman deals with power, with both darkness and light (as well as beyond such constructs), with compassionate and loving beings to the highest degree and true evil, suffering, and matters involving death. Shamans are healers—they do massage, work with herbs, and deal with disease. Many Shamans have a specialty due to their involvement with specific spirits and natural interests. Some Shamans are Psychopomps—transporting souls after death, some do divination or oracle work, and some may be extremely good at working with fertility or wound care. The Shaman plays an integral role in working with the energetic grids and energies that comprise a community. Most significantly, the Shaman is noticed by beings and energies that most people would not want noticing them and has responsibility and power that most people would not want.

So what is involved in a Shamanic Awakening? Beyond the death experience the Shaman will discover that they have spiritual non-physical teachers. They will also have to go through difficult initiations to prove their worth and gain important spiritual understandings. The Shaman will feel the need and pull to be in nature, and is partially nature themselves. There is something wild and non-conformist about the Shaman. The Shaman is said to have one foot in this world and one foot in another world. They are expected to fully function in this world, remain grounded in this world, and be able to interact with this world. They, at the same time, are able to travel through worlds, dimensions, and communicate with energies to bring messages, healing, and barter with the spiritual world for their communities.

There is a current look at the Shaman and Shamanic initiation as if it is marked by mental illness, or that all mentally ill people are Shamans. Although many Shamans go through periods of instability when they are being first initiated, most Shamans are actually incredibly sane. We learn how to work with nature, with the energies of the world, and with spiritual beings outside of ourselves to heal our communities.

Although many people may have access to other gateways, have their feet in other dimensions, doors, or experience "non-ordinary" reality, the Shaman knows fully how to traverse these experiences by making it through the initiations that are set up by spirit so they may learn. Some of us who are being called to become a Shaman do not pass these tests and end up mentally imbalanced or dead. However, it is a far cry to say that Shamans as a whole are mentally imbalanced, or that all or most mentally imbalanced people are secretly failed Shamans.

Shamans in traditional society are often shunned. They are feared, gossiped about, and are outcasts of society until someone needs something from them. In modern society, the Shaman is also shunned. They are outcasts from an early age due to their primal nature. They do not fit in because they are not like the others. This can cause a great deal of pain, especially when the young (or old) Shaman does not realize quite why they are so different. The amount of power that a Shaman has access to can be quite frightening to others.

In modern day, the Shamanic practitioners who are not called form tribes or groups in which they all work on their personal power. They do this to fulfill the modern cultural need for spirituality outside of the construct of modern religion. Often these gatherings mimic initiations that a Shaman might go through. However, those called to become a Shaman are thrown into dangerous initiations and are taught directly by spirit. There are no safety nets and rarely any groups that can help the modern Shaman. It is rare to come up against powers and spirits that are not of the Self, and the budding Shaman will eventually be drawn to an appropriate physical and many non-physical teachers that can assist them. Until then, the spirits that surround the Shamanic initiate put them through tests until they learn whatever is needed to be learned through the particular test they are undergoing.

A Shamanic Awakening involves the ability to heal. This often manifests in present day by an interest in holistic health. The Shaman will easily learn and be able to use their hands, and are natural hands-on healers. Similarly, the Shaman will naturally know or want to learn how to use plants and herbs. They will have a natural aptitude toward herbalism. This can of course be magnified by the specific direction we go with our Shamanic calling.

At some point after the death experience, the Shaman will have dreams and non-physical teachers or physical teachers will appear to guide the Shaman. In tribal cultures, the death experience or a wise midwife while the Shaman was still in-utero would announce that the baby was a Shaman and a formal apprenticeship would commence when the Shaman was of appropriate age. In modern day, many of us have denied for many years the non-physical helpers that surround and try to guide us and our formal spirit apprenticeship has not begun. This creates a great deal of pain and struggle for the called Shaman until they acknowledge and are willing to be a Shaman. A Shamanic call is interesting because when someone is intended to be a Shaman they are unable to do anything else with their lives. Everything in his or her life will fall apart or be in a state of disarray until he or she figures out what is going on and how to get on track with his or her calling.

GEORGIA was a quick-witted, intelligent woman who recently got fired from her third position in the last year and a half. She could cite no reason for her dismissal—she was intelligent, treated others with respect, and got her work done on time or ahead of schedule. When she was four she nearly died from pneumonia, and since that time she has been able to see and communicate with spirits and angelic presences.

Georgia denied anything to do with spirituality. She was a pragmatic woman who had an interest in reading philosophy and painting but thought that her career needed to be something concrete, with a regular paycheck. She began experiencing dreams where she was falling out of the sky, was eaten by animals, and was being taught by strange people that she did not recognize. Gradually she began dreaming about circumstances that had nothing to do with her. The amount of spirits around her increased and she began seeing repeating numbers everywhere she looked. She took a Reiki course but felt out of place. A friend in this course, however, gave her a pamphlet for a workshop in Shamanism. Through this workshop she got the message that she was intended to be a Shaman. She denied this fact and continued looking for jobs. The dreams increased, the spirits around her increased, and she felt like everywhere she looked there was information about spiritual healing and spiritual matters. She began getting sick—stomach pains, headaches, and anxiety that she could not place, eventually resulting in becoming extremely ill with walking pneumonia. When she came to me she was still suffering after a month of walking pneumonia. The amount of spiritual teachers and beings around her was astonishing—I had never seen anything quite like it. When I clearly told her that she was denying her calling to become a Shaman she laughed nervously and began crying. She vowed to start interacting with the spirits surrounding her and learning from them.

The last that I talked to Georgia she was still in a bit of disbelief about her calling but was progressing with a local teacher. The dreams had decreased and she had the appropriate tools to deal with the crowd of spirits that surrounded her.

An interesting phenomena that has happened in the modern day is that with the minimal recognition of spirit or the spiritual realms, the called Shaman will often go through painful experiences and initiations, even going through death experiences again and again until they realize that what is going on is spiritual. It takes years, decades, or sometimes never happens that we realize we are undergoing a Shamanic calling. This is especially unfortunate because when called we will often be unable to do much else with our lives—we are destined to be a Shaman. Every other effort will fail until we realize it. The spirits who surround the Shaman will create painful experiences so that we will "wake up" and realize that something spiritual is going on.

For those of us who are able to recognize or no longer deny that we are undergoing a Spiritual calling, an apprenticeship begins. Beginning Shamans find themselves in new-age workshops and reading until they are able to find the appropriate physical teachers or are able to contact non-physical teachers. Many Shamans today have little training from physical sources since the realization quickly occurs that non-physical spiritual training is more powerful than any physical training and most of the workshops out there are for people with an interest in learning the tools of Shamanism but do not have a calling to it. On a practical level, it is also much cheaper financially to engage with non-physical teachers than fly or drive to a Shamanic group, gathering, workshop, or to a specific teacher.

Those of us undergoing a Shamanic awakening will find ourselves often tested, or going through initiations. These will bring us to new levels of awareness or will create contact with specific energies. Very quickly we will find ourselves in contact with real spiritual energies. Often, the Shaman will be tested by being thrown in the proverbial lions' den with a specific experience to figure our way out of it with minimal help. With the experience behind us and the test passed, we will then learn from our spiritual teachers how to work with the situation the next time it appears. Some Shamans do not pass these tests, and either die, become ill, or are tested again.

For those of us called to be a Shaman these tests are never ending. Initiations are frequently dangerous, illuminating, and are difficult to describe. Once passed, the Shaman gains power and understanding, moving on to the next test. Each moment and decision can be considered an initiation, but initiations come both small and large. The larger ones provide for deep understandings about the world, spiritual awakening, and a general remembering of the Self.

A Shamanic awakening is a call to be a Healer. While Kundalini awakenings are often about the individual, Shamanic awakenings are about a need for some people to fulfill the role of Shaman in society. A Shamanic awakening occurs because the person has genetic, ancestral, or other reasons such as societal or communal need to become a Shaman in this lifetime.

A call to be a Shaman often involves dreams, such as a dismemberment dream, where we are eaten alive by animals or other creatures or our bodies are broken down in some way. This may occur several times before recapitulation, where our body is brought back and becomes whole again. This is often our first initiation as Shamans, and it is an experience that we rarely forget.

We will also have dreams about teachers, about being healed, or about being places we have never been. In some dreams, Shamans will heal others or will teach. But starting out, teachers and other Shamans come to the Shaman in dreams because it is easier to get through in the dream world. There is no (or little) resistance when the Shaman is asleep, no denying that a non-physical teacher is calling us to work with them. Eventually a Shaman will learn how to work with dreams and utilize them as a tool.

During a Shamanic awakening we will desire solitude (or have it thrust upon us), and will have a deep love and need for nature. Eventually we will begin to learn how to communicate with nature, with animals, and with nature spirits such as winds. We will understand how everything is connected and will feel at home in the wild. We will feel called to learn from certain aspects of nature, like specific animals, trees, and plants, and will build a team of spiritual helpers from their energies.

As we become a fully awakened Shaman we will increase our power. We will also become noticed and targeted by others both in living and spirit form—others will want to steal our power or will simply be curious and come to observe. With real and more powerful spiritual experiences will come more powerful spiritual beings. Many of these can be quite fierce, downright dangerous, or bring great knowledge and light. Initiations will become more dramatic as we end our initial training. At a certain point, elements that would be considered dark, evil, and dangerous will come to the Shaman for healing purposes, out of curiosity, to form an alliance or become a teacher of the Shaman, or to steal or latch on to our power. Elements of true light and divine nature, great spiritual beings and other teachers will surround the Shaman. The Shaman will learn about the balance of the Earth, the light and dark, evil and good, and how to play a role in balancing these forces.

It is a popularized misconception that we can have control over spiritual forces and that Shamans only work with "light" or "good." Many of the rules we make up only work when we self-generate the spiritual forces we work with. When we do not we can understand that there are a wide variety of spiritual forces, and that the lightest most-filled-with-love being may also be the fiercest, and the darkest may come to us for healing and comfort. When we are able to move past our own puritanical needs for control over the universe and realize that we have very little control over the spiritual realms or any spiritual beings, we can encounter real spiritual forces. These forces during a Shamanic awakening will guide us, utilize us as tools, and need us because we are in human containers and can interact with them.

There are many capabilities, powers, and elements of the Shamanic life or techniques that are admirable, but a true Shamanic calling is not something you would want to choose for yourself. It is a path that is chosen for the individual. Shamanic tools are wonderful to help heal ourselves and work with psychological constructs, but true Shamans are forces that carry distinct powers, realizations, a certain wildness to them, and the responsibility to work with the community, spiritual beings, and elements that few would wish to.

If you have a desire to study Shamanism, attend workshops, or feel drawn to Shamanic practices they can have a wonderful impact on your life. If you are going through any type of spiritual awakening the techniques learned in Shamanic courses can help you on your path. Shamanic coursework is wonderful to discover subconscious desires, the shadow aspects of Self, and can help you feel powerful and understand your life from a different vantage point. Enjoy your experiences and be sure to explore and pay homage to traditional cultures, understand the history of Shamanism, and learn how to spot ego awakenings so you do not spend money and time on a teacher or organization that is not correct for you. Use your intuition and ask if the workshop, the teacher, and the experience would be right for you. Listen to the answer.

If you have had a death or near-death experience, feel an essential need to be with nature, realize you were called to be a Healer, and have had the initiatory dreams of dismemberment and dreams of spiritual teachers, you are likely going through a Shamanic awakening. Realize that you have felt different from likely a very young age because you are different. Recognize that this does not make you special or better or worse than anyone else, simply different. If you continue to realize that you have spiritual non-physical teachers, feel called to become a Healer, and become interested in nature including plants and herbalism, you are likely on the path of becoming a Shaman. Perhaps the most important differentiating aspects of the Shamanic awakening are initiations and suffering. Initiations are the constant tests that open doors to greater insight and understanding. They also offer power, spiritual allies, and the capability to work with and heal a variety of spiritual issues.

If you progress on this path, realize that being a Shaman is to ultimately balance energies and to keep one foot fully grounded in this world while traveling through others. You will be noticed by darkness, light, good, and evil. If you allow for yourself to constantly open during this type of awakening, you will begin to see beyond your own constructs, your own thoughtforms of dark and light, and the societal appropriation of Shamanism. You will ultimately realize beyond duality and know that it is your job to communicate and work with the whole—darkness and light, good and evil—to negotiate the healing of individuals, communities, and the world.

Occult Awakening

Occult awakenings are where we find a gateway to spiritual awakening through witchcraft, magic, and other occult practices. Occult awakenings allow for us to become aware of the forces of the Universe, such as the elements, as well as to come into contact with personal and spiritual power. In many cases, occult awakenings will eventually allow for us to come into contact with deities and other true spiritual beings, deep spiritual insights, and a unique way of working with the energies that comprise the Universe.

Occult awakenings are strikingly similar in some ways to Shamanic awakenings, especially in the case of witchcraft, where we feel a calling to the practice. Occult awakenings can be low-level understandings in which we create further layers of illusion and obscuration of reality, or they can also be sudden and difficult awakenings into a fully realized or close-to-realized state. In this case we suddenly come into contact with knowledge, understandings, and experiences with powerful spirits and beings that radically transforms our understanding of the universe and our place in it.

Many of us who experience occult awakenings have a unique ability to play with or work with the layers of conditioned reality to our benefit. This type of awakening is not rare, but true, powerful practitioners who have awakened enough to get to the state of understanding and working with the powers and elements that comprise conditioned reality are rare. We discover when we go through an occult awakening that it requires great study and knowledge based in specific traditions as well as focus over many years' time. This is even true for those powerfully or naturally called to occult practices, even though some of us may have natural aptitude and gain spiritual power and knowledge quickly. It takes time to learn the proper rituals, methods of communication, and to develop relationships with the forces that comprise conditioned reality and beyond. During an occult awakening it is important to keep an understanding of the Self and what we are called to do. It is easy to get lost in communities and circles. These circles and communities can be a great way to learn, but as they are focused on group rather than individual need we can find ourselves out of focus from our specific path. Finding ourselves in a safe way and asking consistently why we are being called and allowing for ourselves to go deeper than even the books, groups, or communities venture can create a full awakening.

KANDY was always interested in the occult. She received her first set of tarot cards at the age of 10 and was fascinated by the artwork. She began reading cards for friends and family, experimented with a Ouija board on the weekends as a teenager, and began watching every movie about witchcraft that came out. When she went away for college, she found that her affinity for tarot cards was thought to be odd by her roommate so she put away all of her magical books, cards, and movies to fit in.

When Kandy was in her late twenties she felt a strong drive to begin exploring witchcraft again. At first she read voraciously, exploring all of the Wicca books in her library and purchasing books from her bookstore. She found many of the spells easy and began purchasing herbs and other supplies for her practice. Kandy found a local Wiccan group and began attending their workshop and classes. She deeply enjoyed this group and for many years took part in their functions.

When she was 35, Kandy found herself no longer interested in her group and the books that she read began to seem silly and for beginners. Looking at her group she found that although she had made many friends she wanted to go deeper in her understandings. New knowledge came forward to her in her practices and ceremonies and she found herself at odds with some of the basic tenets of her practice and the group. This was a struggle for her, because although she saw that many of the people she surrounded herself with were beginners and playing with things that they barely knew about, they were her friends and without them she would feel alone. Gradually, Kandy accepted that she was deepening her practice and experiencing an awakening. She began to understand that the knowledge that was coming forward for her and the understandings and books she wished to find were not basic or appropriate knowledge for the group she was in. By opening herself to new knowledge she found the new practices that awakened her fully to her potential. Kandy is now a powerful solo practitioner who is more than happy to guide others who are looking for occult practices that are real or beyond a basic level.

Religious Awakening

A religious awakening is a sudden awakening involving experiences with religious overtones that drastically changes our worldview. Many of us in this category have already had some form of religion in our worldview, however, some of us may have not had any religious practices in our upbringing so the sudden understanding or contact by God, Krishna, Buddha, or other deities will come as a complete shock. Others in this category may go to church, temple, or be involved in organized religion yet be surprised at direct contact with divinity.

This can be an awakening to an aspect of ourselves—such as the God Self in which we see a disassociated aspect of ourselves as divine. We may be stuck in an ego awakening or suffering from mental illness and believe ourselves to be God or another deity. Still for some of us there is a genuine contact with divinity, such as feeling the Holy Spirit, which drastically changes our lives. Direct contact with the divine can be incredibly transformative. Our relationship to a power greater than ourselves is deeply personal and can affect us in a wide variety of ways. Common experiences include a sense of awe, a feeling of renewed purpose or understanding of our place or role in the universe, and anger, grief, joy, or several emotions all at the same time. Drastic changes in understandings, especially spiritual understandings, a deep need and desire to serve God, a changing of bad habits, and evaluation of the life previous to the experience of direct divinity is common.

Beyond symptoms, the actual experience in a religious awakening is deeply individual. Some of us may feel a presence much larger than ourselves, hear God speaking to us, or may feel God or the Holy Spirit within us. The direct experience with divinity rather than going through an intermediary such as church allows us to understand our spiritual path without filter or illusions. We no longer require religious material or organizations but may choose to attend them for the sense of community they inspire.

It is normal to feel a bit crazy undergoing a religious awakening. Hearing directly from God or having understandings about God outside of the appropriate channels is thought of as somehow wrong or a result of mental illness. It is not known that people who are good, mentally balanced people are having direct experiences and religious awakenings every day. When we experience a religious awakening it is likely we will feel a deep call to be of service to the world, to be a good person, and to see God in others that surround us. This awakening fully developed allows for us to develop a personal relationship with God that will inform our decisions for the rest of our lives.

Some of us shut this experience down out of fears of being crazy. It does need to be acknowledged that there are mentally imbalanced people who are simply in a fragmented state and utilizing religious experiences to navigate through their fragile minds and deal with trauma. There are many of us who have gone through religious awakenings who have simply told of our experiences and been called crazy or advised to seek medical care. And there are some of us who have had such a severe religious awakening that we are no longer able to distinguish or deal with everyday reality and the amount of information coming through to us.

When we are going through a religious awakening there might be disorientation or even a history of trauma, drug abuse, or a difficult life. With the experiences of religious awakening there is a clearing, understanding, and reorientation toward spiritual and religious matters, a clarity about path in life, and an awe and humbleness at having these experiences. With understanding and surrender we change our lives and integrate these experiences to become better people and servants of God.

Some of us who experience God through direct experience find the experience too much to handle. We are unable to integrate the experiences or stimuli occurring and require medical care. This is true in cases of feeling of the Holy Spirit, in which the experience creates such a powerful experience and requires a level of understanding that often does not happen. Still others of us create direct experiences with God due to trauma and fragmented aspects of the Self. This is a disassociated aspect of ourselves or an archetype within the confines of conditioned reality rather than a direct encounter with divinity. These are all separate, distinct experiences and must be clearly differentiated so that when we have direct experiences we can feel empowered by our experiences, those of us who are simply overwhelmed are able to integrate our experience and learn how to use tools to work with them, and those of us who need medical care are able to receive it.

If you find yourself experiencing a religious awakening, know that it can be a profound experience. Allow it to inform you. Remain on Earth, humble, and in physical form. Ground yourself. If the experiences are overwhelming, learn tools such as releasing emotions and trauma so you can properly let this energy flow through you. Learn boundaries—there can even be boundaries with God if you are no longer functional due to your connection. If you lack the appropriate filters, have lost functioning in your daily life, or have difficulty with the highs and lows that come from the waxing and waning waves of divinity pouring through you, contact an experienced spiritual guide, counselor, or in severe cases, a psychiatrist.

Walk-Ins

A walk-in is a relatively rare awakening. It may actually be more commonplace than what is talked about, and when we experience this type of awakening we rarely know what is going on. The most common way a walk-in occurs is at a point when someone is in a great deal of pain and commits suicide; although a few people have spoken of car accidents or other happenings where they were close to death or physically died when this has occurred. In some of these instances, a being of some sort will make an agreement with us. This agreement is for the being to walk-in, or inhabit, our body. Basically, we leave and the being gets the benefits of having a physical body. This is much different than channeling, where another being or energy will impart wisdom, or mediumship, where a being may temporarily inhabit our body.

This can be anything from a beautiful being of light to very dark beings. Strange physical reactions and inability to mesh with the human form can also happen with spiritual beings who have a great deal of power or are entirely different energetically from the human energetic grid. When they decide to walk in, these beings would be rejected from the physical form. As humans, we would experience this rejection by either dying or by finding ourselves in rather difficult physical and emotional duress.

A walk-in is for a specific purpose on the part of the being. A human body is fairly small and requires the being to give up a great deal of power to house themselves. Most beings would not want to do so simply because it is uncomfortable and the human body does not deal well with things more powerful or different energetically.

This is not something that is talked about, or even remembered by us when we have made the agreement. It is common that everyone around us will notice that something has drastically changed about us—that our personality, desires, and even physical features, such as eye color, change. Typically this is picked up by those sensitive to energy by noticing that our energy field is no longer congruent, or that there is something much larger overlying or stuffed into our field.

Not much is known about walk-ins. Those of us who have attempted suicide or have had near-death or death experiences are often drastically changed by them, so we attribute our drastic changes to that. However, there is a link to a specific date or time in which in a short period of time we have drastically changed everything about ourselves, including goals, ambitions, interests, emotional outlook, and even physical appearance.

JASON is one of the rare few who remembers their walk-in experiences. He told me in great detail of his prolonged Dark Night issues. A very sensitive man, he had been severely sexually traumatized by several relatives and neighbors as a child. He found himself in several abusive relationships as an adult, and found himself in a state of despair when his boyfriend, who was twenty years older than him and beat him regularly, had dumped him unceremoniously, one month prior.

This caused Jason to go into a tailspin. He was already chaotic and had a hard time functioning, but the breakup was too overwhelming for him to process. He ended up slitting one of his wrists and thankfully had a moment of clarity and called an ambulance. He went through inpatient treatment for two weeks before he was released. When he came out, he was a totally different person. He was happy, realized that he no longer wanted to interact with many of the people he once associated with, and decided to switch his major to nursing with hopes that he could become a psychiatric nurse.

He began losing weight, his eye color changed from blue to green, and he reformed relationships with his mother and sister. He started a relationship with a man his own age and finally felt a sense of peace. About six months after he had been released from the hospital, he began feeling odd sensations on his back. He began visualizing and feeling the physical sensations of wings. He could even twist side to side and feel the breeze from them. Jason began having dreams of not only his suicide, but of a strange room. This strange room became clearer each time he visited until he realized that he was talking to someone in that room whom he called Brian.

Slowly Jason realized that Brian had offered to come into his body and utilize it for divine purposes. Jason would still be there, but the light of Brian would cause all of the darkness to disappear and for Jason to come to a divine purpose. Jason agreed and let Brian in.

This is one of a few examples of walk-ins I have come across. Other people may term this as a sort of voluntary possession. Obviously to most of us it would not be an ideal situation to have an energy take over our body. There also is the question that has not been answered of what happens to the energy of Jason who has been agreed to be taken over. In some situations, this would hopefully be a symbiotic relationship where the energy of something like Brian would transform the energy of Jason. This is not what I have seen in the rare cases that I have worked with, however. What I see is a sort of host/parasite relationship in which an energy is so large that it takes over.

Basically, this situation turns into a possession. To rid someone of this energy would require the host to want the energy to leave, which rarely happens. It is really difficult to convey that having a strong, powerful spirit inhabit your body, especially when you have given up and are seeing drastic improvements in your life is a bad thing. But in the situation of the walk-in, it is no longer the person's life, and eventually the being will likely eclipse the entirety of the person to carry out its own plan and desires. Although this question has never been answered, there is a lack of knowledge about this type of experience and what happens to someone like Jason who has knowingly given up his physical form to another being, no matter how good the desires of the being are.

Possession/Entity Awakening

A possession/entity awakening is somewhat rare, although it is seen more often clinically than walk-ins. We are beings of energy, and when we die that energy doesn't leave. A human being has a period of time in which to visit others and get his or her affairs in order in spirit form before they are no longer congruent with the physical world. At this point he or she is supposed to cross over. Some spirits, due to confusion, fear, anger, or other issues, stay. When they stay they need an energy source to remain here. They then latch onto a human being as a power source to remain in the physical realm.

Other beings of non-human origins such as elementals, animal spirits, or demonic entities also latch onto humans for their own reasons. These reasons could fill an entire book, but common reasons include power, a specific plan that requires a human, being sent by another human or being, or simply as a source of energy to stay in this realm.

The phenomenon of possession is actually incredibly common. We see movies such as *The Exorcist* and picture demons and head spinning, but when we consider possession as simply our energetic body being connected to another energy, we may more readily understand how commonplace this occurrence can be.

When we have an energy attached to us we feel physical symptoms such as the way the energy passed on or diseases the spirit may have had, fatigue from being a power source to another energy, or emotions that are not ours. Occasionally, this energy will cause awakening symptoms. When we awaken by an entity or energy it is sudden. Suddenly we realize how to do complex spells, and we have realizations that are profound about energy work, meditation, and spiritual healing. We know things that we never did before.

So how to differentiate between the sudden awakenings that come from awakening and possession/entity awakening? Feel in your body for something that doesn't feel right, something physically showing up that isn't yours. Notice if your interests and understandings suddenly shift. A famous energy worker who used to be a businessman suddenly realized and was able to perfectly describe different layers of the aura, distinctions between energy fields, and describe entities perfectly when he had an energy attach to him. He previously had no knowledge of anything to do with energy. Another woman I worked with suddenly became obsessed with Haitian Vodou, and was able to accomplish remarkable things while being a Reiki 1/2 practitioner and in the throes of a subtle body/pranic awakening. Another man suddenly was able to visualize himself as a powerful healer and felt the need to fly to Egypt to connect with the energy there. He had never visited Egypt and was previously a Presbyterian with no interest in anything metaphysical or spiritual for that matter.

Although these beings and energies can impart quite a bit of knowledge and understanding, this is not an appropriate method of awakening. This awakening will quickly suck your energy from you, and the entity will simply latch onto someone else that has power. It is somewhat common in these cases (similar to the walk-in) for the person to not want to get rid of the entity. They feel the power and do not want to give it up. I have heard of several instances of death and severe illness from this type of awakening because the host person and their physical body has not built up their power and "muscle" of dealing with such powerful energies in their body so they rather quickly collapse, or at the very least are very quickly drained of energy.

If you find yourself in this category, visit a Shaman or advanced energy worker who can release these types of energies. It can be difficult to find an effective practitioner for this, and you may not want to, but it is best for your health and well-being to do so.

Non-Human Origin Awakenings

It is difficult to know how many of us are awakening as a result of coming from non-human origin. There are many of us on earth who are descended from angels, beings, stars, or are from different planets. Often when we come from this category we will seem different to others. Many of us whose origins are partially from somewhere else will not remember, or will feel despair or a sense of being homesick without exactly knowing why.

Some of us begin to remember our origins. This is beyond remembering past lives, ancestral heritage, or any of the other recollections. At first this starts as a curiosity, perhaps reading or being drawn to materials about a specific group of angels, myths of a certain origin, or a specific planet. There is an immediate click or call to attention when we start reading about a certain being or land. More and more we will be drawn to this material. By synchronicity, the right books, movies, and understandings about our origins will come to us.

At a certain point we will begin to remember our origins. We may dream about situations, myths, and people. As we remember, we may recall our families, our name, and how we came to be on Earth. Often this increases feelings of separation but at the same time the realization that all of the feelings of being different, of always being slightly out of place in this world are now understood.

This type of awakening is much different than the sort of identification that occurs with the archetype level where we may find certain deities interesting, or the realization of a constellation or stars within us during the cosmic level of awakening. This is a full realization that our origins are elsewhere.

As we remember, there can be a connection to the power that we once had. Once we fully release the pain, emotions, and trauma that come from our origin story we can fully learn how to bring the power of our origins through and work with them. This is a beautiful remembering, and can create a huge amount of healing for us. We may have realizations, channel information, come into contact with other humans whose origins are similar, or non-physical beings who can guide us to understand our origins.

This type of spiritual awakening is deeply individualistic, but it is important in all cases to remember and resolve any wounds that came from this layer of remembering. By resolving the wounds that come from our origin story we can claim the power of our origins and learn what that power is. We can then ask for a liaison, a being to help us communicate with the energies from our origin. Remembering our origins, or being taught by a teacher from our spiritual origins, can allow for us to fully awaken and fully remember who we are.

Indigo/Always Awake

The last category of spiritual awakening is that of those born into this lifetime awake. It is widely known that children are more spiritually conscious and aware. As children we are encouraged to have active imaginations, play with imaginary friends, and create our own worlds. Somewhere around the age of six, children become young adults who are encouraged to become an active part of the consensual reality. The grids and conditioned layers of reality descend on us and we no longer are realized as we once were or simply begin to understand to act like other people so others do not think us to be bizarre.

But there are some children—we call them all sort of terms like indigo or rainbow children—who have spiritual knowledge that is beyond understanding. This awakening is different in that we are already born awake in this lifetime, we fully remember our origins, but develop difficulties when we realize or are told that we need to close off our sensitivities, our gifts, and become a part of consensual reality.

Many of us then became double-agents, leading a life of fear that someone will find out that we are awake or more aware. Some of us close down completely and then awaken later in life, rediscovering the things we found out as an awakened child. Imagine what understanding and nurturing of a child who is awake and can see past the collective consciousness could lead to if they did not have to hide or stifle themselves as a teenager or young adult (or even an adult for that matter).

For children who come into this lifetime awake it is important to nurture them and allow for them to realize how they are uniquely special. Allow them to have fun activities that can fully express who they are. Many awakened children will gravitate toward painting, art, acting, singing, writing, music, or other forms of artistry to express their individuality. Encourage this and your awakened child will flourish.

The awakened child comes into this world already remembering who they are. They have very few or no layers of conditioned reality surrounding them. Others will put these layers on the child. It is very common for parents to do so out of fear of their child being different. Understand that everyone is awake, but some no longer remember. The hardest thing to explain to an awakened child is why people do not remember, why their classmates do not experience life the same way they do, and why others are asleep and follow unconscious rules. We can allow for children to maintain who they are but also remain of this world and appropriately find a way to operate in school and community. An awakened child can tend to get lost in other worlds. Encourage them to be a part of both worlds. Get them into nature, playing sports, and exploring the wonders of being in the physical world and having a physical body. Eating good food, looking at art, smelling wonderful scents, and playing in the dirt are wonderful ways to keep an awakened child grounded and present.

If you do not understand what an awakened child in your life is going through, or the child is experiencing distress, a sympathetic counselor who understands working with indigo children, an energy worker that can train you and your child in very basic energy work, or a Shaman who can train or protect your child can be very helpful. Ideally you would experience these things together at an appropriate age level and be open to understand what the awakened child is experiencing. Most of all, if you are a parent with awakened children, do not ridicule them, make them feel bad, or wish they were different than who they are. They are perfect, and if you nurture them appropriately, they can be powerful forces in this world.

PART 4

Common Experiences of Awakening

Physical Sensations

Physical sensations can be confusing because we do not always understand that the spiritual, energetic, mental/emotional, and physical deeply inform and in fact create one another. Even when we do have this understanding there is doubt that the physical stomach pain we are experiencing may be related to something on our spiritual path. So we go to the doctor, who gives us pills and a diagnosis, or pills and no diagnosis. Or we go to the doctor, and the doctor says there is nothing wrong with us, nothing diagnosable at least. Or the doctor tells us to go see a therapist for stress or emotions. These may be all good solutions. It is always wise to see a physician in case something needs to be done drastically, such as a surgical intervention.

But soon we may notice that physical sensations such as nausea or pain show up in our third chakra when we are releasing ideas of the Self. We may be able to link getting headaches to when there is chaos in the world such as political strife, a school shooting, a full moon, or something astrologically happening. Physical issues will remain as long as there are emotions, traumas, and other issues stemming from the Self or any of the other layers of conditioned reality. An emotion or a trauma is like a boulder within our physical body. When we resolve this trauma that created the boulder, the boulder either dissolves or becomes smaller rocks or pebbles. Energy can now move around these smaller rocks or entirely through an area that was once blocked.

Once we have released enough of our own traumas and emotions and those of our family, ancestry, and past lives, we will begin processing societal, global, and cosmic energies. These energies can be intense and difficult to process through the physical body. The force of these energies hitting against even the smallest of pebbles within the physical form creates physical pain and disease. When these pebbles and rocks are worked through and the forces arising within us are surrendered to and even welcomed, the remaining pebbles, rocks, and boulders in our systems will dissolve. The larger energies will simply flow through us. Most of us are conscious enough at this point to know how to release these energies. We now carry the knowledge that we are the world, and we are a release valve for energies from ourselves, society, the world, and even the cosmos.

Dr. John Upledger, an innovator in CranioSacral Therapy, recognized that our tissues show our issues, and that events that we experience—ancestral, past life, and whatever other energies our bodies hold—becomes localized into a specific area and specific pattern in the body. He referred to this phenomenon as energy cysts. By bringing consciousness to these areas of disorganized, chaotic, and walled-off energy, talking with these areas, physically feeling into them and gently inquiring as to what they are, we can release them.

EXERCISE: Part 1—Releasing Energy Cysts

- The next time you are feeling a physical pain, let yourself feel it. We have a tendency to disassociate or not let ourselves feel the areas in our body that are in pain. Do not avoid it. Really feel the pain.
- What does it feel like? Allow yourself to fully describe how it feels.
- How large is it? What sort of space does it take up in your body?
- How deep is it in your body?
- Try to come up with a visual representation of it. Is it a specific shape? Color? Texture? Pattern?
- When you have a firm understanding of how it looks and feels, let yourself sit with it for five minutes and see what else comes up. Any other senses, more visuals, or feelings are all good.
- Now notice what emotion is coming up. What name would you give to it? Sadness? Anger? Fear?
- Now look deeper. How long has this been in your body? Months? Years? Decades? Has it always been there?
- Is it yours (meaning does it come from you)? If not, where or who does it come from?
- When you have gotten all of that information, and have a strong visual, you are ready to talk to it. Imagine that you are talking to a new friend.
- If it feels appropriate, say hello and introduce yourself.
- Ask this body part, this visual image, what it wants to say to you. Let whatever comes up be okay. This may be a visual, a thought, a feeling, or an emotion.
- What does it need from you? Often these answers are pretty simple— release, water, exercise, a change in some way to your life, recognition.
- Ask if it needs anything else.
- Ask if it has anything to say to you.
- Feel free to say anything back to it that you want.

EXERCISE: Part 2—Coming to an Agreement with Your Body

- When you have a good grasp of the first part of this exercise and the body part has said it needs something, ask clarifying questions until you have total clarity on the need.
- If this is something you can give the body, come to an agreement with the body about it. If it wants you to write, offer to write once a week (for example). If it is a past-life energy that wants for you to know how it died or what sort of effects it has on your current life, listen to it. If it is an ancestral energy that has tightened your chest with grief, listen to it, asking if it wants anything. If it is an emotion or feeling that you cannot place, that is okay as well. You do not need to know the circumstances of everything to release it. Simply allow whatever is ready to come up, listen to it, and ask how you can release it.
- Ask if the body will release this energy, in part or in full. Be patient if it doesn't want to change, or if it only wants to release part of the pattern. It likely has more to say, or is waiting for you to realize something another day. If it wants to release in part or in full, allow it to do so. It can do this in many ways, but common ways are through legs or arms, by rising into the air, by breath, or by being incorporated into the body.

This exercise will bring us awareness about our physical symptoms, which will then allow us to release them. Other physical symptoms commonly reported as a result of awakenings are aches and pains, headaches, ear ringing, digestive issues and bloating, autoimmune diseases, chronic fatigue, fibromyalgia, and near-death experiences and "mystery illnesses" not explainable by Western Medicine.

Invariably fear comes up with the experience of processing during a spiritual awakening. We visit doctors to figure out the physical issues that come up with awakening and releasing from the body-mind. When we are experiencing physical symptoms that are worrisome, going to a doctor or holistic healer may be the exact way to move forward on our spiritual path. There is a tendency to throw out physical symptoms because of the spiritual or to not understand that they go hand in hand. I have known several men and women who have thought that their heart chakra was opening who were actually having heart attacks. Whether their heart chakra was opening was a bit of a moot point. Another patient thought her root chakra was opening and it turned out that she was pregnant and had miscarried. There are physical, emotional, and spiritual causative factors in illness. Taking care of all ourselves on all levels allows us to move through physical issues with greater ease.

In the initial stages of awakening, our body releases what is being held in it. When this happens it is a natural tendency to want to stop the process and to resist the sensations. The release of our past traumas and hurts is understandably overwhelming at times, especially if we have no idea why we are reliving old wounds. We live in a culture that abhors anything uncomfortable and it is our natural, base instinct to immediately stop any physical, emotional, mental, or spiritual discomfort. But our bodies are releasing for a purpose—we are processing our traumas so that we can move beyond them and their limitations. We are clearing a pathway so that energy can flow. If our bodies are filled with trauma, pain, anger, and fear, the amount of good emotions and divine flow is limited. We are blocked and are forced to see the world through the eyes of a Self that is wounded and traumatized. When the physical body is clear, divine flow and the force of Kundalini and other spiritual energies can emerge and unfold in the body. This allows for states such as bliss, deep understanding and connection to life, healing of our past, and an awakened state. We are then able to see life not through the patterns and chains of our conditioning and trauma, but through the eyes of clarity and freedom. Each trauma, each emotion or blockage released allows for greater flow.

Spontaneous Movements

Movements that are of a spontaneous nature are common during awakening. These movements can be very subtle, such as muscle twitches or small vibration-like movements in the fingers and toes. They can also be quite large, such as the yogic postures and hand gestures (kriyas and mudras) commonly associated with Kundalini awakenings.

Although not spontaneous, many of us experiencing awakenings feel sudden desires to stretch and open certain areas of our bodies, especially during meditation. In more dramatic awakenings these types of movements are spontaneous and we do not have control over them. These movements can be quite frightening to us because our body is not physically in our control and due to safety issues associated with some of these movements.

These movement patterns allow our body to open up and clear out old energy. Energy often gets locked in joints, tissues, and other crevices of the body. It requires movement to release energy and allow for it to properly flow through the appropriate channels and out of our body. Later in the awakening process the spontaneous movements are a result of the influx of divine energy dancing through our systems. Divine energy is extremely powerful and transformative, and it will release anything that is stuck or remains in the body so we may become a clear channel.

If you are experiencing movements, allow for them to flow through you. Do not resist them. When you resist, it makes the intense energy stagnate, which can become quite painful. Taking up a gentle, movement-based activity like tai chi or yoga is incredibly helpful to allow this energy to flow through you. If you choose yoga, know that hot yoga or Kundalini yoga will likely exacerbate any issues you are having with spontaneous movements. Choosing a more flowing, gentle yoga is often less jarring for the awakening system. You can set an appointment to dance, move, or otherwise release this energy and feel divine flow. So set an appointment to dance in your bedroom, go to a 5 Rhythms, trance or spontaneous dance class, gentle yoga, or tai chi. Have a space without sharp furniture or other objects, an area where you can be without hurting yourself accidentally. Let this energy move through you.

Spontaneous Vocalizations

Spontaneous vocalizations are somewhat less common in the awakening process. These are tones, sounds, chants, words, phrases, and other vocal expressions. Vocalizations happen either spontaneously or we feel an inner urge to express ourselves. The throat chakra is often one of the last chakras to open. As it is opening the tongue may begin spontaneous movements, such as connecting with the roof of the mouth to form a circuit of energy. In cases of sudden awakenings, humming, musical notes, songs, speeches, prose, verse, and poetry may come through spontaneously or be channeled. In rare cases, these may be in different or unusual languages. In such an awakening, expression through writing, song, or other creative pursuits is often necessary to get the energy to flow through the body appropriately.

Chills

Chills can suggest many different things in terms of spiritual experiences. The most common are either the presence of a spirit or downloads or channeling of heightened energies (e.g., chills during Kundalini experiences or the feeling of qi running through the body). Empaths and Sensitives may feel chills when in the presence of spirits; when getting a specific feeling or emotion from a place, person, or object; or when in the presence of higher, angelic type of beings. Specifically noting the accompanying feelings when experiencing with this is important. Feelings of heightened energy accompanied by heightened understandings, pleasurable feelings, and energetic expansiveness accompanying chills may suggest downloading, channeling, or contact with higher vibration beings or spiritual flows. Feelings of anxiety, discomfort, nausea, or other more physically felt issues accompanied by chills may suggest empathic or lower vibration spiritual energies.

Chills can be indicative of nervous system, endocrine, and/or hormonal system imbalances. Looking into both the physical as well as emotional and spiritual factors of an imbalance will allow for full understanding of them.

Spiritual Depression and Cognition Issues

In the awakening process it is common to go through periods of foggy-headedness, inability to think clearly, or inability to handle reading or television. The sheer amount of material that comes into conscious awareness during awakening is more than the mind can handle appropriately. Many of the energies we may encounter are more powerful than the logical capabilities the human mind can handle and are beyond our capacity to assimilate properly. This is especially true once we have reached beyond the archetypal layer of conditioned reality and are accessing cosmic and global patterns. These global and cosmic patterns until resolved appropriately through proper channeling have a huge impact on the ability to have conscious and clear thought processes.

Empathic abilities such as taking on emotions, energies, and thoughtforms that surround us can cause cloudiness or inability to process clearly. Imbalances in the digestive system, which is known energetically as the "second brain," can result in cognitive difficulties, depression, and other issues. Spirits and other beings can attach to our energy field, creating imbalanced thoughts as well as a general lack of vitality.

It is also worth mentioning that hormonal imbalances, such as an undiagnosed thyroid condition and certain dietary and vitamin deficiencies, have large impacts on our brain. If cognition issues are a large factor, there is likely a physical as well as spiritual reason for this issue. Meeting with a holistic physician who is knowledgeable about thyroid conditions, or acupuncturists or naturopaths who can advise on dietary supplements and nutritional advice can be life-saving.

The flickering in between high and lower spiritual states can be a factor in cognition issues, and the general low feelings of depression, Dark Nights, or simply going from downloading or feeling heightened, peak spiritual states, and going back to ordinary consciousness can result in feelings of slow cognition and fogginess.

Stopping studying, reading, and focusing on quiet time, diet, nutrition, and learning how to appropriately channel energy are all that may be needed. If there is a feeling of a presence that is not your own—such as thoughts, feelings, or a spirit, a visit to a spiritual healer may be indicated. Feelings of permanent brain fog, cognition issues, and more significant depression issues are more indicative of a problem that should be approached not just spiritually but medically as well.

Chronic Fatigue and Fluctuations in Energy

It is exhausting to go through an awakening but also remain functional in our daily lives. Most of us who are not going through spiritual awakenings are overextended and relying on coffee or other stimulants to simply get through our day, so adding on the energy required to deal with a spiritual awakening on top of that can be extremely taxing.

Fatigue throughout the spiritual process is extremely common. As we work through the layers of conditioned reality we require conscious effort and energy to process them.

We may also notice periods of heightened energy. When we access divine flow or the deeper layers of ourselves we have more energy. We may also be channeling energies that fill us temporarily with energy. It is extremely common to flicker—going between processing huge experiences with fatigue and then sudden bursts of energy from feeling more flow. This flickering is a remembering and flow of huge proportions with symptoms of expanded consciousness, heightened energy, bliss, love, feelings of oneness, and deep spiritual understandings and then a crash and the fatigue of ordinary consciousness.

As we reach final states of working through conditioned reality there is an overwhelming fatigue that sets in as the body is fully able to remember its divine origins and is able to rest for perhaps the first time ever. After this rest comes continual energy and flow between the heightened states of divine flow and calmer, more reflective states of flow. Even in a fully awakened state we can feel cycles of fatigue and energy. Understanding this process and acclimating to it allows for us to bring simple awareness and acceptance to the process. By accepting the process, we can be thankful or even know when we will feel energized, and during fatigue or low energy we can rest from our experiences.

Digestive Issues and Diet

Digestive issues are extraordinarily common due to the amount of processed, heavy, and difficult to digest foods in our culture, as well as the amount of chemicals and non-food substances we ingest on a daily basis. This is true for everyone, whether they be a "sleeper" or the most conscious person on a significant spiritual path. However, those of us on the path of awakening will have a particularly difficult time with digestion and diet.

Our digestive systems are not only intended to digest food and beverage. They take in emotions, experiences, and are responsible for maintaining our mood and energy levels on a daily basis. When we have a history of trauma this energy commonly gets locked into the digestive system first. We literally are unable to digest what has occurred in our lives and it stays stuck until we are able to process it. In the awakening process our body is attempting to process not only our own old material—traumas, emotions, and experiences that we were not able to previously, but traumas and experiences from our family, ancestry, and so on. In cases of psychic abilities or awakening we are often simply unaware or lack education on how to process all of the stimuli coming at us that is not ours properly so the digestive tract gets overloaded and stops processing.

In either case we return to the analogy of the boulder. When the energy flowing through us hits the boulder (stuck emotions and trauma) more energy will get stuck around that boulder or it will break apart. In the case of the digestive system this is particularly difficult because we need to intake food to survive. When we have a "boulder" in our shoulder of stuck trauma/energy we can lower our usage of that arm. In the case of the digestive system we are constantly utilizing our digestive organs so they have to not only have the capability to digest food on a real, physical level but also deal with the stuck energy attempting to release. In the case of psychic abilities, this would be energy coming in to be processed on top of physical food and previous emotional traumas coming to the surface to be digested.

Although this alone could be the subject of a whole book, the advice for dietary needs is deeply individualized based on the difficulty of the awakening. It is not unheard of for those of us undergoing significant awakenings to simply not be able to eat for periods of time or have very limited food intake. It is common for those of us undergoing milder awakenings to find we need to simply clean up our diet—eating whole, real foods, cutting down on meat intake, and evaluating on an individual basis sensitivities to things like dairy, sugar, corn, soy, and wheat.

During awakening it is common to feel like we are unable to intake any food, or to gradually feel as if we are unable to eat or drink anything. Although this can be very specific to culture and difficulty of awakening, a few understandings may help. Creating a dietary plan that works for you is the key. Although there is a lot of material out there on what a spiritual person "should" eat from all sorts of people, anyone on a significant spiritual path will know that such thoughts are from people still asleep. Anyone else will realize that diet is a deeply individualized thing.

There are, however, commonalities in what might be considered on your spiritual path and diet. It is important to have a diet free from chemicals. Real, whole foods are essential. Small portions of food (such as a handful of food) every two to four hours works much better than having two or three larger meals a day. Cutting off your eating and drinking time after 6 p.m. in order to give your body a rest can be quite helpful. Broths, soups, rice, and other easily assimilated foods that are slightly warming but not too hot are better for the digestive tract than foods that are too cold or hot. Fasting under supervision on an on-off schedule, such as not eating for a day or undergoing an elimination diet to find out individual sensitivities, can be helpful. Eliminating alcohol, caffeine, drugs, and chemicals is often necessary. As you awaken you may find that your body simply does not process drugs or alcohol very well.

Some of us find that stopping eating meat products assists with feelings of heaviness and retention, or we may require meat that is dealt with humanely, is sustainable, or is without hormones. We may find that eating flesh is something we can no longer ethically do. We may realize that everything is consciousness and will eat meat, plants, and vegetables. During flare-ups of spiritual awakening symptoms we may find that bone broth can keep up vital energy while ensuring that our system has sustenance.

It is important to understand what you individually react well to physically in terms of meat, as well as your individual ethics and spiritual considerations of meat. It may be vitally important on your spiritual journey to not eat meat. It may also be vitally important for you to eat meat. Knowing what you individually react to and your own ideology surrounding meat without the propaganda of what others say is important to maintaining your diet and health. Visiting a Chinese Medicine practitioner, Ayurvedic practitioner, or nutritionist sensitive to your individual needs can provide you with educated information about what your body needs to be balanced and healthy.

In significant awakenings, dietary changes and needs may be created seemingly overnight as the system no longer is able to process certain foods that even yesterday you were able to process. Ask your body and pay attention to how your body responds to certain foods on a day-by-day basis. Learning how to work with your individual system and its needs on a daily basis will create a much better result than following specific guidelines from someone who may have no idea what you are experiencing.

For gradual awakenings there is a move away from and inability to process chemicals, drugs, alcohol, hormones, and non-real foods that happens step by step. Typically when we go through gradual awakenings we will become interested in restricted or natural diets before the need is created for them, and we may be restricting ourselves from foods that would be good for our process based on a real need or due to a fad. There are fads in eating, and as the newest understanding as a result of societal conditioning of what is the new "bad" food or the new "super" food is created, many of us can be part of an illusion created by individual companies or society.

Learn about food in an individualistic way—keeping a food diary, noticing what foods make you feel ill right after eating them, how you feel an hour after eating, and then approximately four to six hours after eating can tell you all you need to know. All of these times relate to specific organs and their ability to digest. Bringing this information to a qualified professional can allow for you to come up with an individualistic, realistic plan of what works for you. Relying on your inner guidance and ability to discern how you are feeling immediately and some time after eating will allow for you to understand what foods your body enjoys and which foods your body is resistant or even allergic to.

Energetically, the digestive tract is supposed to separate the clear, good energy from our diets and let it flow through the channels of our bodies. Our digestive tracts are also intended to dispose and process what we no longer need—waste products, experiences, energy, and emotions. On an energetic and spiritual level, what is needed for the digestive tract is the free flow of energy and processing of all physical and emotional materials that are clogging it up. This requires grounding to process both emotional energy as well as physical waste material. Learning how to utilize the tree meditation even on a basic level and receiving body work and herbal support from a caring, experienced professional is essential if the digestive tract is in a state of being frozen or overwhelmed. Visceral manipulation (abdominal massage), Arvigo Maya abdominal work, Chi Nei Tsang, acupuncture, and herbal recommendations from a certified and knowledgeable herbalist can help your body begin to process and work with the stuck energy in your abdomen. Energy work and spiritual healing can allow for you to regain power and vitality that has been lost after this center has been offline for a period of time.

EXERCISE: Tree Grounding Exercise

This is a fairly well-known grounding technique. It is also excellent at releasing any sort of stuck energy in the body, and can pass stimuli through in periods of overwhelm. There are many different variations of it, however this version is very specific to opening and allowing larger energies to move through your physical body. If you are ungrounded or having difficulty with these types of energies, you may find that doing this outside, or next to a tree, to be enormously helpful.

- First, place your feet on the floor. You can be sitting or standing.
- Feel the bottom of your feet and their contact with the floor.
- When you can feel the soles of your feet, imagine roots coming from the bottoms of your feet. You are a tree, and are growing roots as thick and wide as you need. At first this may seem like a visualization, but as you do this more you can actually feel the sensation of the roots growing. Over time they will become permanent, and will not require much effort to maintain. For some of you, this may seem at the beginning a Herculean task. You have not felt your feet, your legs, or been embodied for a very long time, if ever. So be patient.
- When you feel like your roots have grown, you can now use them.
- When you feel energy that is not yours, or even energy that is yours, see this energy as a color and breathe it down or allow it to flow down your legs and through your roots into the Earth.
- When you are ready, you can also use this pathway to take in Earth energy. Imagine the color of earth energy you would like to receive, and allow for it to flow through and up your root system as high up into your body and as deeply as it will go.

202

Although simple, this work may be deceptively difficult at first. The more you do this exercise, the more permanent the roots will be and the easier it will be for you to let go of energies. The key to this work is to understand when an energy is within you that you wish to let go of, surrender it without creating a story or seeking the logic behind it, and breathing it down your legs and out down your roots. If you are blocked, this energy may get stuck in your physical body somewhere. Keep on working at it—bringing energy down and out and bringing Earth energy up and in. Gradually, energy will begin to move and your physical symptoms will lessen.

For those of you who have done this basic exercise you may wish to work with this exercise on a deeper level. Only do the Advanced Tree Work when you can clearly feel the root system when you bring your attention to it and can feel energy flowing both down and up your body.

EXERCISE: Advanced Tree Work, Part 1

- Allow yourself to do the basic work, if needed.
- Grow your roots as deep and as wide as they will allow.
- Allow for your roots to go to the center of the Earth—going through all of the layers. Start at the crust, working your way through the rigid rocky layers, the smooth ocean layer, the plastic layer of the lithosphere and upper mantle, and the rigid lower mantle filled with silicate rocks and minerals that composes the biggest layer of Earth.
- Go even deeper, breaking through the rigid lower mantle to the fire of the liquid outer core. Take a breath and feel your roots access this energy.
- Go deeper into the rigid inner core of the Earth. Feel your roots become at home and at peace at this depth. Allow for them to find their appropriate place at this depth.
- Feel them settle in at this depth.

If you are able to make it to this depth your roots will be permanent and you will be able to draw on energy from any of the layers of the Earth. When you choose to do so, simply allow yourself to recall the position of your roots and journey upward, eventually meeting your feet. Draw energy from any or all of the layers. Eventually you will feel permanently anchored to the inner core of the Earth and will no longer need to visualize.

Energy exchange will be automatic, and larger energies can circulate through you with little issue or need for direction on your part. There will simply be a noticing on your part of a large energy coming through you and then a flow through your roots to the appropriate depth for the energy to disperse in. This exercise is successful when you can feel a strong flow of energy through your crown all the way down through your feet and into the Earth permanently.

When you are ready, you may go to Part 2. It is not necessary to completely feel yourself in the deepest layers of the inner core to do Part 2. However, each time you achieve a new depth in Part 1 I suggest redoing Part 2 because the results will differ.

EXERCISE: Advanced Tree Work, Part 2

- Once you have completed the initial tree work you may notice that your roots feel the need to grow wider or larger. Let them do so.
- Widen your roots as much as they feel comfortable. Allow for them to open. They may engulf your entire feet or may spread underneath you.
- Allow your root system to grow. It can do this in a wide variety of ways, however, commonly you would go from a single root to a system of roots growing from the single root out of your feet.
- When you feel a system of roots, allow for them to connect with the layer of depth you are at. This may be simply the Earth, rocks, dirt, liquid, etc.
- Allow for them to drink in sustenance from the root system you now have in place. This may be a natural feeling or you can imagine a color or allow a specific mineral or liquid to rise up within you as far as it can go before meeting blockage. Do not force this energy to rise further than it is ready to.
- If you are ready, allow for your root system to connect to humanity. Allow for it to entangle with other people, animals, and plants.
- Breathe in this collective energy and feel the connection through your root system up your body as far as it will go.

When practiced regularly, there will be a feeling of permanently having not only deep roots and grounding but a feeling of being connected and embodied at a deep level. Even energy from the largest and highest sources can pass through you. In time, this simple tree exercise can allow for you to release every single pattern that you have to release, for you to feel deep levels of spiritual flow, and for you to work with energy in a very conscious and significant way.

Headaches

Headaches are another common occurrence during awakening. Top-down awakenings are notorious for resulting in headaches, as the energy that is filling the crown and the third eye is bottlenecked. Emotional issues and past traumas can create headaches when the body is attempting to process them, particularly feelings of rage and anger, which are in Chinese Medicine known to have an upward, fiery motion, and result in headaches on the side of the head as well as in the eye system. Kundalini can cause headaches in the occiput (back of the head) or in the whole head due to upwards flow of energy. Global patterns can create headaches, as world events are processed through us as a release valve, and many of us are not skilled or clear enough to process such large energies. Sensitives and psychics, particularly Empaths and Clairvoyants, often get headaches from massive influxes of energy that is not theirs that results in headaches from the body attempting to process so much energy.

Working through the blockages within the physical form, including emotions and traumas, and transcending the layers of conditioned reality to become a clear channel allows us to move past headaches and migraines. Letting go of the identification of being someone who has headaches is also important. An illusion of or wish to control the energy coming in and the sheer amount of overwhelm that creates headaches and migraines, can be surrendered to allow for the energy to properly process. Learning how to work with energies so they can flow through the meridians properly in a downward instead of upward fashion is crucial to allowing for this energy to dissipate. Understanding what the migraines or headaches provide for you can also be a revelation—acknowledging if they give you time alone when you are overwhelmed, for example. Acupuncture, bodywork, and meditation focusing on grounding and understanding what the migraine or headache is saying to you (essentially why it is there) will allow for the headaches to be minimal, or disappear altogether.

Eye Symptoms

The eyes show how awakened a soul is. These eyes are clear, sparkly, and full of humor and joy. There is a light to these eyes that others can see. Eyes are the window to the soul, and they can reveal the emotional depths, pain, sorrow, anger, or degree of openness in a person. It is rare that people look one another in the eyes because the eyes can rarely hide our wounds.

Eye symptoms during awakening can vary greatly and can be ingrained in the physical as well (as in, get an eye exam). It is common during a clairvoyant awakening to have eye symptoms including feelings of cloudiness and during a top-down awakening to have eye pain that can be quite severe. Other symptoms during the awakening process include a feeling of seeing from the third eye (sixth chakra), from the back of the head, from great distances or watching ourselves as if we were on television (common if we are disassociated), or seeing from the heart instead of the eyes.

Other physical symptoms include astigmatism, floaters, ocular migraines, and feelings of constriction, heaviness, cloudiness, or being able to see film or veils over the eyes. When the layers of conditioned reality become thin it is possible to see the remaining layers of conditioned reality as a film or veil over the eyes.

Eye symptoms should go away if we are willing to work through the blockages on a spiritual level. If they are deeply ingrained in the physical we may need physical intervention. Many eye symptoms come up because we are blocking seeing on some level. Questioning what we do not want to see or what would happen if we did not have symptoms will allow for us to consciously process what is creating pain and dysfunction. Recognition and awareness that we may have fear of our clairvoyant capabilities opening, or we may be blocking seeing the issues of ourselves and our surroundings and taking personal responsibility for this, will allow for us to work through the spiritual causes of eye issues.

Dreams and Sleep

A common experience in awakening is to have vivid dreams. The dream world is a place where we remember who we truly are. We have now removed enough of the conditioned layers of reality to get a glimpse, a peek at what is at the core of us. This begins to show itself through being fully awakened in dreams. We are not there yet in our daily lives. But a part of us now remembers being fully awake, and knows who we truly are. We are able to see what is to come in full awakening in dreams—at our core we are a servant of the divine, a helper, a light, and a God or Goddess in our own right.

Dreams are a way that our body can process large amounts of subconscious material and larger patterns, such as societal energies. Sometimes during dreams a feeling of the presence of non-physical beings in the room occurs. These presences appear because we are becoming more aware of the non-physical world, and in sleep we are even more open and awake. If we find ourselves being drained by energies while sleeping or while awake, boundaries, shielding, and the use of herbs and crystals can assist us. Before sleep, we can say out loud or to a spirit guide that is specific for the purpose of protecting us from being drained or attacked that we wish to remain here—and that no other spirits are welcome in the room with us while we are resting. Further work in developing a spiritual "bouncer" can be learned through experienced spiritual healers. We should not feel bad about setting limits, or stating that we need a night off from helping in the dream world. We all need to have energy and be functional in our daily lives.

If setting basic boundaries does not work, shielding ourselves by imagining a giant bubble of light forming around us before we go to sleep can be very helpful. We can facilitate this by imagining the bubble being created by divine light or by a particular spirit guide blowing a bubble of light around us with the intent that anything that is not of light will not be able to enter. When we are asking for this bubble, we do not create it from the inside out. We have a force outside of us do this. Otherwise we are creating it from our own energy and may wake up tired from having to keep this bubble going all night.

Herbal preparations can be extremely helpful. Burning herbs such as sage, copal, or palo santo on a regular basis to clear our space is a good energetic clearing method. Spiritual oils and floor washes can help protect us in dreamtime. One of the simplest preparations can be lemon and salt in water sprayed around the bedroom before sleep. It leaves the room with a wonderful scent and is repellant to many energies. In more severe cases, putting a protective border of salt around us, around the room, and in the windows can keep energies at bay.

In acupuncture there is a concept of not having the appropriate energetic boundaries. If our wei qi (protective energetic boundary) is weak and we are too open we allow too much energy outside of ourselves in. Finding an acupuncturist can help us become less porous, or let less energy that is not ours into our physical body.

When we find that we are drawing extremely negative or strong energies during sleep or otherwise, we may need to find an outside practitioner such as a spiritual healer who understands working with protection, guarding, or depossession who can help on a case-by-case basis.

Our sleep can easily become fragmented and we may go through periods of insomnia, waking at certain times, or somnolence. These periods of lethargy and increased sleep are important to process the experiences we are going through. Insomnia or need for little sleep may occur due to divine energy pouring through us, resulting in a diminished need for sleep. Insomnia may also occur because we are sensitive and are having energies bother us, or because we are awakening and are having a hard time dealing with the emotions and energies that are arising.

Sleep Healing and Learning

Being healed or healing others during sleep is a common occurrence. During unconscious sleep healing we begin to have strange dreams in which we are being healed or we are healing others. It is also common to experience being taught or learning something during dreams only to forget the lesson once awake, or to only partially remember the experience. These experiences begin happening when we have worked through some of the issues of Self and family enough so that we can access our true awakened selves.

In dreams we fully remember who we are. We are awake. The conscious mind is only ready for as much information as we can process and handle in waking reality. As we awaken in our daily lives we remember more and more of our dream states and they go from something that we have happen to us to something that we actively participate in. When we become more awakened we begin to remember our experiences during dreams, will draw more healers to us for healing purposes during dreams, and will go from student to teacher in the spiritual realms.

When enough of the layers of conditioned reality have been worked with that we can handle the understandings that come through in the sleep state, the intensity of the dreams will increase as will the memories or capabilities to recall lessons and experiences from the dream state. This is conscious sleep healing, and this can be a big leap forward in consciousness, as the dream time offers experiences with spiritual beings, divinity, and spiritual teachers that is not to be had for most in the physical world. It is difficult for many beings to want to or be able to come through in waking reality. Many prefer to interact in the dream state, which is an intermediate ground for all types of energies, including us. The memory of healing others, or being healed by experiences in dream time, can be a big step forward in the personal evolution of healing and becoming an awakened soul. The memory of who we truly are that is afforded in the dream time and the readiness of teachers and healers who inhabit the dream time result in understandings that affect our ordinary waking reality.

At some point there becomes no divide between the spiritual and physical realms, the dream time and the waking time. In an awakened state we will feel called to heal, to learn, to experience both in sleep and non-sleep. As awakened and conscious souls we can learn to use the dream time as a tool. The results are quicker because we do not have to battle with the blocks and wounds of the people we wish to heal or interact with, and we are outside of the timeline, location, and other constructs of conditioned reality.

Sleep Paralysis

Sleep paralysis is a sudden inability to move the physical body right before going to sleep or right after coming out of sleep. Although there are neurological and emotionally based reasons for this phenomena, it can be spiritually based. During this experience, visions of everything from extraterrestrials to demonic activity occur with feelings of terror or anxiety. It is important to note that many of these feelings of terror or anxiety are body based, meaning that they come from the lack of control that occurs and the inability to move the physical body rather than the visions, even if the visions are scary. In some cases the physical body is engaged in sleep but the switch-off to the awakened soul in dream time has had a malfunction and we find ourselves fully awake without the benefit of the layers of conditioned reality surrounding us. The fear, anxiety, and other emotions at finding ourselves in this state turns the energies in our space from non-threatening to those of demons and monsters. In some cases we are going through an experience that is genuinely scary, but in many cases the fear of finding ourselves in that state is enough to project or misunderstand the situation.

There is not much known about how to work with this condition. Ideally we would work through our fears, anger, and other emotions, and for some of us this experience is about control. Surrendering of control or the illusion of control is one of the most difficult things to do on the spiritual path. For those of us who are genuinely experiencing issues with frightening visitors, checking in with a spiritual healer, learning about spiritual bathing practices, and learning how to protect the bedroom before sleep is essential. Unfortunately, if there is something quite complex happening with an energy that is beyond simple protection measures, working with a very experienced spiritual healer who can rid you and your house of these issues is necessary. As reasonable, rational people we should rule out the logical before we move on to theories about abductions and demonic energies. We can then find the appropriate healer to work with us through this experience—whether it is a therapist, neurologist, or a very experienced Shaman.

Astral Projection

Astral projection is something that is commonly experienced and often opens up without us fully knowing—we will simply relate strange dreams or feel out of our body without knowing why. Others of us who are consciously able to astral project utilize this skill to gain knowledge, do distance healing, and explore different planes of existence. Some of us utilize this ability to have spirit families, partners, or meet others in astral form. This comes with great skill, and it can be difficult for even the most experienced astral traveler to become fully embodied again or want to integrate back with the physical body. Many of us explore astral projection out of curiosity. Astral travel often comes with other psychic abilities and is a common interest for many of us. Often our capability of traveling this way is rather minimal unless we have gone through significant awakenings, or have a natural aptitude for it.

Emotional Fluctuations

The uncovering and bringing into consciousness of traumas, and issues that may not be known to us is difficult, especially if we are not aware we are going through a spiritual process. Sharp transition between the highs of feeling heightened spiritual states and the lows of crashing into a lower spiritual state create difficult emotional experiences.

Emotions once understood as part of a spiritual process can be worked with systematically—releasing each trauma, emotion, and experience that comes up through surrender. Some of us have events in our past that are too traumatic to process alone and we require counseling. Others due to biological or genetic predisposition are unable to handle the awakening process and end up medicated, in psychiatric units, or as drug abusers.

As we stop flickering (going back and forth between spiritual states) our emotions even out. Once we have worked past the first few layers of conditioned reality containing the energies of Self, family, ancestry, and past lives, the deeper layers can be emotional and overwhelming but as they are more impersonal can be easier to process.

There is a psychoanalytic nature in our culture that feels as if we must examine and logically figure out each emotion, memory, and experience that arises. When we are dealing with an awakening process much of that is not necessary and can even be detrimental to the process. Surrendering the need to know and letting emotions release is the fastest way to work through surfacing emotions. Not hooking oneself into the story or creating further illusions surrounding the story—simply allowing the energy to clear—will allow for us to become free from the emotional fluctuations that occur. When we are able to release the emotions and experiences that come up out of our physical bodies without having to know logically why things are coming up, we can move past them. We are then free from them, able to release the patterns and restrictive energies created by them.

Awakening is difficult, especially if we have learned to shut down or numb our emotions because they are not appropriate. Learning to process these emotions through meditation, body-centered therapy, working out, being in nature, or in your own unique way will allow for them to clear. Surrendering the need to know, especially with larger societal and group energies, or the need to create a story or attach an importance to them will allow for the pattern and emotions to fully clear instead of simply change into a new pattern that needs to be changed at a later date. Letting go of emotional baggage is difficult. We like being the victim, and our stories create our identity. We fear who we would be without our wounds. Not all emotions have to release at once. Allowing for some of the experience to process, part of the story to release, and partial healing so the body can adjust and still feel safe works well when releasing difficult emotions.

Alteration of Belief Systems

It is normal for us to change our belief systems over time. Every one of us will expand during our lifetimes—changing our belief structures in some way. In the awakening process this can happen gradually or quite suddenly. In sudden awakenings our belief systems may change drastically within a few minutes. The influx of cosmic energy, or the rise of Kundalini, can create a rapid change in understandings and beliefs very quickly. This is quite disorienting and takes time to readjust and integrate the powerful experience that created this rapid change. The release of patterns in a fast manner leaves us quite aware of the patterns and beliefs that we just released—creating relationship, friendship, family, and job existential crises that can be profoundly life affirming or leave us shell-shocked.

One of the common adjustments of belief structure is the letting go of physical and materialistic forms of beliefs for more spiritual understandings. Letting go of physical possessions and shedding of the belief that we need designer cars, new clothes, a large house, or to "keep up with the Joneses" can be a profound shift.

Another common shift in belief structure is the understanding and letting go of personal and societal rules and conventions. Awakened souls may conduct themselves appropriately for whatever conventions necessitate, but it is a conscious decision to do so. Letting go of religious rules or definitions for personal contact with the divine; of puritanical views on sexuality; rigid rules of what sex, race, class, and culture mean; of books, teachers, gurus, and the opinions of others to create our existence occurs. It is no longer necessary to quote teachers, to have physical gurus, to have others tell us what their truth is and define it as our own. The awakening process is a freeing process—we are freeing ourselves from belief structures. It allows for us to understand who we truly are and what we truly believe without the confines of conditioned reality. We are able to see through the belief systems of others and the grids that make up such unconscious belief systems and form our own based on what we personally know to be true. There is freedom that comes with awakening—and this freedom allows us to examine and question our belief systems, adjusting them if necessary.

It is common in awakenings to create a huge amount of rules based off of ego of what enlightenment means and how to achieve it. Enlightenment is personal freedom—the ability to create the life and understand our truth without the chains of our wounds and the layers of conditioned reality. There are no rules. We do not need to become Vegan, listen to only certain kinds of music, not watch TV, only interact with certain people, or any of the other emotional, sexual, physical rules that people concoct. Awakening is individuation. It is freedom. There are certainly commonalities in experiences and similarities in path. This does not mean that awakening means that you never eat Twinkies or stop listening to heavy metal if that makes you who you are. In shedding the belief systems that are illusory or told to us by others we can discover what our own belief system is free from conditioning.

Release of Behaviors

During awakening we will find ourselves letting go of behaviors that no longer serve us. We may find ourselves unable to take in certain foods or drink, go into places that no longer resonate with us, and will no longer wish to participate in drama and chaos over inconsequential things. Once we resolve our wounding, we naturally release negative behaviors and find what foods, activities, and experiences truly nourish and make our souls peaceful or joyful.

Time

Throughout the process of awakening the concept of time may begin to change. At first, this is an intellectual understanding brought forward by books and other spiritual materials. The concept that time is non-linear is understood by the intellect but not really experienced. When experiences (like peak experiences) occur there begins to be an understanding about how the boundaries of time itself can shift and change. A place of great beauty that we were standing at for just a few moments felt like eons, or a lunch in a café that went on for hours feels like just moments.

After the personal experience of the expansion of time, the deeper understanding that our personal timelines and time itself is non-linear can occur. At first this awakening is to our past timeline. This may be an understanding that a part of ourselves is still in the space of being an unhappy six-year-old child or that our ancestors and their timelines live within us in the current moment.

For some there is an expansion and understanding of the future timeline. This may be anything from a knowing of what is to come, such as in precognitive and other psychic states, or an actual meeting with some version of our future Self. Dreams about the future that appear realistic, an understanding and processing of our own death, and realizations of the varying paths we could take present themselves.

Beyond the future and past, in a fully awakened state there is knowledge that every time, place, and understanding is in the now, the present. Other dimensions, times, belief systems, realms, are all in the present moment. To some this appears with imagery of a big eye or a dot on a page. By accessing the Void (the layer beyond conditioned reality) we can work with time as we can any other created construct.

Drug Abuse and Numbing

It is entirely normal for sensitive people to want to numb themselves. We live in a society that engenders numbness. Drug abuse, drinking, television, shopping, food—these are all ways to numb to make it through difficult situations. Unfortunately, these become a pattern of abuse as we quickly discover that it is easier and quicker to get a drink or to watch television to suppress our grief and rage rather than process them. That discovery then becomes our biggest tool for dealing with the major and then the minor hiccups in life. We then become numb, simply playing out the motions of our own life and lacking the tools to deal with any bumps in the road.

While this is a societal epidemic, drug abuse is rampant in the awakening process. So much so that it is considered as part of the criteria for defining states of spiritual emergency. Significant spiritual experiences or high sensitivity levels create a feeling of isolation or inability to express spiritual experiences to others. Feelings of being crazy, unable to relate experiences, or just plain overwhelm create circumstances in which we use drugs in order to cope. Spiritual experiences are not yet accepted by the mainstream, and true spiritual experiences are difficult to describe to others. Psychic abilities and sensitivities are often so overwhelming that we turn to drugs simply in order to cope and shut down the amount of stimuli coming in.

Many of us are sent through hospitalizations and psychiatric or even general allopathic practitioners who prescribe antidepressants, antipsychotics, or other medications that stop or slow down spiritual awakenings. While there is need for these medications for some of us, many doctors lack the understanding of spiritual experiences and give medication out of ignorance or disbelief of the spiritual factors of illness.

Finding out how to work with spiritual experiences and the proper tools to process energy is crucial to our survival. If addicted, allopathic communities offering detox and medication to work through the substance withdrawal is necessary. Consideration of the reasoning behind the addiction and whether or not it is a part of the spiritual process will hopefully be explored by ourselves as well as through holistic and traditional medicine in the future.

Initiations

Initiations are tests that bring us from one state of being to another. This can occur in a very conscious way, as when we are going through spiritual rites of passage such as a graduation ceremony. Initiations into adulthood, sexuality, graduations, and other rites of passage are sorely lacking in our modern day. Many of our initiations have lost their spiritual significance, and passing on of teachings from elders no longer occurs. This has created generations of adults not initiated or unsure of their adulthood, and generations of both women and men not properly initiated into matters of sexuality, procreation, and becoming a man or woman.

When we are on a spiritual path there are spiritual initiations both large and small. Some of these initiations are quite difficult, such as Shamanic sickness, where we die or come very close to death to be able to work with and see beyond the physical world. Initiations can be overwhelming physically, emotionally, and spiritually, and can involve a wide range of symptoms and experiences. They are so individualized that although each one takes us to a new level of understanding there is no solid criteria for what one may contain. This is because many initiations are self-generated and are as difficult or complex as we make them. Initiations are necessary to allow for the logical capacity of our brain to make sense of the experience and understandings in the spiritual awakening process.

Many initiations are spirit-led. The initiation of releasing death and identification of the body is commonly a severe illness or even death. The merging into oneness is a feeling of bliss and joy that is unable to be contained. An initiation may lead us to be accepted by a new spiritual teacher. At the stage when freedom, bliss, and love come pouring in, it is common for us to retract because we do not feel worthy. Once we feel worthy we pass through the initiation. There are always further initiations as we continue to unfold into divine flow. By simply flowing through initiations the best we can rather than resisting or self-generating physical and emotional scenarios, we can gain the knowledge and experience from them without the pain.

Mental Illness vs. Spiritual Awakening

We are all spiritual beings, and every human being on earth has trauma. Even awakened souls feel a full spectrum of emotions and must process their experiences. In modern society we have medicine that takes care of the physical. We also have the mind—the realm of psychology. Within the last decade allopathic medicine has just begun understanding that the mind and body are not separate. But the suggestion that a physical illness may have spiritual roots, or a mental imbalance may have spiritual causes is still considered ludicrous for most health-care practitioners, even holistic ones.

If we are undergoing a spiritual process, while counseling and medication may help the mental and physical, the spiritual layer is not taken care of. Unfortunately our current medical paradigm does not understand spiritual experiences, thought processes, or physical or mental processes that do not fit into what is considered "normal." Many people who go to receive help for spiritual illness are treated through drastic and unnecessary means because the spiritual dimensions of illness are not understood or considered.

Many of us are truly going through a spiritual experience that does not fit into any medical paradigm. We need spiritual instead of biomedical assistance, which we may not know about or may be unable to find. If we are going through a spiritual awakening and are not able to function, medication or hospitalization to stop or slow the process and ensure our safety may be necessary. Ideally, those of us who are temporarily overwhelmed would be given tools so medication could be titrated and we could learn to process our spiritual experiences in a more gradual and embodied manner.

Some of us during spiritual awakenings want very badly to hold onto our traumas and victimhood so we let the material coming up to process define us. We create illusions and delusions centered around our past lives, our childhoods, or ancestry and go from practitioner to practitioner with an odd delight in the fact that nobody is able to help us.

In certain cases we are seemingly genetically predisposed to have a type of awakening which will create a situation of long-term hospitalization and medication. Even with tools and guidance we would not be able to make it through the awakening and be functional in the world.

Although we all are going through a spiritual experience, some of us are self-creating angels, gods, demons, and everything in between out of our own wounds and disassociated aspects of ourselves. This disassociation is necessary for the mentally ill to survive. In this category hopefully we can move closer to wholeness, to healing those disassociated aspects of Self, but the delusions are simply that. There are some people who are truly in the stage of becoming divine and realizing their divine origins, some people who have a direct link to God, and some people who claim to be Jesus because being themselves is too painful. It is easier for the traumatized person to have a demon chasing him or her than to see an abusive parent for who he or she really is.

Although it is a popularized notion that every person who is mentally ill is going through some sort of spiritual awakening, things are unfortunately not that simple. Although we all are going through a spiritual experience, careful and pragmatic differentiation of the spiritual dimensions of illness along with a treatment model that gives appropriate care to those who need long-term medication and hospitalization, those who might need those things for the short term, and those who might need a spiritual counselor to learn tools would be an ideal standard of care. It is doubtful this will happen in the near future. The numbing of painful experiences, the medicating of traumas, or the stopping of an awakening process may be necessary for people to simply survive intact. However, once people are stabilized and functional enough to learn tools and question their experiences there should be a frank discussion about letting go of the numbing materials and an in-depth questioning of the spiritual dimensions of illness. Until this is a standard of care, we can only inform ourselves and make choices based on our own understandings and available resources.

Epilogue

The path of awakening is the path of freedom. It is a path of casting off the rules, belief structures, and understandings that we have given ourselves or that we have been handed by various sources. The awakening process allows us to finally understand who we truly are as individuals and how we can uniquely be of service to the world. This path allows us to directly feel the entire flow of the ocean of divinity and the singularity of being one drop of that ocean simultaneously. This is a beautiful thing, and a rarity in this world.

It is easy to get caught up in complexity, in intellectualism, in ego, in the memes, books, religions, spiritual paths, and gurus who seek to sell us or tell us what our truth should be and what our awakened state should look like. As we progress we are able to let go of the teachings and rules of others. We all need teachers, mentors, books, and even gurus. But when we have direct experience of the divine we no longer need these resources to define our Self and our reality. In an awakened state, we will always be learning, always unfolding. But when we are fully awakened, we are no longer seekers. We have sought.

There are many paths to an awakened state. There are millions of us awakening in small or large ways in this world. This book should provide the understanding that there are common ways to awaken, common symptoms and guideposts that can let you know that you are making progress on your path. It should help you to know that others have had similar experiences of awakening over hundreds, if not thousands of years. You are not alone. Although there are commonalities, awakening is a direct revelatory path, and one that is deeply individualized.

It is easy to get caught up in the tragedies, the negativity, the issues and difficulties that arise in the awakening process. Because awakening is difficult – even the most gradual of paths requires us to face our truths and discount our illusions, to let go of the lies and the stories we tell ourselves. For all of its difficulties, awakening is a path of extraordinary healing, embodiment, and realization. Each layer or trauma that we work through allows for us to experience greater flow, realization, and personal and collective healing.

For all the complexity that may come with arriving at an awakened state, being awake is exceedingly simple. It is knowing who you are and acting from the place of knowing who you are. It is realizing that no matter who you are and how "enlightened" you are that you are not that important. It is understanding that being awake is simply an illusory ending point. It is the letting go of competitive spirituality and the hyper-fixation of attaining more than you already have and being more than you already are. It is realizing that the divine flows through your life and your human form and that it is not separate from it. No matter how awakened you are you still go to the grocery store, pick up your kids from school, and clean the litter box. You watch television, eat good food, and have sex. People still cut you off in traffic. The difference is that life becomes simple. You either do something or you do not. You no longer have mental chatter and layers of trauma magnifying and distorting your experiences. You have patterns and issues and arguments come up and you have the embodiment, the presence, and the ability to deal with them in the moment. You no longer believe the thoughts and patterns that remain from the distorted or traumatized Self. Your life becomes simpler and simpler as you continue to let go of the chaos and the varying traumas and beliefs that once defined you.

By realizing that an awakened state can flow through the physical form we can be awake in our everyday lives. We are meant to live in this world. We are meant to have physical bodies. They are not an inconvenience or something to stop identifying with. Spirituality and enlightenment is not separate from our physical world and our physical bodies. It is in our work place, at our local coffee shop, and at our family dinners. Our senses, our experiences, and our physical bodies are unique and magnificent creations and we can, as awakened or awakening individuals, be of great service to humanity and to ourselves through the vehicle of our physical form. By becoming more awakened and embodied in our daily lives, our world can be more awakened and embodied as a whole.

About the Author

MARY MUELLER SHUTAN is an Acupuncturist, CranioSacral Therapist, Zero Balancer, Herbalist, Spiritual Healer, and Artist. Through her own intense spiritual awakening process she discovered simple, clear ways to help people with psychic abilities, Kundalini, and other spiritual awakenings navigate their experiences. She has a worldwide practice and currently resides in Arizona. For more information please visit her websites: www.maryshutan.com and www.lotusbodywork.com

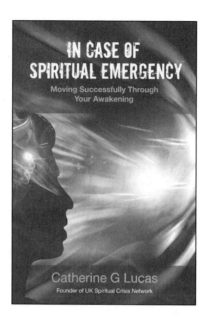

In Case of Spiritual Emergency
by Catherine G. Lucas

PERSONAL STORIES OF SPIRITUAL CRISES are presented alongside practical and effective guidance in this exploration of a fascinating phenomenon. When spiritual emergencies, such as mystical psychosis and dark nights of the soul, are understood, managed, and integrated, they can offer enormous potential for growth and fulfillment, and this book offers three key phases for successful navigation. Encouraging, supportive, and life-saving, this resource is essential for avoiding the mental, emotional, or spiritual paralysis or exhaustion that can result from underestimating the current age of increased individual and global emergencies.

978-1-84409-546-9

True Angel Stories
by Diana Cooper

THIS INSPIRATIONAL BOOK offers a multitude of angel stories from everyday life, which show how these light beings can truly transform lives on Earth. In addition, Diana Cooper has designed exercises and visualizations that help the reader to open up further to the wonders of the angelic realms. Stories discuss guardian angels, feathers, signs, rainbows, prayers, numbers and names, unicorns, orbs and much, much more, making this the ultimate angel compendium.

978-1-84409-612-1

Also of interest from Findhorn Press

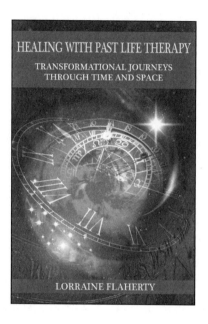

Healing with Past Life Therapy
by Lorraine Flaherty

PROVIDING EVIDENCE to the validity of past lives, this self-help guide
delves deeply into past life regression and offers a thorough understanding
of each step of the process. Through detailed transcripts of actual sessions,
ordinary people speak candidly about their experiences with this form of self-
discovery. Confirming that she has gone through the same journey to healing,
Lorraine Flaherty incorporates stories of her own past lives to illustrate the
ways these insights can aid in clearing away mental clutter, help to form better
decisions, cause one to become more empowered, and put one's life on the
right path. With a compelling and down-to-earth approach, this remarkable
discussion illustrates the ways that any reader—from the idly curious to the
serious spiritual seeker—can develop a greater understanding of who they are,
where they come from, and where they are going.

978-1-84409-634-3

Lorraine Flaherty

All the tracks on these CDs take you into a deep state of relaxation allowing you to let go and achieve each of the stated objectives.

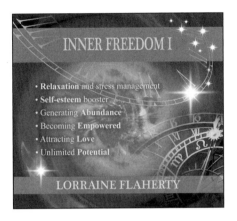
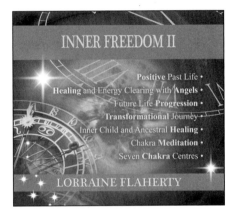

Inner Freedom I

CD1
- Relaxation and Stress Management
- Self-esteem Booster
- Generating Abundance

CD2
- Becoming Empowered
- Attracting Love
- Unlimited Potential

Inner Freedom II

CD1
- Positive Past Life
- Healing and Energy Clearing with Angels
- Future Life Progression

CD2
- Transformational Journey
- Inner Child and Ancesteral Healing
- Chakra Meditation
- Seven Chakra Centres

978-1-84409-640-4   978-1-84409-641-1

FINDHORN PRESS

Life-Changing Books

Consult our catalogue online
(with secure order facility) on
www.findhornpress.com

For information on the Findhorn Foundation:
www.findhorn.org